24. JUN 97   TONBRIDGE LIBRARY   NOV 02

NOV   16. OCT   25. MAY 94

30. APR 90   08. JUN

26. MAY '90   10. AUG   03. AUG 94

08. JUN 90   28.

08. AUG 90   16. JAN 92   19. JAN 93

18. AUG 90   04. FEB 92   25. FEB 93   AUG 95

07. APR 93   13. SEP 95

21. SEP 90   19. MAY 92   05. MAY 93   11. OCT 95

31. DEC '9   8/11/95

26. JAN 9   24. JUN 92   13. SEP 93

21. SEP 93   22. AUG 96

12. SEP 96

TONBRIDGE LIBRARY
TEL: TON. 352754

KENT

COUNTY

LIBRARY

942.25

Books should be returned or renewed by the last
date stamped above.

02. MAY 97

WILLARD, Barbara

The Forest
— Ashdown in E.Sussex

D0538876

THE FOREST
Ashdown in East Sussex

By the same author

The Mantlemass Novels

The Lark and the Laurel
The Sprig of Broom
(Runner-up for the 1972 Guardian Award for Children's Fiction)
The Eldest Son
A Cold Wind Blowing
(Runner-up for the 1973 Guardian Award for Children's Fiction)
The Iron Lily
(Winner of the 1974 Guardian Award for Children's Fiction)
A Flight of Swans
Harrow and Harvest
The Keys of Mantlemass
(Short Stories)

The Queen of the Pharisees' Children
(Winner of the 1984 Whitbread Children's Book Award)
Ned Only
The Miller's Boy
The Grove of Green Holly

THE FOREST
Ashdown in East Sussex

Barbara Willard

SWEETHAWS PRESS

Published in 1989 by
Sweethaws Press
Owl House
Poundgate
Near Uckfield
Sussex TN22 4DE
Telephone Crowborough (0892) 653722

All rights reserved

British Library Cataloguing in Publication Data
Willard, Barbara
   The forest : Ashdown in East Sussex.
   1. East Sussex. Ashdown Forest, history
   I. Title
   942.2'51

   ISBN 0-9511795-2-7

Text copyright © Barbara Willard 1989
Photographs copyright © Ashdown Forest Centre 1989
                  © Hugh Clark a.r.p.s. 1989
                 © Chris Marrable 1989
                 © Dulcie Parkhurst 1989

KENT COUNTY
LIBRARY
942.25

Printed in Great Britain by
BPCC Wheatons Ltd
Hennock Road, Marsh Barton
Exeter EX2 8RP

C130294749

'At about three miles from Grinstead you come to a pretty village called Forest Row, and then, on the road to Uckfield, you cross Ashurst (*sic*) Forest, which is a heath, with here and there a few birch scrubs upon it, verily the most villainously ugly spot I ever saw in England. This lasts you for five miles, getting, if possible, uglier and uglier all the way, till, at last, as if barren soil, nasty spewy gravel, heath and even that stunted, were not enough, you see some rising spots, which instead of trees, present you with black, ragged, hideous rocks. There may be Englishmen who wish to see the coast of *Nova Scotia*. They need not go to sea; for here it is to the life. If I had been in a long trance . . . and had been waked up here, I should have begun to look about for the Indians and the squaws, and to have heaved a sigh at the thought of being so far from England.'

WILLIAM COBBETT
Rural Rides
22nd January 1822

These Alpine hills of wide expanse,
(That fill the heart with wild romance)
Far distant from the town's loud hum,
Where courtly guests but seldom come;
A heathy waste of huts and dens,
Where human nature seldom mends;
No polish'd schools, but turfy fires,
Far away from village spires;
And should the chime of Sabbath bells
E'er reach these dark, benighted hills,
Few heed the call—here all is wild,
Their Sabbeth pass'd their time beguil'd
Idly (far from example's sway).
In groups among the fern they lay,
Or in some hidden nook, where reigns
Confusion to distract their brains,
At some sly gin shop, sick'ning sight,
Profane the day, meet, drink, and fight.
Yes, ages thus have witness'd long
The truth of this, my uncouth song.
Then O my harp! wail with the winds,
Nor cease till Ashdown yet amends . . .

THOMAS PENTECOST 1852

It is a tract of singular loveliness, one of the few surviving vestiges of primeval England . . .

PETER BRANDON
The Sussex Landscape 1974

For William George Salvin Bowlby
The Story of Where He Was Born in 1988

'And all sway forward on the dangerous flood
Of history, that never sleeps or dies,
And, held one moment, burns the hand.'

W. H. AUDEN

Contents

*Re-printed from the Ashdown Forest News

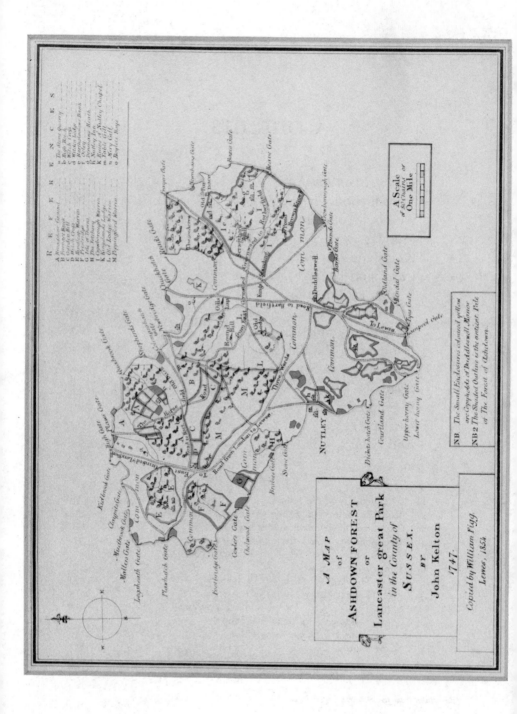

A MAP
of
ASHDOWN FOREST
or
Lancaster great Park
in the County of
SUSSEX.
BY
John Kelton
1747.

Copied by William Figg
Lewes, 1854.

A Scale
of 80 Chains or
One Mile

REFERENCES

A Broadstone Ground.
B Forest or King's
C Birch Grove
D Welch Lodge
E Bearlfoggy Warren
F Bartholomew Barch
G Inn or Bounds
H The Factory
I Cranborough Warren
K Kensland Warren
L Old Lodge Warren
M Fryeningford Warren

a The Stone Quarry
b High Rock
c Birch Grove
d Welch Lodge
e Bartholomew Barch
f Duddy
g Pippingford Heath
h Nutley Inn
k Remns of Nutley Chapel
l Rabit Gill
m Mary Gill
n Old Gate
o Boyles Ridge

NB The Small Enclosures coloured yellow
are copyholds of Duddleswell Manor
NB2 The Shaded Outline is the antient Pale
of The Forest of Ashdown.

List of Illustrations

From the terrace of Pippingford Park.
The Pageant: The Stars.
The Pageant: The Players.
The Pageant of Ashdown Forest.

Introduction

Two writers of children's books have found their inspiration on Ashdown Forest.

Barbara Willard, exchanged Sussex Downs for heather, pines and greater solitude, came to live on the edge of the Forest in 1956. Thirty years earlier, my father, adding rural to urban, had come to half-live a mile to the north of the Forest in what today would be described as a second home. He was a Londoner and continued to live in London. But the four of us—he, his wife, his son and his son's nanny—would pile into a large, blue, chauffeur-driven Fiat and travel down every Saturday morning and back again every Monday afternoon. And we would spend a whole, glorious month there in the spring and two months in the summer.

Barbara Willard, inspired by her new surroundings, made them the setting for ten of her children's historical novels (eight in the Mantlemass series and two others). The first of these books was written more than ten years after coming to the Forest. One of them won the Guardian award and another the Whitbread award. My father, equally inspired, made the Forest the setting for two of his books, finishing the second little over three years after his arrival.

I wonder if anyone, buying a house on or near the Forest today, making it his or her first or second home, could be so powerfully influenced by its magic—that feeling of continuity, that link with the past, that remoteness from the present that bring imaginary worlds, dream worlds within easy reach. Is it quite so easy today to sit on the heather, alone with your thoughts, listening while the Forest talks to you? I hope so, but I am not too sure.

Cotchford Farm is where the London road crosses the Medway. From our front lawn we had a view across a meadow to the line of alders that fringed the river. Behind these the ground rose through more trees, and above them, in the faraway distance, crowning the view, was a bare hilltop. In the centre of this hilltop was a clump of pines.

Of course we went there. Of course we made many expeditions to the Forest. But Chuck Hatch, where the Forest began, was a mile away, and in those early days our one car had only the one driver and both lived in London. So those expeditions had to be on foot.

My father had been a great walker in his youth, but he needed both a companion and a purpose. My mother, too, was a great walker, but she was happiest walking alone. So I suspect that most of my father's visits to the Forest were family expeditions—to make yet another attempt to count the pine trees on Gills Lap or to search for the marsh gentian. Later, in the 1930's, my father bought a Morris Oxford, and when he had learned to drive it, we were able to travel further afield—he alone to play golf, or perhaps a family outing with me in the dicky. As I read Miss Willard's book names kept echoing up out of the past: Kidds Hill, Newbridge, Pippingford, Sheffield Park. But why we went there and what we did I cannot now remember. Only one name has an event attached to it: Kidbrooke Park, scene of that great pageant. It took place in 1929 and here on the grass arena I played the part of Christopher Robin for the last time. Pooh was then left behind; I went on to become a schoolboy; and the Forest became a place where I might watch a bird or find a nest. I would go there alone now, up through the Five Hundred Acre and back through Posingford. And while there I would never see another person: the Forest was all mine.

'Don't you ever go back?' people sometimes ask me today. No. Even if it had remained as it was when I knew it, it would give me no special pleasure to see it again. For it would not look the same to me. And in any case it is not as it was. Even the Forest, which has changed so slowly over the centuries, has changed much since I walked there as a boy. More and faster cars. Litter bins. Car parks. Ramblers. Riders. Picnic parties. Only twice, of necessity, have I been back.

The first of my visits was in 1978 and was in connection with the memorial to my father and to Shepard that 'the Pooh Trustees were proposing to erect. Miss Willard refers to it, and though she reassures me that it is being 'well managed', she seems a little doubtful about whether or not it took the most appropriate form. If it didn't, the fault was entirely mine.

One might well have expected arguments and disagreements, with the Conservators or the Commoners entrenched on one side and the Trustees on the other. But in fact all here was politeness and cooperation. The arguments took place between the chairman of the Trustees and myself. I have been re-reading the letters and memoranda that passed to and fro. What an immense amount I had to say! Perhaps we had both caught something of that stubbornness, that 'don't you dare try and get the better of me' that we are told has always been found among those who have lived on the Forest. Our Chairman favoured the commemorative seat. Three seats on a raised stone platform, backed by a screen of shrubs, and the whole thing sited where nobody could miss it: that was his proposal. How fiercely I opposed this! Shrubs? What shrubs? Heather and gorse are the only two shrubs that grow on the Forest. Seats? Why seats? With the short grass or the heather to sit on, who wants a seat? So what, then, did I want? Very briefly: what is there now, and what (apart from the inscription) looks, I hope, as if it had always been there, so that visitors (sitting on the grass) can feel themselves to be where my father sat, where Pooh sat, seeing what they saw.

My other visit was in connection with the attempt by BP to get a licence to drill for oil. I heard about this when I was rung up and told by a reporter from a Sussex newspaper. I was told that East Sussex County Council in their proposed

Structure Plan had forbidden the exploration for oil or gas within the Forest but that the Secretary of State for the Environment (*for* the environment?) had overruled them: exploration would be permitted provided the land did not suffer 'serious harm' (as defined by the Secretary of State?). In consequence BP were able to put in their application. Did I know about this? And what were my views? I did not know, and I said, in a rush of words, just what I thought.

It says a lot for the diligence with which the national press scans the local press that from then on it seemed that our telephone never stopped ringing. We even bought a whistle so that I could be summoned from the top of the garden.

It was lucky that the proposed sale of the Forest followed so closely on the heels of this threat. The two merged into each other; and when I was invited to take part in a press conference at the Forest Centre, I was not too sure exactly what its purpose was and what was expected of me. To those who had invited me the sale was the greater of the two threats, the need to raise the necessary money their top priority. For me, coming up from Devon, this was a local matter, which Sussex, a rich county, could surely solve without any help that I could give. But drilling for oil was altogether different. For if Ashdown Forest, with so much in its favour, was unable to resist, then nowhere in England was safe. If a battle had to be fought to prove that there were at least *some* places where what lay above the ground was of greater value than what might lie beneath, then here was the place to fight it. Nor was that quite all. How many are the requests for help that come through our letter box! How worthy they are! And how determined are we to fill in that form and enclose our cheque! But somehow we don't, and in the end the form gets lost and we console ourselves with the thought that one small voice, one small cheque would not really have made much of a difference. But here, with me, for the first time, it *could* be different. To my own small voice could be added, if I wished it, the infinitely louder voice of a teddy bear. And it is perhaps an indication of how strongly I felt that, although I have spent sixty years of my life trying to escape from Pooh Bear, here I was positively inviting his help. BP versus PB. How I relished the contest!

I met Barbara Willard both in 1978 and in 1987. On the first occasion I had come down to discuss the memorial with Leslie Hope who was to carry out the work, and Miss Willard lived just next door. The second occasion was at that press conference. But in a sense I had known her before then, through her books. For a while she was writing them and I was selling them. She has made a name for herself—a very considerable name—as a children's novelist. And it is precisely because she is a novelist rather than an historian that her history (one could almost call it a biography) of Ashdown Forest is so very readable. She brings the Forest alive and we share its many emotions. We laugh when it laughs. We suffer when it suffers. And in one place we are near to tears.

I suppose that nomads like being nomads, wandering from place to place. But I am not a nomad. I like putting down roots and feeling that I belong to where I am; and this makes me feel immensely superior to the person who only arrived a year or two ago. I have lived in Devon now for thirty seven years, which makes me superior to quite a lot of my neighbours. But I was not born in Devon. I was born in London, and this, I suppose, makes me a Londoner, something I have always felt rather ashamed of. So when, in 1924, we moved—half-moved—to Sussex, I was quick to put down new roots. Here, among fields and woods and muddy lanes, was where I really belonged. And I considered myself a Sussex man (or is it a man of Sussex?) until just after the war, even though, what with school and army, I had really spent so little of my life there.

This makes me jealous of Barbara Willard. She is so *totally* Sussex. It is not just that she was born there. Both her parents were born there too and both sets of grandparents lived and worked in Sussex. Although Brighton was her first home, she was, in those faraway days, within easy walking distance of the South Downs, and names like Truleigh, Duncton, Firle, Caburn, Blackcap, Balmer Down and Plumpton Plain thrilled in her blood as they had thrilled in her grandfather's. But sadly, with the end of the war, the South Downs began to change. Sheep and shepherd vanished and houses took their place. In 1956 she fled from Kingston under the Downs beyond Lewes—having survived years of London-dwelling—to seek solitude elsewhere. It must have been a wrench after so many years; but she took with her one of the two great loves she had inherited from her grandfather—a love for Sussex (the other was a love for Shakespeare). Where better place could she have found to put down new roots than the very edge of Ashdown Forest? She had visited it as a child. Now she began to see it properly and to understand it and love it as deeply as once she had loved her Downs. As the years went by and as her Mantlemass books were written, so she became more and more enmeshed in Ashdown affairs. She joined the Board of Conservators at the time of the 1974 Act and stayed for ten years. For a long time she had resisted writing openly about the Forest (she had never named it in her books), but eventually she became tantalised by the realisation of how little most people knew about what they were looking at. And what with that and the various recent disasters and their attendant publicity, coupled with the fact that very little had been written about Ashdown since the early 1960's, she felt that the time had come, both for her and for the Forest, to put this right. The resulting book has taken her two years of researching and writing, and, as she tells me, 'I doubt if I have ever enjoyed writing as much.'

When a highly skilled and greatly admired professional author says this, there can be little doubt that her readers will be sharing her pleasure.

Christopher Milne
Devon October 1988

Author's Apology

The tale of Ashdown Forest is so long and so crammed that it cannot all be told in one modest volume; in fact, to write adequately about the place may well be an impossibility. What follows here can only be a digest and it was not easy to select from such seductive material. I have probably left out almost any reader's favourite anecdote or aspect of the Forest, and for that I offer my apology.

Every forest in the land has its history of origin, custom and tradition; and of those influences, gathering with time, which have too often been allowed to whittle and chip at both custom and legend. Here on Ashdown we may thank two circumstances for what we so happily retain. We thank the roistering royalty of the 14th century for realising that the thrust of land clearance could destroy their favourite sport— for where might the game shelter when ploughed acres replaced deep woodland? And we thank those *customary tenants*, latter called, as now, *commoners*, for their stubborn insistence on their ancient rights of grazing and *estover*, which was strong enough to retain the *Right of Common* against all threats. That Right still stands, and because of it so also does Ashdown Forest.

A tale that stretches over six hundred years needs a host of talents to do it justice. For this reason, hoping to avoid an impression of having 'mugged up' the specialist subjects, I have begged, and most generously been given, the help of various experts, for all of whom the Forest is a strong and living entity; their essays appear among the *Appendices*. A great many people have helped with the production of this book—some have recommended sources, others produced personal recollections and anecdotes. I cannot possibly name them all and at first I thought it would be better to mention none for fear of some shaming omission. Gratitude, however, must be allowed to surface. For the honour of the Administration, I thank in the first place John Nicolls, Forest Superintendent and Clerk to the Conservators, who allowed me the run of the Forest archives; his lieutenant, Janet Ruxton, forever turning up bits of invaluable interior knowledge; and the Rangers for their general interest and their generous help over particulars—some of those particulars include photographs for the illustration of this book.

I thank two good friends, Anne Sheldrick, Chairman of the Board of Conservators, and Margaret Tebbutt, for reading and correcting an idiosyncratically typed manuscript; and D. M. Meades, Brian Herbert, John Gent, Chris Marrable for those technical essays which needed expert handling. I thank Alan Morriss for letting me into the past of Pippingford. Personal records of Forest life come from Fred Kirby of Nutley, whose father, also, is remembered here; Bill Coleman of Fairwarp; and Barnett Field and his sister, who recall their time at Ashdown Park Memorial school. And I thank Frances Howell for taking on the nail-biting job of preparing the Index. Does any author thank the publisher in these circumstances? If not, then let me be the first. Not every forest-dwelling writer is fortunate enough to have a forest-dwelling publisher.

If there are still omissions here, may I be forgiven.

Apart from the collected papers and the Minute books of the Board of Conservators, practically every volume of the Sussex Archeological Collections offers up some item of information about Ashdown Forest; fascinating detail, too, may be combed from parish guides and handbooks. Gathering these scattered pieces has been rather like collecting for some charity, and I hope I may have done at least a little justice to an exceedingly worthy cause; indeed a noble cause. Whatever else, *The Forest* has been compiled not only from records and recollections but from years of deep and daily-increasing affection. Personal reactions to change in such a place are bound at times to be regretful and some suggestion of nostalgia is probably unavoidable. This is no lament, however, but a recorded thanksgiving that such a place as Ashdown Forest still exists in a countryside increasingly harried and cramped.

It is perhaps foolhardy for a writer of fiction over fifty-odd years to attempt such a tale as this one. Inevitably, speculation was forever twitching and nudging. I have honestly resisted it—or if I have allowed myself to be mildly tempted I have always added a warning *perhaps*. Fiction is a lot easier to manage than fact. In a clash of imagined characters there are always ways of escape. In retailing the recorded past there can be none.

B. W.
Nutley *October 1988*

CHAPTER ONE

Monday

Beyond the garden gate the Forest begins. It fans out immediately over six thousand-odd acres of heath and scrub and woodland. These acres are all that is left in the Sussex Weald of that great forest said to have stretched a hundred miles from east to west, thirty miles from south to north. According to legend, a squirrel might then travel from tree to tree over three counties without ever touching down. A traveller in present time heading west, perhaps with the Hampshire forest in mind, may come upon a remnant or two of ancient woodland—Worth Forest, St Leonard's Forest are two such Sussex survivors. These, except for some stretches of defiant common, are privately managed by now. A royal whim in the 13th century preserved what is today the Sussex forest of Ashdown by enclosing it for a hunting ground. The outline that was drawn then remains pretty well the same as the outline drawn by modern map makers. Within that outline much has changed but much, almost miraculously, remains. Above all else, the Right of Common.

The maintenance of this ancient custom, the dominant force over all this Forest during six centuries, has been the unbroken bond between past and present. We can thank a distant king for what might be called an early act of conservation, even if for the wrong reason according to modern opinion, but throughout the accumulating years the commoners of Ashdown Forest have developed a pig-headed power that has prevented total disaster more than once. There are few signs that the power has been relinquished, though its direction has inevitably changed. In the earliest Forest records, commoners are called *customers*, or *customary tenants*. Inheritors of long custom they most certainly were and the custom is preserved by their descendants. It takes a crisis to bring it to fruition in these somewhat quieter days, but crises loom pretty often.

When I was a child I picnicked with cousins on Ashdown Forest; then I lost it for years. A holiday in a village nearby and the place swam back easily and strongly. A later picnic, on the final frail edge of war's beginning, is remembered as the last time my young brother and I walked together in the countryside. Now I have no need to picnic, unless for a change of view, for I have lived with the Forest at my gate for something over thirty years. It is beyond every window and has come to surround my everyday life as it surrounds the garden—to which it contributes honeysuckle, bluebell, dog rose, wood anemone and, less welcome, bracken and birch seedling. It supplies birds in variety though not in such variety as once it did; squirrels but no longer hedgehogs; and badgers, delightful but messy. And, as at the outset when the great seal was set on the Forest's future, there are deer.

Once there was a half-gate at the foot of the lane, that could be closed to keep cattle contained, and this was confirmed by a second such gate at the end of the neighbour lane. This is the waste edge of the Forest, a little outside the actual pale. Cattle are not at this time grazed on the Forest, though they might well come again; sheep have been pretty well withdrawn over the last year or two, probably only temporarily. In thirty years the Forest has changed in many ways. Living on the Forest has changed, too. Below this house, sharing the same track which led once to a small farm, there was in the 'fifties one car in use and that only at weekends. Nine or ten now shuttle up and down; reason, I fear, for the disappearance of hedgehogs. It is hard to believe that petrol was in short supply thirty years ago and all traffic round and about the Forest, even on the main London road, delightfully gentle. A dog prone to wandering could visit chosen friends without necessarily being slaughtered . . .

Love of place, which seems to develop mostly in later life, may hold less actual anguish than love of person, but it is painfully possessive. Unavoidable sharing calls for a generosity which the place-person often finds hard to encompass. The pressures are great on such a place as this Forest, a bare fifty miles from London, a posting-stage on the way to the coast. It can be a struggle to accept the inevitability of what seems invasion. Sometimes I feel like declaring myself—why not one of those rear-window stickers: *I love Ashdown Forest?* There is really no need. The sticker is invisible, but a lot of people know it might just as well be there.

At any season I find the Forest best of all on a Monday morning, for the totally unworthy reason that it seems to have been given back. The visiting strangers have gone home. Their purpose was no more malign than to enjoy themselves, and encourage the children to enjoy themselves, in the simplest possible way. A walk in the country! What less harmful? Only the meanest spirit could think otherwise. How merrily on a summer Sunday the assorted vehicles come spinning into the car parks, doors bursting open almost before the wheels are still, children tumbling out, dogs running in wild delighted circles, mums and dads organising—he a bit bossy, she wondering if she remembered to put knives into the picnic basket . . .

They arrive early and depart late in summer time. Gradually, though, the light changes, the temperature drops, the noise is all of car doors slamming, engines starting. Then a bit of grousing, weary young quarrels—'You did it!' 'It was your fault!'—wheels spitting in a rather too determined way on the gravelly surface of the car park. Soon of the cars remaining the owners may be seen at a distance, hurrying their return to base which must carry them to the start of a new week. The sky holds a hint of lemon, as though even at the height of summer frost reserves some right. Two cars remain . . . One

. . . Then the place is clear. The rooks and magpies fly in and
pick about for prizes; the jays watch warily from litter box
lids where squirrels will take their place. And when it is
totally twilight, though before the lovers whose cars slide in
with quite a different air, the rabbits arrive. Then deer. The
scuttling rabbits, the poised yet wary deer make nonsense of
all earlier occupiers . . .

When the tide of visitors washes back and Monday
morning offers its replacement of solitude, the mood for those
of us so fortunate as to call this place home is bound to be a
heady one. If time, weather and fatigue could be controlled
there need never be two days together when the same ground
is covered. Six thousand and a few acres may make a modest
forest, but they yield unending profit to any walker, particularly the inquisitive walker. The days when I have been
prevented from stepping out onto the Forest would make a
pretty small muster over the years, but there are still places I
do not properly know. Vistas are mostly very grand, remote
and unobtainable, but there is no lack of smaller matters and
little difficulty in adjusting from the immense to the minutely
particular. The argument over the felling of a respected tree
easily gives way to curiosity over the appearance of some
non-indigenous plant—will it colonise to confuse future
botanists? Topsoil brought in to repair a track can set up
many anomalies. One year there was a mass of early crocus in
bewildered clumps, and in the same summer two handsome
roots of *alchemilla mollis* appeared unsuitably on one of the
riding tracks. These probably arrived in some load of garden
rubbish—masses of it gets dumped perpetually, weeds, grass
clippings, rose prunings, dead leaves. Daffodils, too, appear
frequently near car parks, not exactly garden escapees but
garden rejects. Since the long years of propaganda have at last
stopped people grabbing at every flower growing in the wild,
the stranger-daffodils are able to settle down and multiply.
Unpampered, living rough, they decline in size and splendour, growing a little pale, too, each year until, after several

springs, they look almost genuine, almost what daffodils should be . . .

In the quiet of Monday morning the Forest is like some vast room whose windows have been flung wide. If there is a problem it is merely that one of choice—which outlook, which best loved tree-line or twist of running water? From the high ground the views are of surrounding hills, the south downs, the Surrey hills—or there is that one spot where you may rotate to identify four counties. I would always favour the southern aspect, probably because I was there before I was here. It is best on a day with big clouds, none darker than a mild grey, the rest blinding white and gently bowling across the sun. Against such a background the downs are sharp and clear though without that sharpness that brings them close and foretells rain. Heads can be counted from Wilmington to Firle, by Blackcap, by Ditchling Beacon to Truleigh, Chanctonbury, Cissbury. On certain rare October evenings when the light is changing it is possible to see still further west—though I may have been indulging myself once when I imagined Duncton.

That is a rare and exalting light, while on a chosen Monday morning in summer there is a workaday light. The wind at that season is probably a little south of south-west, soft on the cheek, comfortable. It carries, or seems to carry, a reminder of the sea. That may be the scent of bracken, which has a slightly briney tang to it. At this season it spreads such a dense green sea of its own that the smaller paths, those that are little more than deer runs, are pretty well swallowed. Any walker who knows them can just about push through waist high, more than waist high. The thought of adders, however, brings caution to the native. Leave them alone and they slip smoothly on their way; but in a brackeny situation it is too easy to step on the creatures, or for the dog to step on them, and they will not accept rough treatment without retaliation.

Summer, even on the acclaimed Monday morning, is by no means the best season for the Forest. Autumn cannot fail to offer more than any other time. Spring is just spring, exhuberant, delicate and a bit silly, following the inevitable pattern, an infinity of subtly differing greens, bluebell, wood anemone—few primroses here. When the bracken first breaks through it has some charm, acres of mock asparagus far removed from that later sea, so heavy and unvaried, so downright boring. The initial hint of better things comes after the orchids, the first-footer among the heathers, delicately pink and immensely welcome. There is a fractional pause, then, almost a change of light. The purple heathers take up the theme, with *erica tetralix*, the close-leaved heath, surely the winner for its exhuberant colour and dark sharp leaf. The less well coloured ling then takes over, swamping all. Sheets of the stuff are spread like tented cloth. As if infected by the basic dye, the bracken begins to turn. When this happens it is difficult to understand why one has ever supposed it a mere invader. It complements all, not least the marsh gentian which is the Forest's pride. Impossible, when bracken is at the peak of its colour, to have too much of it—or so many of us claim. It is not only autumn, either,that gives it so long a splendour—wet winter restores colour to the battered rows and they glow again.

But from February onwards the ground is covered not only with dried up humps of bleached and battered brakes, but with dead deer-grass, tattered sedge-grass. The wind blows these strands in dusty whirls, piling them against bushes of skeleton gorse and broom, laying a fuse which needs only a touch of flame to rush forward and consume acres.

In earlier times, the ground was burnt off to improve grazing—it was an acknowledged practice of the commoners, though not one, I believe, that ever had any outright official sanction. This purposeful firing had developed, by the time I came to know the area, into more or less a local sport. The little lads set about it when they came out of school, their dads on leaving the pub at closing time. There are several traditional ways of organising the business. The most satisfactory for the incendiary is to set a fuse and be away to some nearby height to enjoy the results from the first moment of rising smoke. When a knot of boys and men stand together to watch as the flames sweep forward, it is not impossible to recognise a fire-raiser by the self-satisfied glances he throws around the rest of the group. He probably left a stump of candle burning in a jam jar half filled with paraffin—the classic method.

The children, in the days when I learnt to sniff the very first hint of smoke, were less sophisticated but very determined, and a local storekeeper might or might not oppose a ten-year-old's demand for a dozen boxes of matches. The first time I looked out and saw a forest fire with a number of young attendants, I telephoned the local police sergeant, expecting him to take some action, however mild.

'There are quite a lot of boys down there. I can see them deliberately spreading the fire.'

'Oh no, madam. Those are mice. We've a lot of mice with matchboxes in these parts.'

This was the moment at which I realised that living on Ashdown Forest was likely to be very different from living in a quiet village, beautifully and placidly set under the downs near Lewes. And I remembered a neighbour of those days exclaiming in horror when he heard of the proposed move— 'You can't go there! The Forest is full of savages!' A bit extreme, no doubt, but at that moment as the telephone clicked into silence and the flames began to race up the bank side, I wondered if he could be right.

The fire-brigade could of course be summoned. Then as now the service depended to some extent on volunteers and members were summoned to the station by the wailing of an old air-raid siren. By the time they had either wrenched themselves from their beds or laid down whatever tools they were wielding, got to the station, mounted the tender, clapped on their helmets and driven bell-ringing to the scene, the fire had very often been put out by sweating neighbours employing beaters in great variety—brooms, rakes, sacks. This household ruined numberless besoms in the cause; they cost about two shillings each in those days. One year I enlisted a number of nearby children as fire-fighters. When they saw smoke or heard the siren they were to come pounding down the lane and snatch up a broom from the row we kept by the garage doors. But they enjoyed it too much. It became apparent that one could very easily light a fire to ensure the rest the fun of putting it out. Not a doubt that it was fun, not least to see the faces of the firemen as they arrived too late. To make the turn-out worth while they sometimes decided things would be safer if they burnt off a bit more—which was when the joke ended . . . One year the malice of the fire-raisers was such that it began to seem impossible to continue living on the Forest. Then gradually things improved, though there can be no positive cure in an area that invites incendiaries.

There can be black Mondays, therefore, as well as those others. Sunday fires are often the result of nothing more sinister than a dropped cigarette, since they happen most often in that spring weather when the forest floor is littered as with straw purposely spread. In summers of long drought, of course, the Forest is much at risk. Then the warning notices go up along the roadsides, in the car parks. But the words—fire, danger, hazard—blurr into commonplace far too quickly. One excessive summer the word was changed to *peril. Fire Peril,* or *Peril from Fire,* I forget which. The public response to the word seemed to be a casual 'What's that, then?' as they continued to use the forbidden, indeed the perilous, picnic-stoves. One such, overturned by wretched accident on a day of high gusty wind, rushed over many hundred acres, leaping roads so that the traffic had to be diverted.

Fire is beautiful as well as cruel and, particularly at night, fire is dazzlingly exciting. In those spring fires the flame is blown from mound to dead mound, creating long furrows.

Those brittle strands of sedge-grass, dipping themselves in flame, then spiral in the heat's self-perpetuating draught and are carried like tapers, scattering fragments, to ignite where they fall. Utter desolation follows. The birds are gone. The squirrels and the foxes are charred bones. The black ground retains its heat for many hours and it is not unusual to see wretched mice dragging their scorched feet and bellies towards safety seldom found in time. Once, when fire got into tall trees, an owl swooped and cried above its nest until, overcome, it dropped into the blaze. And once I saw a cock pheasant running up and down, up and down, in a fruitless search for its vanished nest.

Between the true fires of autumn and the false fires of early spring, the Forest winter holds horrors and delights. Snow is a bonus, not merely for its good looks but as a plate for a million prints—of mice and other small mammals and the slinking trail of foxes, of small birds and large, from big-footed crows and jays to the tripod print of the woodpecker; and so to neat rabbits, clear-stepping deer. The identification of deer slots is a skill on its own, they are so varied by age and kind. Then there is the delight of bright sun melting tree-snow into icicles which ring faintly as a breeze takes them. After a few weeks of handsome winter, however, come the bitter casualties, starved birds feebly moving, rising with difficulty; wood pigeons frozen to high branches; a fishing heron trapped by ice. The sun at midday lasts too briefly to help any of these victims. Only the release of the ground can offer any hope. When at such times a slow thaw frees detached patches of ground they are quickly crowded and full of quarrelling. They are like soup kitchens for the needy but, as in other contexts, help comes too late for many. One fierce winter years ago the village was cut off for a time. We walked on free and silent feet feeling as though we had somehow escaped the world.

There come also in a Forest winter days so bleak they are probably best forgotten. The chill and the wet take all colour from sky and ground, the place exists without strength to do otherwise. Such moments are so vile they are endured only by a few connoisseurs; they are collector's pieces . . . And so, too, may be days when mere mist becomes fog and the most familiar trees seem strangers, often with a hint of threat in their blurred outlines. The absolute stillness seems a challenge. The calm is curiously alarming and the Forest itself appears as a vast stage obscured by gauzes that may or may not part on a solution, a climax to unseen action. I know of people, born in this place, attached to it through several generations, who do not care to walk on the Forest even in good weather. What they fear they could never define, but there are certainly days when their anxiety is an easily transferred infection, for some kind of baleful magic is abroad.

Night time offers an altogether different impression, a far more subtle sensation—and not simply because it is dark instead of light. The beauty of summer nights of full moon may be enjoyed in a million places—the Forest surely cannot claim any priority. Only as one stands at the gate, or by an open window, or moves quietly down the track to where the Forest expands as though to no horizon, familiarity, affection, ensures that the enchantment appears unlike any other. In the dark the Forest is taken over by those who know it best, whose right is supreme. The deer move swiftly, heard only when their fine hooves tap on hard ground, or when they push through undergrowth which does little more than sigh as it closes behind them. Fox or vixen cry out after their own seasonal custom, some far and faint, some startlingly near. Hot summer brings out the nightjars, though not as many, I think, as once were. So many insects to whirr or whine, frogs in converse, at one time hedgehogs grunting on the way; sometimes badger joining in. There are at present few nightingales and the glow-worms have shifted from beyond the gate, where they used to line the path, but they are still about. Immediately outside the house in dark and half- dark, bats once skimmed and swooped; these have not appeared here for some time. But there is still a huge variety of moths . . .

These are split-second images of the Forest, its mere physical presence; this is what anyone can see and hear, even if not always with wide-open eyes and ears. There is another Ashdown, locked away as the past must in some manner always be. The place's history, once released, colours and gives contour to all the rest. Six centuries of variable turmoil, a tale of grandeur, conflict and long-lasting strife which reached its official climax a hundred years ago and should surely then have been stilled. But struggle seems bound up in the composition of the soil. Authority is likely to be slyly dealt with by stubborn men and so it has been here. The commoners were accustomed to niggle and rebel even against such as John of Gaunt, or the powerful Sackville family in any one of its many guises in these parts. They still rebel, though the voice has most often dwindled to a 20th century grouse. Ironically, it is the Board of Conservators, set up a century ago 'to protect the Rights of the Commoners', which now appears in the role of tyrant when a tyrant is felt to be needed.

CHAPTER TWO

Kings and Consorts

However the tale of Ashdown Forest may be told it is bound to be a story of conflict. The protagonists remained the same officially until that day in the 1880s when a law suit, sharp and sour with accumulated acrimony, set a seal on the past and pushed the Forest into its future. This was to be the healing of old wounds, the culmination of those six centuries of quarrel between the Lord of the Manor and the commoners. The Lord held from the King until such time as land became democratised; the commoners, or *customary tenants,* had 'by custom' certain grazing and other rights with set limits strictly maintained; there was a right to *estovers,* that is the right to take certain sorts of wood for fuel and repairs to land used commonally. It is uncertain when these rights were instituted, but they certainly trace back to William the Conqueror; reasonably enough, since the word *estover* comes from Norman French. It could, though, have been a contemporary name given to a more ancient custom.

At the time of the court case which eventually laid down in modern terms the rights of Lord and commoner, two great volumes of documents connected with the past of Ashdown were assembled, from a far larger collection, to be used as evidence by the commoners' lawyers. Volume I. takes us from 1297, the last years of Edward I's reign, to William & Mary in 1693. Volume II. carries the tale into the 1880s. The case turned on a further commoners' right, which was to cut *litter*—mostly bracken—which was used extensively for over-wintering stock, since it was a great deal cheaper than straw.

This right had caused trouble for years, and though the commoners had long been confirmed in their right to cut as estovers birch, alder and willow, and to graze their beasts according to acreage, the Lord of the Manor in the 1880s asserted that he alone was entitled to the Forest litter. Low growing herbage, it was claimed for him in Court, could only be taken by 'bite of mouth', or grazing.

When Volume I. of the Ashdown Forest documents is opened, that case is the best part of six hundred years ahead. Many matters concerning the area go back yet another century, and broader issues at least to the Romans. Practically every page of the carefully collated documents offers some clue to events not merely long past but trailing their peculiarities into the present. Known as the *Raper Papers*, after the solicitor who acted for the commoners and combed his evidence from the fuller source, they are a model of selective skill and make totally absorbing reading.

Before plunging into these Forest papers, certain practicalities had better be looked at—as for example:

'The first thing to be said about Ashdown Forest,' states a contemporary writer on Sussex, 'is that it is not a forest at all.'

Many might consider this apt, since Ashdown features more heath than woodland. Interpretation of the word *forest* has been much discussed by experts, particularly over recent years. First, they say, we are to consider the vast, blanketing forests of the distant past, how they were rolled back gradually by the increasing thrust of cultivation. In this context, it is considered, the word came to apply to the ground itself, the out-of-doors. Peter Brandon, in his book, *The Sussex Landscape*, favours the theory that the word is derived not from *foresta* but from *foris*—meaning land outside the common law, free of man's intervention, unploughed; a place of trees, certainly, but less and less so as building called for felling and the open countryside with fields and farms came into being. It is well to recall that Dartmoor is designated a forest. There it is on the ordnance map, *Dartmoor*

Forest. Opinion is at liberty to follow dictionary definitions, which quarrel and overlap. *An extensive area of land covered with trees* will be the most popular choice. R. M. Lockley, in his editing of *The Natural History of Selborne,* uses 'an uncultivated waste, often without trees'. *A large unenclosed area of wasteland* is a variant that comes near to the present learned concensus. *Unenclosed woodland district kept for hunting and usually owned by sovereign. An unenclosed royal hunting ground*—these last better define what we know of Ashdown Forest, but it still has factors and features that make it unique among forests, and its past is very much its own.

'The forest' features in a thousand ancient tales. 'Once upon a time, on the edge of the forest . . .' It is always *the* forest, as much an accepted part of the natural world as *the* sea, *the* mountains. How many noble knights, riding from castle or city on their quest for love and fortune 'come to the forest'. It is a place by implication strange and dangerous, concealing skulking beasts and violent men; the end of civilisation.

When the Romans annexed Britain they must have had a hard time of it clearing forest as they marched. When Ashdown was a part of the much larger forest they called Anderida, they pushed through their great road from London to Lewes, carrying it over high ground by what is now Duddleswell. The foundations of this road were laid in many places with slag and cinder from ancient iron workings; later, the colonisers worked the iron on their own account, notably at the suitably named Oldlands, by Heron's Ghyll. Some years ago, firebreaks were ploughed over various parts of the Forest; heavy rains then washed out fragments of furnace waste that had been disturbed by the plough. My own memory of this is very keen because it came at a moment when the place finally took me over. I had only just begun to learn about the great local iron industry of the 15th, 16th and 17th centuries. There lay these recognisable fragments, waiting to be harvested by initiates. Picking up the fragments, balancing them on my palm, I was the one who was initiated.

These were the years, the early 1970s, when the public came increasingly to visit the Forest. The administration felt a need to assist in their enjoyment of the place but also to deal with suddenly proliferating motor cars. One thing they set about was a parking area near the only easily observed strip of the Roman road, which they enclosed within a neat paling. A map, engraved on metal, mounted in a solid stone block of the local stone and showing the course of the road, was duly installed. Although this inovation caused many qualms, it is a job well done and tells a great deal to anyone interested enough to take a look at it.

That small stretch of the Roman road, which anyone can find who wants to, is placed ideally for absorbing the true smell of the Forest. The ground drops on the westward side into a deep well-watered ghyll, then rises to obscure the south save for a long vista carrying to the furthest line of the downs. In the right conditions, right weather, right time of day—which should be early or late—this site is almost absurdly evocative. The effect is not entirely transcendental, however, since it depends on what one wishes to believe may lie on the other side of the road—still called the High Road. During the last war a tract of land running from the nearby crossroads was given over to the government for a radio station. The place was constructed underground and legend has it that its builders, or excavators, uncovered a Roman posting station which, in the urgency of the time, had to be covered and forgotten. There is absolutely no shadow of evidence that this ever happened. The fact remains that the nearby crossing is ancient, that the nearest farm was called Streeters, easily 'the farm on the Street'—a name unfortunately now lost by translation into one more mundane, a sad break of continuity.

The BBC's World Service operated from these quarters for many years. They had a cluster—or forest—of pylons and when they were still upstanding it was an amusing exercise to

pause down in the bottom where the water drops over a great
stone block, and discover that their siting was so exact that
they could be lined up one behind the other to appear as a
single. A lot of us believed that when the radio people pulled
out, the ground would revert to the Forest. Now we know it
was requisitioned outright and today has a different function.
You can stand up there when no one is about and the omens
are right and surely hear something other than remembered
call-signs. Perhaps this Anderida of the Romans is particularly
equipped to lure the fanciful. 'It is not to be proved,' said
Daniel Defoe of Ramsgate's claims to Roman origin, 'either
by them or anyone else; and is of so little concern to us that
it matters nothing.' Indifference in such an inquisitive writer
seems almost offensive, but perhaps we are becoming over-
concerned to record the past, to nag away until we suppose
we understand.

Three hundred years after the Romans withdrew,
Ashdown, by then called Andredswald, appears in the
writings of the Venerable Bede. From his cell in the
monastery at Jarrow he must have sent scouts in every
direction collecting information and impressions, which were
then woven into the dense texture of his great book *A History
of the English Church & People*. The work was concluded in 731
A.D., and it is obtainable in paperback well over a thousand
years later. The wealden forest is described by Bede as 'thick
and inaccessible', the haunt of deer and fox and badger, the
lingering wolf and the wild boar. Which is the place to note,
perhaps, that Woolpack Farm near Fletching is reputed to
have been originally Wolfpack . . . Centuries after Bede,
Henry VIII is known to have hunted the boar within easy
reach of London—perhaps on Ashdown? Certainly he was
among the monarchs who sported here, though perhaps not
merely in pursuit of deer or boar; romantic conclusions are
often drawn from the fact that Sir Thomas Boleyn held high
forest office at the appropriate time . . .

The forest still covered a vast area, stretching to Pevensey, as late as the reign of Edward I. At that time it is noted as part of the Honor of Aquila, Ralph de Saurel is its Keeper and it is called the Forest of Esshedon. Already the commoners were making themselves known to the administration. At that time the *Master Keeping the Forest* was paid 4d a day for 'himself, his man and his horse'. Humble foresters in his employ, cutting wood for palings, erecting fences, digging ditches were paid 1d. There were of course deer to be poached, wood over and above the allowance to be secretly cut and carried—one man is accused of purloining 'ten backes burden of wood'. There are no records that I have found of fearsome punishment at this time, perhaps they are so obvious that they are not noted down; the administration would have been very far from a brief period in the 19th century, when it was agreed that if a man admitted his offence and said he was sorry, honour would be satisfied. Quarrels over wood, whether wind fallen, branch fallen or root fallen, appear endlessly recorded over the centuries. The names of the culprits being so often the same as local names today, I feel that I am at the trial of neighbours.

The documents of the Ashdown Forest archive that make up the two volumes dealt with here, are by now, happily for this writer, translated where necessary and have recently been indexed—an exacting task. They are a mine of information for any ardent local historian and any such may study them and the originals from which they are culled, on application to the Information Centre by Broadstone on the Ridge road, or at the Records Office in Lewes. The language is a bonus and the spelling worth enjoying—as in John Sac Kerville and other variants. The granting of favours is set out with courteous pomp and even stern rebukes have grace. Here is an extract from a patent roll of 1350, issued over the seal of Edward III:

'The King to all to whom etc. Greeting. Know ye that whereas Philippa Queen of England dearest consort by her

letters patent lately granted to our beloved Thomas son and
heir of John de Berkhame and to William Fitz(h)ide and the
heirs of the same William ten loads . . . of a suitable
brushwood to the Manor of Berkhame near and convenient
each year for the term of the life of our same consort within
the Forest of Asshedown in the County of Sussex to be taken
and carried by view and livery of the Keeper . . . of the
Forest whenever the said Thomas and William shall
choose . . . '

   The instruction continues with rights of free ingress and
egress to and from the said Forest. It grants common right of
pasture for 13 cows and 1 bull through the whole year
'wheresoever with their issue they shall suck'. This mention
of the whole year suggests that the custom of the *fence month,*
when does were dropping and suckling their fawns may have
been introduced some time later—for during that month all
other animals were excluded from grazing. Thirty hogs were
added to the Berkhame bounty, with an assurance for the
future even after the royal consort 'shall come to the end of
her life.' Queen Philippa held the Manor of East Grinstead.
Over the years names change and presumably Barkham
Manor, which stands by Grisling Common, off the Newick
road, is today's Berkhame.
   'Witness the King at Westminster,' this order concludes,
'on the 20th day of October. By writ of Privy Seal.'
   Today, when as a commoner I seek to cut wood, I
telephone the office . . .
   Asshedown or Eshdon or Esshesdown, the variations are
more or less endless, still retained at this time its old form,
many thousands of acres encompassing several parishes. But
what was to become the core of the place may have seen most
of the royal hunting, for it was in the parish of Maresfield that
Edward II built himself what is variously described as a
palace, a castle or a hunting lodge. To narrow the issue we
have a letter headed 'from the Palace at Notlye'. The actual

location of the long vanished building has never been established, though experts over the years have claimed that it was here or it was there. There still exists, though in altered form by now, a property that has been claimed as the farm that supplied the royal holiday home, and an antiquarian clergyman in 1902 declared that the ruins of 'the castle' were there for all to see in a neighbouring wood. The adjacent ground is high and unusually flat, so flat that in war time it was used as a landing strip after clearing and levelling by Canadian troops. Perhaps matters might be the same here as are claimed for the site by Duddleswell cross roads; perhaps there were discoveries during hasty preparations which the urgency of the moment put out of bounds to the curious

Between felling and ploughing in those early days, the King's game must have been hard pressed, retreating of necessity, the deer increasingly a menace to crops, descending by moonlight on nearby villages and appearing not the least picturesque to small and struggling farming men—though they could kill them on their own ground without facing charges of poaching, so the situation cannot have been entirely disastrous. Then came that early act of conservation, though it was certainly without our own specialised good intent. The King decreed the enclosure of 13,000 acres of the vaster forest to be designated a *Royal Chace*. It touched on the parishes of Maresfield, Hartfield, Withyham and Buxted, portions of each being within the designated pale. As the work went into operation there was gradually drawn that curiously shaped entity which we see on our maps still. Gates and hatches were eventually sited and the few survivors, though now only names, are names we use daily—Chuck Hatch, Greenwood Gate, Poundgate, Plawhatch . . . From that time forward the name Ashdown was applied only to the enclosed royal acres. The rest of the far wider external forest was gradually eaten away by the demands of later ages and the various commons that remained outside the pale, Horney Common, St John's Common, Stumblewood Common are examples, lost their identity as their use declined, as they became merged with remnants of manorial waste.

It was only a few years after claiming and organising his royal chace that the King granted Ashdown to his third son, John of Gaunt, named for his birthplace, Ghent in Belgium. It was a gift that may not have been willingly received, a gift mis-named since it had to be paid for. There may have been some conflict over this arbitrary change of ownership but it does not emerge whether father or son considered himself the gainer. Did John, Duke of Lancaster, long for a tidy little hunting place within easy reach of London, or did King Edward see the Earldom of Richmond as a convenient base from which to keep an eye on the turbulent North—for it was the Earldom which John was to give in exchange for Ashdown. According to the proclamation and the deed of gift, 'the said John . . . like a grateful son preferring his Father's pleasure and convenience of the Kingdom of England to his own private advantage' relinquished the earldom 'of his own pure will and free accord'. John promptly made his mark by re-naming Ashdown—it became Lancaster Great Park and so remained in popular usage for nearly three hundred years, though it was still referred to as Ashdown *or* Lancaster Great Park in official documents. For many years these came from the Savoy Palace, the Duke's London residence, and were so stamped. 'Given at the Savoy,' is written alongside the seal . . .

The change of ownership led to inevitable problems. There appears no positive date for the setting up of the pale—its physical entity, that is, with ditch and bank, fence and gates and hatches. Until this actual barrier was raised, those gentry accustomed to enjoying the area as a hunting ground continued their pursuits. But under the new lordship there were sure to be new rules; for one thing taxes in the area rose by £15 a year. Even less convenient was the fact that in becoming Lancaster Great Park, Ashdown was no longer open to all comers. Authority had stepped in and such as the

Earl of Arundel, based at his castle in Lewes, found little to please in the new regime. But it was Sir Edward Dallingridge—or Dalyngrudge or Dalyngridg, or indeed any other conceivable spelling—who prepared to fight the new order. In the feudal tradition, Dallingridge was a retainer of Arundel as well as being attached to other noble families, such as the Despensers. He was also quite a politician—which he had proved at the time of Wat Tyler's peasant revolt against Richard II's imposition of a poll tax. Sir Edward's daughter Margaret married a Sackville—Bolebroke in Hartfield, some of which still stands, was one of his properties, as was Bodiam Castle. He was a rich and vigorous man and through him an organised opposition to Gaunt and all his followers came into operation. Not only was the Forest mysteriously and extensively fired, but Dallingridge drove away stock from land of Gaunt's in Fletching—4 cows, 6 oxen, 30 sheep. He or his followers broke into courts being held by Gaunt's stewards, snatching away their papers of commission and in one case burning them under the unfortunate steward's very nose. A scholarly, if perhaps slightly muted, exposition of Sir Edward Dallingridge's buccaneering behaviour by Simon Walker of All Souls, Oxford, can be read in Volume 121 of the *Sussex Archeological Collections*.

Gaunt's handling of the affair was masterly. In the accepted poacher-gamekeeper tradition, he appointed Sir Edward Master Forester. Unfortunately, this skilful move misfired. Dallingridge took the job to be one that provided license for all his friends to hunt whenever and wherever they pleased within the pale. Unsurprisingly, Gaunt sacked him. In due course, Sir Edward Dallingridge was brought to trial. He made the most of the situation, striding into the court room, flinging down his gauntlet in accepted chivalric tradition and demanding to meet his accuser in single combat . . . He was fined, he was imprisoned for non-payment, he was released, he was re-arrested . . . At the end of it all, Gaunt re-appointed him to his old job and as far as can be learnt the two settled down fairly amicably.

The commoners, too, found problems under the new regime. They had been in trouble long before the pale was set up and now saw themselves threatened with ultimate exclusion. There were also properties that were suddenly cut off from accustomed haunts and sources of wood supply and so on. The whole enterprise seemed to threaten such as Sir Thomas Lodelowe (Ludlow?) who held the property called Parrock in the parish of Hartfield. Sir Thomas spoke up for his rights in council and those rights were upheld. The instruction in the matter is addressed to 'our Chief Warden of our Chace of Ashdown, who now is or for the time being shall be'—a suggestion of impermanence that might well have caused the Chief Warden to brood. Sir Thomas's rights of estover—his wood, grazing and pannage—are granted in perpetuity and his beasts are to have free access to the royal chace 'peaceably without impeachment'. One item to note is that he is granted two beech trees to burn 'at the feast of the Nativity of Our Lord.'

Not only the rights of neighbouring gentry and commons appeared jeopardised by the enclosure. The Prior of Michelham, some miles to the south-east, made claim that his predecessors since the Priory's foundation had been allowed pasture for 60 large beasts, pannage for a hundred hogs and a good deal of timber. These rights would have covered a much larger area and must surely press hard on the new, reduced Ashdown. The monks of Salehurst also held rights here—awarded to the Sidneys of Penshurst at the Reformation. There were more such claims from further afield, for the Abbot of Gerstein was also accustomed to enjoy pannage for a large number of hogs; and was the new Lord, royal or no, to rob the Church of its perquisites? On a smaller scale of disapproval, grumble and alarm, were those monks who had always been free to cross the forest, moving over the countryside from one religious house to another. Presumably this was allowed. They would have needed guides on their forest travels. A few years before the enclosure it was said that sixteen or seventeen guides were needed to see a traveller safe through Ashdown, each one taking over from his fellow to lead the traveller the next few miles, the length the guide claimed as his perquisite.

Over the years, the various allotments of timber, a number of them fairly obviously made as *douceurs* in some slightly awkward situation, give an extraordinary picture of felling and destruction of mature trees. It is not until later, the reign of Henry VIII that much is heard of this. Then there is a claim from authority that 'great waste' is taking place within the bounds of the hunting ground, the deer and other game are short of cover and the situation is one to cause grave concern. The commoners, the customary tenants, are not slow in replying to this accusation of ill-usage of the Forest. That is, the complaint from above is dated 1519 and the aggrieved response comes a little over a year later—not bad, really, given the period and the local conditions.

Time out of mind, the commoners cry, since long before the pale was thrown up, it has been their privilege to exercise their rights within the King's Forest of Ashdown, or Lancaster Great Park—to cut wood and to graze their beasts, to take heather for thatch, turf for fuel, litter for bedding . . . This is a very long document, full of bold protest, complaining that the rangers and other Forest officers do as they please and harry the poor commoners. There is, too, an early note of the effects of iron working on the Forest, one item being a protest that the wood grove on the common of Quabrook is cut down and made into *cole* by one Will'm Muggleweick 'and sold to the stele forge.' The curious name *Quabrook* is still in use and an eye on the map shows that Will'm Muggleweick would be well placed to cart that timber to the Newbridge forge, or a bit further to the works at Pippingford—then called Pippingworth. It is also particularly interesting to find complaint of lands on the south side of Chelwood as being in some dispute. This is an area which has only recently been absorbed into Ashdown Forest. It was until then a part of the lands, along with other commons in the area, Piltdown, Grisling, of the Manor of Maresfield, belonging to Sir John Gage. The rest of Ashdown has lain within the Manor of Duddleswell since the 16th century. At the end of the long document of protest and grievance comes the statement:

This is the true copie of the said presentment taken by me Robert Marchant on the eighth day of June 1614.

By that date the *copie* was needed as evidence in another quarrel.

We are still dealing with the 1520s when there were complaints and naggings from all sides. The occupiers of 'a manor called Paroke' are said to have no right whatever to common within the Forest. This is gall to a present day reader who knows perfectly well that at the time of the enclosure Sir Thomas Lodelowe was confirmed in his rights in perpetuity, and that was in respect of Parrock.

John Pope of Hyndall—nowadays Hendall—was accused of similar unlawful behaviour. Popes remained at Hendall and are referred to a hundred years later than this document of 1520. They became iron masters and the remains of their enterprise have been explored and documented.

Some of the details given on Forest affairs are detailed and homely. The pale was clearly in constant need of repair. Having regard to the uninhibited behaviour of frustrated commoners it is not difficult to see why this should have been so. In one area 'a myle or more a flyte short* of the seide pale is almost p'strate to the ground'. Order is given for wood to be cut forthwith for repairs. And as the years pass and in almost every document we learn of great beeches, well-grown oaks, tall birches being systematically felled for use or gift, the wonder is that Ashdown today can show any part at all that answers to the popular conception of the word *forest*.

*(possibly *shot*)

CHAPTER THREE

Lords and Ladies

There are constant distractions for any but a dedicated scholar in attempting to decipher a little of the Forest's past. Items on the ground demand recognition—like the three handsome yew trees which stand today by Duddleswell crossroads. They are not immensely ancient but must surely be heirs in direct succession to venerable ancestors. Three yew trees traditionally marked those farms ready to overnight drovers and their beasts. There is Streeter's Farm conveniently at hand, while from Nutley to a nearby point runs 'the old drift road'. This existed primarily for the annual *drive* of grazing beasts for counting and inspection—and impounding if need be. A drove road ran all the way from London to Pevensey Levels and the Welsh drovers themselves came to these parts on their own routes, with their little black cattle, called *runts,* for sale at various fairs; at East Grinstead in November, at Nutley in April, when beasts were bought to fatten for the following Christmas. To imagine them resting near Duddleswell surely indulges a fairly reasonable fantasy . . . And factually, one of the many Forest surveys, that of 1564, the reign of Elizabeth I, maps a parish boundary employing a 'ewe' tree as its marker. The boundary line takes its course by the still standing Beggars' Bush, which is a few hundred yards from the crossroads and the yew trees of today. The highway authority has from time to time displayed a strong inclination towards butchering our three 'ewes'. They stand under a preservation order and in any case there are at least two other ways of improving visibility for traffic using the crossroads. If the road-safety card is played cunningly enough, the slaughter might be sanctioned—the trees must be watched . . .

Distracted yet again, quite early in the records I pick up the name of a neighbour's ancestors. Impossible not to sacrifice the general to the particular and follow this intimate lead, chasing them through the centuries. The name changes spelling with time and varying scholarship but reaches its present day form as early as 1610, when they vanish—but reappear in good fettle in 1671. At times they are claiming their copyhold lands, or seeking new such land; establishing their right of common over however many acres; or they are pledging their word among many other 'honest tenants' in some claim to or against authority, perhaps a grouse against the Rangers. A concourse of such honest tenants makes bold on one occasion to say that the King *ought* to ensure that this or that custom should be upheld; or has the word changed emphasis with time? These commoners of Tudor times are as jealous as ever of their rights, even after three hundred years of royal dominance of the area that affords many of them their entire living. Perhaps surprisingly, the various local courts incline to sympathy with the more humble commoners. Often, when their faults are recorded the word *poor* marks them for mild treatment. Not all commoners were poor men, however, right of common on Ashdown attaching to many prosperous manors, some a considerable distance from the pale. David Middleton, gentleman, is hauled before a wood-mote in the reign of James I, accused of cutting and carrying three hundred cartloads of wood valued at £300, which sum he is to pay in fine. By that time more and more wood was being felled to supply, at a good price, the increasingly active iron-workings. The risk of illegal felling would have seemed worth the taking—though we do not know what ideas David Middleton had for the wood he poached.

Of the various immensely detailed surveys of Ashdown over the centuries, none is more particular, more thorough, or nearer to the kind of official report we know today, than what was undertaken during sequestration by the Commonwealth. By that time the place was dis-parked and neglected, the pale was down and the deer fled. The survey of 1650 is particularly solemn, and so detailed that it is even more impressive than the flourishing declarations under royalty. The surveyors confirm the area of Ashdowne, or Lancaster Great Park, or Chace, and value the 13,991 acres 27 perches somewhat unimaginatively at £13,991 plus some odd change. In their findings at local courts, they appear both stern and fair, with that bias towards the humbler sort which it would have been sad indeed not to find maintained by their kind. Nathaniel Browne, however, though clearly no gentleman, is described with some distaste as 'a great destroyer of deere'— though since the pale was in ruins this must have been more by luck than any poacher's judgment. His punishment is not detailed, but fines were unpredictable, or so it seems to a present day reader, ranging from 2d to the £300 taken off the transgressing David Middleton.

Quite why there should have been a further Parliamentary survey only seven years later is difficult to fathom, and no reason for this has apparently been discovered. Truly the Forest at that time had reached that disordered state that makes such miserable reading; perhaps the measuring and the prying was an attempt to bring it back to some sort of shape and purpose. In spite of all, it still offered grazing and somehow there remained trees to fell. With the deer at large, it would have seemed folly not to take advantage of the fact. They are great destroyers at any time and to rid oneself of a marauder while at the same time stocking up the larder sounds like good management.

But between earlier surveys and those undertaken during the Commonwealth more than the pale had decayed. Houses used for administration, the White House at Duddleswell, called also the New Lodge or the Courthouse, was more or less tumbling down. The Old Lodge, where Sir Henry

Compton had had his dwelling when he was Steward, was in
the same state—largely, it is suggested, through his own
fault; perhaps he could not accept the new regime. Horses
grazed where horses had never grazed before. In the years
1632, '33 and '34, no court had been held of woodmote or
eversfald—evesfald—avesfald according to period scholarship. There had been a lack of jurors as well as a failure to
respond to summons. The commoners seem almost to have
gone to ground, to be dealing as they chose, to have clenched
their stubborn teeth and taken what was available, in the face
of what seemed to them injustice and neglect . . .

Before even the earliest days of the royal hunting ground,
when the enclosure was not yet thought of, in the time of
Edward I, the Sackville family had been a part of Ashdown's
story. In 1605 Thomas Sackville, Earl of Dorset, was Master
of the Forest under King James I; the title was confirmed to
his son in 1609. Understandably, we hear nothing of this
during the Commonwealth. When the monarchy was restored, in the person of Charles II, a third Earl of Dorset was
back in office; by favour of his King, Master of the Forest for
his lifetime, and to his heirs thereafter.

What happened next could have been curiously relevant to
our own times. The King granted the Forest on a ninety-nine
year lease to George Digby, Earl of Bristol. The rent was to
be £200 per annum, due to the Earl of Dorset, and the new
tenant could do pretty well what he pleased. He could
'plough up, divide and enclose and erect houses', gathering
for himself 'all rents of freehold and copyhold customary
tenants and of all free tenants and all quit rents and customary
rents and custom monies and other payments whatsoever and
all fines'. The woods are his 'to cut down and grub up' and
the ground is his to split into parcels. Ashdown, in fact, is his
to dismember.

The King was indebted to a great many followers who had
supported him in his exile and in the struggle to regain the
throne. Bristol, what is more, had been one of the first to

attempt the removal of the King's mentor, Lord Clarendon, whose solemnity in later years fitted very ill with the free ways of the Court. Bristol, then, surely deserved his reward; and having discovered the simplicity of discharging debts with grants of land, the King was ready to take full advantage of what might offer, and grant again. The results of his policy appear in rents to be paid to Bristol. What the Earl of Dorset felt about all this is not too openly revealed.

It is not at all unpleasing to report that things went very ill for the new regime. As fast as land was enclosed the fences were thrown down, the new young hedges grubbed up, the cattle turned back on to land it had been their right to graze. The commoners mustered to protect their customers. Garth Christian, writing in 1967 his book on Ashdown Forest, calls the quarrels that followed a 'tedious series'. And so, of course, they are. They are also open, noisy expression of revolt against tyranny. It was not only the little men, with their scattered parcels of land, their modest herds, who set boldly about the authorities. Those many small outlying manors with forest rights were by now richer, larger properties with sturdy and thriving owners. The iron industry, for one thing, though by then in decline on Ashdown, had none the less proved the basis of many modest fortunes. Prosperity leads to louder voices. Besides, it may not be too fanciful to suppose that the days of the Commonwealth had left a liberalising mark on such men as these. Maybe they had lost some sense of awe on discovering that a King, even a King of England, could be tumbled and destroyed—and perhaps they were not all such happy followers of the monarchy's restoration. This part of the south-east had long been non-conforming. Even Christianity had had to struggle for a foothold in Sussex, and the area has always sprouted out-of-the-way religions. Not very surprising, then, that popular opinion hereabouts had largely supported Parliament. In the higher echelons they set about their convictions politely, not too willing to call old friends new enemies.

TF—D

During the actual Civil War, as an example, Colonel Morley of Glynde, hot for Cromwell, none the less sent a warning of promised action to his neighbour across the fields, Lord Gage at Firle. Lady Gage was about to give birth and the Colonel was anxious that she should be taken to some place of safety. Gages, whose seat is at Firle, have been Lords of the Manor of Maresfield since the reign of Henry VIII. Maresfield lands run cheek by jowl with those of the Manor of Duddleswell which has the freehold of Ashdown; which is how it came about so recently that the parcel of Maresfield land jutting against the Forest by Chelwood Gate, changed hands to make one with the Forest itself . . .

By 1661 the Earl of Bristol is well behind with the rent. Dorset, as Master of the Forest, complains bitterly, sounding most irritated and aggrieved. In a money-raising effort, no doubt greatly aggravated by disgust at the treatment he has received from the commoners, Bristol contrives a somewhat specious exercise, leasing his land to Dorset for a yearly rent of £100 'to hold for 97 years from the 25th March 1664'. It cannot be a straight re-fund, Bristol already having done some sub-letting—among others to Thomas Culpepper, a respected enough name in Sussex and one already in the records of the Forest—in 1318 Thomas Culpepper was Master and also Maresfield's Lord of the Manor.

Reverting to 1664, the court at Duddleswell in that year appears concerned almost entirely with the non-payment of dues by commoners and with rent default. Commoners hit back at strangers who have blatantly infringed the accepted rights, particularly in the matter of wood cut and carried. So the charges shift and the commoners are attacked for over-grazing—too many cattle in all the wrong places. Nor have these beasts been accounted for in the proper way by 'one or more droves or common pound drifts every yeare in the Forest.' Why not? By neglect or default? 'What inconveniences have grown or happened thereby?' The names of those charged appear again and again throughout that 'tedious series' of quarrels.

One of the watersheds in the relations of landlord and commoners came in 1678. Sir Thomas Smith, who had become possessed of several hundred acres of Ashdown, announced a 'Bargain and Sale of 500 acres' to Simon Smith, presumably a relation. At the same time, Sir Thomas attempted to free the land 'from several claims and pretences of several persons'. A year later came a notice proclaiming the King's pleasure 'concerning the inclosing of Ashdown Forest to such as claim common pasture there.'

This was indeed disaster, the threat of age-old custom eaten away and the Forest's character changed for ever. Thousands of its acres would be enclosed—and, indeed, the notice suggests, the commoners will surely do much better with an allowance of 4,400 acres today than in yesterday's deer-ridden wilderness. For then the King, as lord and owner of all the land, took every year '3 or 4000 head of Deer Red and Fallow' and '3000 head of cattle at least' were maintained at pasture. So that, the deer having dispersed when the place was disforested, the commoners will fare much better, for the acres remaining unenclosed will be theirs alone, with twice as much grazing for their beasts 'as they ever had or enjoyed' in the past . . . So, *God Save the King*!

Clearly it was assumed that such reassurances, firmly expressed, would be accepted with quiet gratitude and the pulling of forelocks. The King and his advisers should have known better. The King, it is true, had spent most of his life out of England, but by the date of these events he had had time to catch up with his own countrymen. 'The severall persons who claime common in Ashdone Forest' once again proved tough and resistant. They spoke up with firmer voices than often in the past, they had become newly articulate in this 17th century. They had several hundreds of commoner-years behind them and a number of them were those men of modest substance already mentioned. Sir John Pelham was appealed to; Sir John Fagg was appealed to. They acted as negotiators between the commoners and his lordship of the manor, who was very obviously increasingly frustrated by the Ashdown business, his failure to escape his responsibilities—and the fact that nobody answered his letters. Two months, he complained, since he had written to Sir John Pelham, who seemed forever to prevaricate—as if playing for time could assist the circumstances. Meanwhile, he was being paid none of his rightful dues so the affair must be settled 'as soon as maybe'.

It was not settled until the 1690s, after a further twenty-odd years of tussle and ill-feeling. Then John Newnham, holder of fifty acres assigned to Nutley Inn, with the support of his son and other commoners to the number of 51, pleaded at law for the rights of the commoners, so long threatened by the vagaries of authority.

Thus there began on 7th May 1689 a lawsuit that was to change the face of the Forest for ever, though it took another four years to settle. The case, *The Earl of Dorset & his Lessees v. John Newnham & Other Commoners*, was heard in the Duchy Court under the Lord Chief Justice and a representative of the Court of Exchequer. Both sides, no doubt, proved eloquent. Out came all the familiar arguments—that the newcomers had only one desire, which was to improve the Forest by modern methods, not only for themselves but for those whose claims—mere pretence—had brought about the present sorry state of affairs. And up came the well-worn but useful theory about the deer, and how their dispersal could only be to the advantage of those who had been forced to share their grazing and take their estovers—the wood often ruined by antlers' fraying—all under the eye of those marauding beasts. The future improvement in wood and grazing they certainly did not deserve, having absolutely no true rights over the ground.

I think often of how John Newnham of Nutley Inn replied to all this, speaking up for himself and the rest with great resolution and fortitude in the presence of men far above him, obstinately proclaiming that rights of common had been his and his fellows' accepted prerogative through time unmeasured. And such rights had nothing whatsoever—as had been suggested—to do with services rendered or recompense for damage of one sort and another. He spoke for many who would not have found it easy to make open contribution to the controversy. Of those who, at the least, lent their names, many were illiterate. 'His mark' comes often enough in lists of protestants; and in one document a slightly different form appears, a mark actually made on the parchment and above it the description 'his ink'. No doubt there were some defaulters, too timid or too *dunch*, fearful of reprisal by fines they would not be able to pay. As one grows accustomed to their names so one watches for them, and some are missing in the final reckoning.

All this did at least mean that the case was not dismissed out of hand. It was given a decent hearing. The court found in favour of the Earl and his fellows, which was to be expected. The area set aside for the commoners was seen as sufficient for their needs, the original 4,400 acres having been raised to 5,000. A commission was then set up to enquire into the shape and size of the enclosures and how they should be sited to the best advantage. The commission surprisingly increased the acreage of commonable ground to 6,400—which is where it stands three hundred years later. It can only have been a dreary and a dismal conclusion for those who had so boldly and hopefully set out their claims. True, they had increased their land allowance by fighting for it and would have absolute grazing right over their own, open parts of the Forest. The rights of the Earl to cut litter on that ground remained undisputed, which debased the favourable clauses in the verdict.

Looking at the map of Ashdown Forest as it is today, you are looking at it as it was drawn in 1372, then re-drawn in 1693. There lie the infuriating enclosures with the Forest girdling and green. Those enclosures must have seemed like

the slammed gates of paradise to those who could no longer
wander freely—for they can seem just so today. Yet how
many, waking to realisation of what had been taken away,
truly believed that the last word had been spoken? How many
consoled themselves with the knowledge that had they lacked
courage to make their stand they could have lost everything—not only for themselves, either, but for us coming so
far after . . .?

The commoners retained less than half of what they knew
they were owed, and this could not be forgotten. The fire was
damped down, it was certainly not finally dowsed. It broke
into fresh and vigorous flame when the moment arrived—
which was not until another two hundred years had made
their mark on the Forest.

The costs of Forest litigation over the centuries would add
up to a fortune. The complaints and resultant legal struggles
proliferated in the years following the 1693 verdict, with its
realignment of the long familiar. Claims and counter-claims
shift back and fore, the commoners increasingly aggressive,
the Lord of the Manor and his tenants haughtier by the
minute. With what skill the lawyers deal and at times with
what apparent deviousness. During these years there are
recorded alarming sales of timber. In March 1727 there was
advertised a sale of 'All the oak trees with the tops and lops
of the same That are now standing growing or being on all
and every the waste ground or uninclosed land that is lying
and being within the Manor of Duddleswell.' This does not
include young timber, but what a terrible and sweeping
order. A survey five years earlier had claimed 4,991 mature
trees standing on Ashdown Forest. Nine hundred and ninety
one seems to be some sort of code number, recalling the
acreage noted in the Parliamentary survey of 1650. As usual,
there appears no record of the re-planting of oak, or indeed
of any planting at all at that time.

The Lord of the Manor's tenants who had been granted
their enclosures and would make the most of them, now took

up the matter of coney breeding. In medieval times there had been warrens for the breeding of coneys, or rabbits, in several parts of the Forest and the practice continued for many years. These warrens or *pillow-mounds*, can still be identified in various places—one is on the Old Lodge boundary to the south- east of the property and another on ground belonging to The Pheasantry, off the Ridge road from Wych Cross to Coleman's Hatch. Several such warrens were said to have been illegally set up, but others were duly licensed—Broadstone Warren, Hindleap Warren have the official ring. If the coneys escaped from the warrens they became automatically the property of the Lord and their poaching could be perilous.

In the first two decades of the 19th century the Forest had a Lady of the Manor of Duddleswell. She was Arabella Diana, Dowager Duchess of Dorset. Her husband, the 3rd Duke, died in 1799 and she re-married in 1801, retaining her title but sharing the lordship with her new husband, Lord Whitworth. Her son by her first marriage was killed in a hunting accident, so she remained the Forest's Lady. Either she or some lively adviser recalled the useful fact that the Forest having originally been enclosed for sport, sporting rights must still obtain and should be applied for. Hunting had dwindled from its original splendours with the decay of the pale and the dispersal of the deer, but there was still some game and more should be bred.

The Lady makes her application and it is granted. One thing swiftly leads to another and enclosures are set up for the breeding of such as blackcock. The commoners are warned, as in other centuries, against the cutting of litter, which provides cover for the birds. As they are constantly abusing the ban, the warnings become increasingly tough. They disturb William Sewell Esq of Twyford Lodge, who in a long letter pleads for forbearance all round. 'My wish,' he writes, 'is for amity and liberality.' He is one of very few to express any tolerance. The earlier years of the 19th century are not

distinguished, save for the opinions of a few advanced
thinkers, for any particular leniency towards the petty offences
of underlings. In the early days, when the classes were divided
by a mighty chasm, king and commoner, there could be a
kind of warmth towards the lovable villains who behaved as
they did because they knew no better. It was different in the
days of Arabella Diana. The commoners to her and her peers
could only seem to be 'above themselves'.

The continuing business of enclosures for the breeding of
game birds was to some degree settled at a meeting held in
August 1816. It was proposed that agreed areas should be set
aside for breeding. The commoners were to 'cut no litter
upon the Forest between the 31st December and the 31st
September in every year, and to abstain from exercising their
right of cutting litter altogether within any of the 'places
undermentioned which are now marked out by post.' There
would be five of these—the Five Hundred Acre Wood,
King's Standing, the Crow's Nest, Gill's Lap and Hollies
Down. All but one of these are distinguished today by car
parks. These forbidden areas amounted to 270 acres. There
must have been a preponderance of gentry at this meeting,
which could be one reason for the somewhat spineless
acceptance of the resolution.

In order to see the statute carried out, The Most Noble
Arabella Diana Duchess of Dorset and The Right Honb'le
Charles, Earl Whitworth appointed a gamekeeper, Richard
Avis, with really far-reaching powers. He was given 'full
power and authority to seize within our said Manor all and all
manner of Greyhounds, Setting Dogs, Spaniels, Lurchers and
other dogs, Ferrets, Guns, Nets, Wires, Snares and other
instruments or Engines used or kept for the taking, killing or
destroying of Hares, Pheasants, Partridges and other game
. . . ' This was worse than the days of *The Laws of the Forest,*
when a commoner might, at the least, still keep a dog—
providing it was lamed.

The building of gentleman's houses around the outskirts of

the Forest had continued over the years and there were many fine residences to supply enthusiastic sportsmen—places like Kidbrooke and Maresfield Parks, like Twyford Lodge, Lavertye and Holly Hill. It was the mild-mannered William Sewell of Twyford Lodge who claimed that he had killed forty hares in a year . . . London was creeping nearer, the Forest and its affairs increasingly taken over by those the locals were bound to see as foreigners. More and more unfamiliar names appear on the ever increasing pile of legal documents concerned with Forest matters. The disputes will surely never end. The commoners remain stubborn and restless—and not only the commoners quarrel with the Manor. Courts are convened and no one appears. Intruders put up cottages on manorial waste and these must come down. Nothing has happened by the next summons, so there are fines; and the cottages, little doubt, were thrown down.

What were these dwellings like? Presumably their builders claimed squatters' right, though this does not appear at the time. Their destruction might account for some of those scatterings and clusters of stone that may be found, not only in the waste, but some little way within the Forest. Were they just hovels, a room with a hearth and a chimney? Some such rough shapes form the core of many present-day houses about the Forest. In fact, the business of illegal dwellings had been going on for years. In the previous century, John Brett, 'a loose idle disorderly fellow', 'put up a hut for himself on the King's Highway leading from Witchcross to Nutley.' John Brett was further charged with taking holly, lopping timber and committing 'other wast and spoil'. It was all most inconvenient for the then Lord, who felt himself 'injured in his property'. The hut came down for John Brett could certainly never have paid the alternative fine of £20 at a time when 20/- was a respectable sum.

This case, with its allusion to holly, precedes by almost a hundred years a grand row between the Lord and Lady of the Manor and the Rest about a similar matter. Holly had always been a forbidden crop, the property of the manor since the beginning of time. It would still be so today, save that the timber rights on Ashdown were made over to the Board of Conservators some years ago. Holly has always had a price on its head for in winter at least it is fodder for deer. The first Christmas I spent on Ashdown I went merrily to cut holly for the house, only to be shouted at by a Ranger of those days. It was the first time I had cried 'I am a commoner!' It did me little good. I was no more to be favoured than John Brett or the others—and rightly so.

The holly and its cutting be-devilled the 1820s, calling forth quite passionate expressions of outrage. Many of those described as persons of inferior standing were hauled again and again before the magistrates, to be dealt with 'according to their station in society.' The magistrates, however, were prepared to do little more than threaten and it was very clear where their sympathies lay. This tiresome leniency becoming well-known about the Forest, holly thieves took the hint. In April 1825 a stern notice was distributed throughout the neighbourhood: *All persons detected in cutting, damaging or destroying any of the Hollies, trees or underwoods, on Ashdown Forest will be prosecuted.*

Whether or not this had any effect, complaints switched to other activities. This was a generally lawless time, though smuggling may have passed its height. There was an immense amount of trespass and fingers were pointed at others than the commoners. It would be a hard heart that failed, at this period, to feel almost as much sympathy for the men at the top, or near it, as for those one sees as the true heroes of the piece—those for whom the Forest stood as a traditional means of livelihood. The exasperation of Sir John Shelley, indeed his wretchedness, writing from his home, Maresfield Park, in 1826, is very nearly touching. The building of cottages must have lapsed after that case of John Brett, though isolated instances are mentioned. What came now to bedevil the locality was true squatting, building from dusk to

dawn, at which hour the chimney would be seen smoking and
the right would be established. Then as now, squatters took
a lot of shifting. 'If this goes on I shall have an Indian town
close to me of some of the greatest rapscallions that ever
existed,' writes poor Sir John. And he concludes plaintively,
'Let me have a strong letter from you on the subject. You
know how pig-headed your honest Sussex fellow is.' On
second thoughts, his *Indian town* suggests in this case tenting
rather than building.

   In spite of the various diversions, the cutting of brakes for
litter remains the foremost issue over the years. It is not easy
to feel altogether patient with them over this. Why did they
fail, on both sides, to get it settled one way or the other?
Certainly for the commoners appeals to higher authority had
had no happy results in the past; to dare all, in such
circumstances, could have been to lose all. Yet how curious it
appears now that there should have been such ambivalence on
all sides. The confusion never properly clears. The exercise of
a timeless tradition had been denied any right by the Award
of 1693, when it was so forcibly presented that the right of
cutting belonged totally to the Lord, that for commoners it
merely implied grazing, the taking by 'bite of mouth'. Yet in
1816 when the preservation of game on the Forest was being
organised, the commoners were ordered to 'abstain from *their
right* of cutting litter' at certain specified times. Four years
later, the right of commoners to cut litter was openly declared
illegal.

   Other cutting came under scrutiny at this time. The taking
of turf was long discontinued except by parish officers for the
benefit of their poor. There was much argument over this,
but in 1830 it was agreed that 'poor industrious persons'
would be allowed turf for fuel after applying for a ticket
authorising however many turves at 1/– a load. Perhaps the
parish paid, for a shilling is still a fair sum to be found by
poor, however industrious, persons of that time. There were
also tickets for poor non-commoners for the grazing of one

cow, between given dates. 2/6 was the fixed price in this case
and each ticket had to be signed by two members of the
Committee—a body fairly recently set up to attempt some
checking and ordering of Forest affairs.

It was the Committee which appointed four *Lookers* to
patrol the Forest and watch for marauders. Maybe they, too,
were pig-headed Sussex fellows, for nothing very startling is
seen to emerge from their activities. Their situation somewhat
matches that of vigilantes in later years, who were employed to
warn of fires and inform on incendiaries. But it occurred to
them, we are told, that it could be more profitable to start the
fires and then do the notifying for the agreed remuneration.

Those first Lookers were also empowered to arrest sheep
illegally straying. In April 1832 Robert Ashley 'of
Withingham' is in trouble for 'removing his sheep from the
Lookers'—presumably by taking them from the pound. The
Committee meets at *The Chequers,* Maresfield, and Robert
Ashley's misdemeanours are first on their list. It is explained
that he signed a paper acknowledging his guilt in the matter
of the sheep, expressing his contrition and agreeing to pay
poundage and expenses of 2/-. That was back in September
and now it is April. No monies have changed hands. He will
receive a solicitor's letter. The tone of this meeting, however,
was benign; though certainly it was pointed out by one
thoughtful and far-seeing member of the Committee that
about 160 poor persons' cattle are grazed on the Forest
outskirts, and if all these were to be paid for, agreeably to the
regulations, they could produce an annual revenue of £20.
There is no recorded reaction to the suggestion . . .

The Manor of Duddleswell now gained a new lord. The
title passed through Arabella Diana's daughter, who had
married a De La Warr; her son, George John, Earl De La
Warr inherited the Forest. He was, of course, still a Sackville
on his mother's side, and his home was Buckhurst Park in
Withyham. He emerges in his early days as Lord as possibly
a shade reluctant when it comes to manorial affairs. A letter

written at Buckhurst in 1833 shows him as very much a family man and a country lover. 'Again I am sorry to say that I shall be absent from the Forest Meeting on Monday. On that day I must go down to Hatfield to put a little boy to school, and on Tuesday I am going to Rotterdam with Charles—putting him so far on his way to Dresden.' The letter shows him troubled by the assortment of local conflicts. It has been suggested to him that if those commoners who had once enjoyed litter cutting were actually licensed to do so they might be converted from secret enemies to open allies and the constant nagging of one side against the other be put to an end. Would this be a possible notion? 'The countryside is looking so enchantingly beautiful,' he concludes with an almost audible sigh, 'that I am miserable at the thought of returning to the strife of the Metropolis . . . '

Bracken is just as much a problem today, though for the exactly opposite reason that it is not cut enough. Even as recently as twenty-five to thirty years ago, it was cut in great quantities and with considerable style. It was scythed or swopped into tidy rows, so that a long bank could look as finely terraced as a vineyard, and loaded into horse-drawn carts and carried away. It was a pleasing family activity, the children helping with the raking and loading, the smallest riding home as they might on a load of hay. When that generation of children grew up they often moved away from homes without a proper water supply or electricity. The practice fell into disuse except in a very modest form. Few gardeners round about seem to realise the potential of bracken cut and spread over winter beds; a shelter and a compost in one.

Time after time through the first three-quarters of the last century this age-old business of cutting is argued and battled over. It is sometimes possible to wonder if the commoners really wanted it all settled. Certainly it gave them some power over autocracy, but at a price. On one occasion the Reeve reports how he tried to arrest some men quite openly helping

themselves to the controversial crop: 'They laughed and went
on cutting'. One commoner, similarly accused, remarks
largely that 'five or six thousand men could cut without being
caught.' Allowing for his style, how wild and lonely a place
the Forest must even by then have been . . . The penalties
inevitably grow tougher, for there are many trespassers who,
though their names are familiar, have in one way or another
lost their right of common. As the building of large houses
continued, estates were built up which swallowed small
holdings, so that a man might become beholden to a new
landlord and no longer, in his own person, directly to the
Lord of the Manor. It was for these newer resident gentry to
speak in matters of entitlement and their sympathies varied.
Also the attitude of the courts began to change as they came
under newer rulings. Though at one time they had been
inclined to favour what one could call hereditary delinquents,
now they grew tough and uncompromising. There were
several prison sentences—twenty-one days for Dan'l
Heasman, four months' hard labour for the vividly named
City Bannister. 'The result of these convictions,' writes one
troubled gentleman to another, 'was to create a defiant feeling
in the Foresters. They fancy they have rights and they cannot
be persuaded they have not.'

A few more years of squabbling and then came a very
significant letter from the Lord's solicitors to William Wallis
Esq, a member of the Committee, who lived in Hartfield
parish.

'We are instructed by Earl De La Warr to stop the cutting
of Brakes and litter on Ashdown Forest . . . We can assure
you that it is a complete act of trespass to cut the Brakes or
Litter even by a Tenant and we hope therefore that with this
explanation you will not only make amends for the past but
prevent a future occurrence of the Acts complained of.'

Mr Wallis did not reply.

CHAPTER FOUR

A Man to Remember

In August 1874 a meeting was held of that Committee that had come into being some years earlier in an attempt to organise Forest affairs. It superceded the Association, set up many years before, which, to quote a reeve of the 1870s, George Edwards, 'fell through because some of the commoners wanted to make it a stepping-stone to enclosure.' It was at the 1874 meeting and not, as often concluded, twelve years later when a further court case had been dealt with, that the Conservators of Ashdown Forest came vigorously into being; they were, of course, self-appointed. They called themselves then the *Conservators of the Commonable Rights of Ashdown Forest.* This move led to a turning point in the affairs of the commoners, though it seemed for some time that planned developments might not go quite the way these early Conservators had hoped.

Let it be acknowledged right away that practically speaking every vital move in Forest affairs rested from this time on the sympathetic tenacity of one man: the remarkable William Augustus Raper. He was a partner in a firm of Battle solicitors Messrs Ellman, Raper & Ellman. He may well have known little of Ashdown Forest when, in the early 1870s, his firm was employed on one of those uncountable conflicts between Manor and Common which appeared set to continue to infinity. Mr Raper was the partner who took over the job of representing Robert Edwards, a tenant farmer of Hartfield, along with the several others concerned in Edwards' alleged trespass. Needless to say, that trespass concerned the cutting

43

of litter. He had cut, it was claimed, where litter must not be cut—indeed, it had to be stressed, that litter must not be cut anywhere, ever, by any commoner. Edwards was tenant of land at Lynes Farm and Little Parrock, and had other holdings in the Manors of both Maresfield and Duddleswell. He was no novice in such affairs as now encompassed him. It had been his habit, he declared, for forty years and more, to cut litter in the places named in the indictment, and none had ever said him Nay. In this he was vigorously upheld by the collection of witnesses assembled for his support.

The case was dismissed, to the frustration of the Lord of the Manor, and no less of his solicitors, the London firm of Hunt, Curry & Co. From this moment they are seen to be fighting a running battle with Raper, who was surely the best thing ever to have happened to Ashdown Forest. His work on the Robert Edwards case, highlighting the situation of the commoners over centuries, must have filled his imagination and ordered his actions. Whether consciously or not, he dedicated himself to the Forest and its foresters. When he set his hand to this particular task he was taking up a challenge and a cause that he would not escape for the next forty-three years. But for his efforts, the history of Ashdown might well be lying uncollated and jumbled—it was he who brought order to the archives.

To read the letters of William Augustus Raper, sharp or mild, according to necessity, is to encounter a man of fairness, firmness and a considerable, often caustic, wit. From the very beginning, though champion of the commoners, he never fails to be seen weighing the claims and certainties of the other side before quietly demolishing them. It is fascinating to chart his progress into prominence among the several prestigious gentlemen of the neighbourhood. At a time when a lawyer was very much the servant of a rich client, he is never brusquely alluded to; he is always, politely, *Mr Raper*. His exchanges with Hunt, Curry & Co. reveal, it must be owned, a shade of sardonic satisfaction with his own

Near Twyford. Spring.

Autumn in Five Hundred Acre Wood.

Trekking near The Vachery.

Greenwood Gate from the rim of Wren's Warren valley.

Gill's Lap, a high point on the Forest.

Near Gill's Lap.

Early morning in the Old Lodge Nature Reserve.

Ashdown Park. Approximately three hundred acres of the Forest's woodland were destroyed by the great storm of 1987.

Morning. The Wealdway through Five Hundred Acre Wood.

Sunset. Camp Hill Clump.

Four Counties Dial looking towards the North Downs. The dial was put up to commemorate the Silver Jubilee of Queen Elizabeth II in 1977

The Airman's Grave. 'This spot is sacred . . . they died that you may live.'

'. . . and by and by they came to an enchanted place on the very top of the Forest called Galleon's Lap . . .' Here at Galleon's Lap are commemorated A. A. Milne 1882–1956 & E. H. Shepard 1879–1976 who collaborated in the creation of *Winnie the Pooh*.

Early morning walkers.

'Iron Flush' at Three
Wards on Millbrook.

The number of animals
grazed on the Forest
was once in excess of
2,000. This has declined
dramatically in recent
years, but new methods
are being tried to
encourage grazing.

An alert but not over cautious fox cub (*Vulpes vulpes*).

Only about two pairs of the dashing hobby (*Falco subbuteo*) succeed each year in rearing their young on the Forest.

The adder (*Vipera berus*) is not aggressive and its natural instinct is to avoid detection.

good-tempered self-assurance. Rightly so; his letters are a
model of biting good manners. The Earl's men, by com-
parison, appear flustered and tetchy. It should be noted that
the Lord of the Manor just then was Reginald Windsor, 7th
Earl De La Warr, who before he inherited had been Rector of
Withyham but must none the less have lacked something in
the way of Christian spirit—he had instigated a case against
his brother for possession of Knowle, the Sackville strong-
hold in Kent. He appears to have been well versed in the
delights or torments of litigation and perhaps his employees
had become slightly infected—most particularly a keeper
named William Pilbeam.

In 1876 the conflict between land owner and land user
reached a satisfactorily dramatic crisis when Pilbeam
approached John Miles, a commoner tenant of Bernard Hale
Esq. of Holly Hill, Coleman's Hatch. John Miles was
diligently cutting litter on Mr Hale's account. Pilbeam
appeared over the horizon, strode up to John Miles and
ordered him to stop cutting and be off. John Miles, in
accepted Sussex fashion, answered briefly. He became one of
the principals in the case that eventually came to court. When
asked what he had done about Pilbeam's command, he
replied, as plenty of others had in such circumstances: 'I went
on cutting.' The four words summarise centuries on
Ashdown Forest.

As is usual in such matters, the case was a long time
coming to court. That time was needed. It gave William
Augustus Raper opportunity to compile his evidence. For a
start he combed through all documents concerning the Forest
since its enclosure in the 13th century, extracting those that
bore directly or even obliquely on commonable customs over
the years. He gathered and copied what he found into those
great volumes already alluded to here, which have become
known as *The Raper Papers*—surely a best-selling title . . .
Raper knew as well as any commoner that the right to cut
litter, however challenged, remained a justifiable practice, but

he was equally aware that its legality rested on a knife-edge. He needed more than ancient documentary evidence; he needed living experience fully recorded. He set himself to collect more statements than there were commoners, since his older witnesses would be the fathers and grandfathers of those still working. He had to face the prospect of approaching some who would shy away from any suggestion of giving testimony, and others who would have reached an age of less-remembering. It was the long memory he needed most, however, and as he proceeded with his task he contrived to coax from old men and women memories in amazing detail of the Forest they had always known. He had to deal with the reticent and the garrulous—some statements are several pages long, others amount to no more than a terse line or two. All, read now, are valuable.

Quite apart from the value at that time of such recollections, these statements give the sharpest possible impression of a poor man's life in this countryside during the first quarter or so of the 19th century. The present day reader's sympathy and interest is caught and held as the old foresters relate, not only stories of litter cutting, but of many other details, general and personal, of their early years. How often they speak of their childhood—at school from the age of ten to twelve; walking to school from Legsheath to the poor-school at Sackville College in East Grinstead. In one case this happened only when the child was not well enough to help with the farm work, in which case he got no dinner that day. Working as carters' boys, as post carriers, message carriers between the big houses; most of them moving all the time, even as they grew into manhood, from one employer to another about the Forest, as work ceased in one place and became available at another. And often out of work altogether and turning for help to the family home. Or—as one such forest dweller says—'. . . went to Hartfield workhouse for a short time, times being very bad.'

'Went to work at the age of eight,' says one old man to

Raper. 'I began to drive a plough before I was twelve years old,' says another. John Marchant tended his grandfather's cattle on the Forest 'for days at a time when they were first turned out until they got used to it . . . Terribly lonely work it was.' This man later became a roadman, which cannot have been much more sociable than his childhood occupation . . . Then there was John Brooker, telling how 'Three months before I was eight year old I went as farm boy to Major Faulkener . . . At fifteen I was entrusted to sell—and sold—bullocks at Crowborough Fair to the value of £75.' At the age of seventy-odd, he describes the word *litter* as 'anything that comes to the scythe.'

Sometimes the foresters tell of work so scanty they are obliged to seek it away from the Forest—in West Sussex, in Kent. Even at a great age—lucky to reach seventy in those days—they recall the details of their moves; six months here, a year out of work, three years in an unfamiliar place—or, of course, the workhouse. Interestingly, those who quit ordinary forest work to become gardeners and the like to the new breed of estate-owning gentlemen were much more likely to settle and stay for the rest of a working life; ten years, twenty years. One of these speaks warmly of how he was given a cottage when he grew too old for outdoor work.

We cannot reckon how many of those forced to seek work elsewhere actually stayed away. The tales told to William Augustus Raper are the tales of those who came home. 'I returned,' is heard, time and again—and it is heard in varying forms today. Many local men who took themselves off between the wars to Canada and other helpful places, will tell you that they 'had to get back to the old Forest'. In the case of Raper's people it is just this attachment that gives power to their statements. As Raper encourages confidence their claims expand until litter seems held to include anything taken from the ground; not only brakes but turf, heather, peat, as in far distant days; marl, stone. Perhaps there are moments here, too, when one feels a certain sneaking sympathy with the Manor . . .

Lord Colchester, as Charles Abbott, Speaker of the House, living at Kidbrooke Park, took a considerable interest in Forest affairs and believed in exercising his rights, deciding for himself what some of these might be. He is recorded as being a great taker of stone. This may not have been what Raper needed to hear but he recorded it faithfully even if he would not want to use it in evidence. George Tester worked for Colchester. He was 93 when Raper talked to him, and 'baptised at Horsted Keynes' so his mother told him. Lord Colchester, says Tester, 'made an artificial cascade in the brook (presumably the young Medway) and took all the largest stones he could find on the neighbouring Forest for this purpose. 'I helped (with) one stone weighed 9 tons, and we dragged it down in a truck made on purpose at Forest Row and drawn by 7 pair of oxen. We also took many loads of green turf off the Forest to make his lawns and gravel to make his carriage roads.'

No wonder his lordship spoke up for rights of common when the appropriate moment came.

He was not alone in stone stealing. Raper's informants tell of Sir Spencer Maryon-Wilson who built his house, Searles, near Fletching, entirely of Forest stone. Sir Spencer started building in 1870 'and in that year took 574 waggon loads of stone, and in 1871 36 loads, and in 1872 120 loads and about 4 or 5 since.' No payment had been made, Raper was assured, and though the Lord had grown rather restive, Sir Spencer remained uncooperative, at least for many years. In the distant days it had been the humble self-supporting commoner who had proved stubborn; by the 19th century the comfortable gentry landlords did not hesitate to stand firm. By no means all Sussex men, they saw none the less the advantage in practising how not to be *druv*.

Raper's relationship with the various old people he inter-viewed is characteristically pithy, but warm and concerned. Edward Killmer 84, of Forest Row, is 'rather vague'. Edward

Heaver, 76, is a 'first rate witness. Pretty robust.' John
Brooker is an 'intelligent good witness but waterworks
wrong.' Then there is Gilham, John; suffers at times from
bronchitis. 'Not safe for another winter,' mourns Raper. It is
John Gilham who recalls the old commoners' custom of
putting out hay in winter for the deer. In return, allowance
would be made for two grazing cattle, or some other
reward—accounts vary. One almost hears the helpful, per-
suasive voice of the 'lawyer gentleman' as he sits by smoky
fires in forest dwellings and with the greatest patience and
humour wheedles their stories from one after another.

One Forest family, the Edwardses, appear on both sides of
conflict. Abraham was one who spoke up readily for the right
to cut litter. 'I have often seen the teams of the late Stephen
Langridge carrying litter to Upper Parrock Farm . . . the old
gent used to have a wonderful sight of litter.' Mention of
teams gives an impression of how much was claimed.

Robert Edwards was the Hartfield farmer whose case first
brought Raper to Ashdown; but another Edwards, George,
was at one time Reeve, and is spoken of somewhat crossly by
Edward Heaver of Legsheath—Raper's 'first-rate witness',
whose testimony covers a good deal of ground and grows
freer and more rumbustious as it proceeds. One day, he
relates, he was cutting litter when Reeve George Edwards
appeared and told him he must not take litter off the Forest
unless he had the permission of Lord De La Warr. This was a
time when the Lord of the Manor was trying hard to assert
his authority, and George Edwards told Heaver he could if he
wished have a ticket signifying the approval of the Lord and
acknowledging him as a permitted litter-cutter. 'I told him I
could do without.' It very obviously gave Heaver some
satisfaction to tell this tale. What was more, he then, probably
with a self-congratulatory chuckle, told of other prizes taken
off the Forest. 'I had five loads of stone and sand . . . to repair
my cow hovel . . . I also took a few of his holly bushes for a
fence.' No comment, from Raper.

Heaver's nephew, whose name was Buss, has memories of the eccentric Mr Fuller of Lavertye, whose hare hunting proclivities appear and re-appear throughout the records of the Forest during these years. His private pack of harriers is most often spoken of with respect amounting almost to affection. 'I remember one occasion when the hare was so hard pressed that it fell dead in front of the hounds.' On another occasion, having failed to find a hare, Fuller offered anyone 1/– who would put him in the way of finding one. Buss had seen a hare 'sitting' just before. So off went the hunt, to check this claim, taking the shilling with them to the spot. Fortunately for Buss, if not for the quarry, the hare was quickly put up and the reward handed over.

Practically every one of Raper's skilfully conducted interviews adds something to the picture of the Forest in the first years of the 19th century and even earlier in the case of the oldest men. As with Buss and the hare, the game is spoken of again and again. John Brooker—he of the faulty waterworks—tells how they 'used to shoot anything that got up, including pheasants, partridges, black game, hares, rabbits, etc.' Plenty of blackcock in those days, he claims, particularly mentioning The Mount and King's Standing. 'I have seen as many as 80 in a drove.'

One wonders if Raper felt his researches in any way hampered by these diversions. Was he at times pulling his gold watch from his waistcoat pocket, or did he find even the trivialities as useful as we do in building up a fuller picture? Some of the depositions cover pages, so probably his patient interest never flagged. But the main issue of litter cutting easily gets lost in the mass of often repetitive detail, and litter cutting, after all, was his quarry. One William Hobbs lived by Brown's Brook and meandered a bit about conifer planting. 'I heard 3 or 4 years ago of Lord De La Warr planting fir trees on the Forest, but I never heard of his predecessors planting except the clumps which was done years ago.' But he has a tale of litter cutting, too. One day in his own neighbourhood a load of litter 'coming round a corner, was turned over into the pond, horse and all.'

The case of John Winn is mentioned more than once. He had been in gaol for litter cutting—but he had also been poaching, which was probably what counted with the Bench. The whole issue of taking litter had been prominent for so long that it had had years before Raper to become a Cause. 'He was a great man of litter' is said admiringly of many a prominent commoner long dead.

Countless small points of interest emerge from these encounters of Raper's. The word *brakes* for bracken takes over from the *fern* of some early writings and is today's usage. Heather for thatching is called *long heather* but is no more available, they seem to suggest. Long heather is sometimes called *leggy* and it is tempting to decide that this must be the origin of the name *Legsheath*. Names chop and change here as in other Forest records—Gill's Lap is sometimes Gill's Cap, Ghylls Clump, Gill's Leap. Hardened by an 'h' as in one of these instances, the word lines up as it should with Heron's Ghyll, Mirey Ghyll, Breakneck Ghyll and the rest. In early documents the spelling of names is most often phonetic; in these personal accounts, these 'live interviews', the sound is always one of dialect. Even today you sometimes catch Scotchford for Cotchford.

Farm names in general are evocative, picturesque and sometimes funny, and the farm names attached to Ashdown make a goodly selection. Some remain, all are worth remembering. Pleasant Farm rivals Heaven Farm; Workhouse, Pest House, Hospital and Fitness speak for themselves. Peculiars Farm presumably has an ecclesiastical connection—and there are many such left from the days when religious houses claimed common rights—Paternoster Wood, Ave Maria Wood, Monks Farm, Priory Road are all reminders. In Nutley, the name Chantersell appears in a parish survey as *Chantry Soyle*.

Through all the pages and pages of personal recollections

few women find a place; a poor legacy from those days when
royal wives were granted the Forest as some sort of extra
benefit. It was John of Gaunt's wife, Blanche, who brought
him the title of Lancaster, so her influence, or her memory,
remained as long as Ashdown carried its alternative title of
Lancaster Great Park. And Gaunt's third wife, Katherine
Swynford, held the royal chace in her own right during her
son's minority. Earlier royal ladies are all named in the Forest
papers of the 13th and 14th centuries—Eleanor, Margaret,
Isabella, Philippa, are all 'beloved consorts' with a finger in
the Forest pie. And there is certainly ample evidence of
Arabella Diana's importance to 19th century Ashdown. One
of her particular interests, according to one Jenner, father of
the Nutley smith, was the keeping up of the Nutley pound.

The humbler sort of woman gets scant recognition from
Raper's interviewees. ' I married at twenty-one' they say; or
'Then I got married.' When their families are mentioned, it is
the sons who get named. Here and there, a daughter
inherits—to the general benefit of her husband, but at least in
these parts this is a rarity.

One woman interviewed in her own right is Susanna Rice.
'Infirm', Raper notes; and she is seventy-eight when he
consults her. She is of particular interest because she lived for
twenty-seven years in a house with six acres of land, called
then as now *The Goat*, once an alehouse. Whether or not
it was originally *The Goat & Compasses*, standing, it is said, for
God Encompasseth, does not emerge. The word *gote*, in Sussex
dialect means a watercourse and there is certainly a stream
nearby. In its sociable days *The Goat* was a destination for
smugglers using the still traceable track that enters the Forest
below Twyford Lane. The Goat crossroads, a few yards from
the still-surviving house, are the junction of the Forest-Row
West Hoathly roads with the smaller road that runs from
Wych Cross past Hindleap and then on down the hill past
Legsheath to Weir Wood and eventually East Grinstead.
'Never saw a goat on the Forest,' says Susanna—and indeed

they were not commonable animals.

Then there was Sophia Constable of Ruttingham Farm along Down Street. She 'had had a paralytic stroke but has got over it.' Sophia must indeed have made a very good recovery, for she obviously delighted in the idea of being a witness in the case, whenever it might happen. 'She says she could travel very well,' notes Raper. Sophia Constable made the bold claim that she could 'distinguish Forest litter from any other.'

Another woman who testified was Martha Baker. Her fluent evidence and total recall has been quoted often enough—by Garth Christian, for one. 'Capital witness,' says Raper. She told him how she went to help with litter cutting as a child, and how she and her sister carted along the baby in its cradle. Between them they managed to tip the little creature out on to the grubby Forest floor. They got a hiding, she recalls cheerfully, when they arrived home. She, her sister and what she calls 'the other children' cut nine loads of brakes and were paid 1/– a load. 'I had a new frock out of the money.' When she was older she used to go to a shop then at Marsh Green which sold drapery and grocery. Not the only shop to appear about the Forest. There was another near Duddleswell, at Campfields Rough.

Had Christianna Cogger lived in the 19th rather than the 17th century she could not have failed to make Raper a good witness. As wife and widow she was forever bunching up her fists against authority. Her husband, John, was in trouble time and again for grazing animals above his allocation. These were of course impounded. Christianna always knew the right moment to steal them away from the pound and avoid the fine. Poundage fines vary enormously over the years, not always in the expected direction. In 1607 Christianna failed for once and John was charged £3 for twenty steers—but in 1811 Colonel Young of Holly Hill got away with 6d poundage for ninety-seven sheep . . . By the time Mr Raper was making his enquiries, the custom of the

annual drift had died, so none of his interviewees had tales to
tell of the matter. It had come to an end when various young
farmers unofficially took on the job of driving commoners'
beasts to the pound—where they appropriated the poundage
fee and treated themselves to a fine dinner at the inn.

Letting the family animals out of the pound seems by
tradition a woman's job and it would be good if more of
these lively souls appeared in Raper's great collection of
valuable evidence concerning litter cutting. The many personal irrelevancies which he must have found a little time-
consuming make wonderful reading today . . .

With so much suitable evidence of long practice comfort-
ably in hand, Mr Raper must have gone fairly confidently to
the first day of the court hearing when at last it arrived. Once
again, the commoners were to be pitted against the Lord of
the Manor—this time, surely, they must prevail.

Though the incident which sparked off the case brought by
Earl De La Warr against John Miles, and therefore against his
employer, Bernard Hale, took place in 1876, the case did not
come to court for a considerable time. It was heard eventually
in the High Court of Justice under a stern and apparently
rather prejudiced judge, Vice-Chancellor Bacon. As the bulk
of documents held at the Public Records Office in Lewes
readily suggest, it all took a very long time. It was a test case
of its kind—a rising against long-established authority but a
battle for the protection of ancient custom. The protagonists
formed a highly assorted gathering, some no doubt travelling
to London for the first time to give their testimony, some
bold, some easily intimidated. John Miles, the most obviously
important, was also illiterate; Martha Baker was there and
may well have enjoyed her spell in the witness box. This was
a very different affair, though, from the case of 1693.
Increasingly the commoners had come to include men of
considerable name and substance, prominent people whose
rights of common were vigorously and profitably engaged.
The most prominent was the 15th Duke of Norfolk, Earl

Marshall of England. Others included Sir Spencer Maryon-
Wilson, whose reliance on the Forest has already been
reviewed. The Earl of Sheffield was well established at
Sheffield Park and had considerable property round about
which entitled him to Forest perquisites. Sir John Shelley, of
Maresfield Park, had died, but his widow was ready to
participate; and Bernard Hale whose employee John Miles
had been instrumental in bringing matters to a head, was
Deputy-Lieutenant of Sussex. A pretty fair swathe of local
society had much to lose or gain.

They lost.

The fatal flaw in the Decree of 1693 had been the omission
of any final ruling on the cutting of litter and in spite of all
Raper's magnificent work, this was bound to be the stum-
bling block. They were back in no time to the 'bite of mouth'
argument. The judge could see nothing whatever in the
business to justify the commoners' extraordinary claim to a
right which quite clearly had never existed. They were not
only disturbing the quiet process of the Earl's affairs, they
were wasting the time of the Court in fruitless delays and
offensive argument, disturbing the even tenor of country life
in a most ungentlemanly fashion . . .

The Lord of the Manor, therefore, made his point, won his
case and returned home in triumph.

It is difficult not to let the imagination off its hook just
here. Feelings must have run so high! What arguments and
worse would surely have taken place in the local drinking
places, what attempts at burning and uprooting in traditional
style . . . Thomas Pentecost knew of such matters when he
wrote censoriously of Ashdown in 1852 as 'A heathy waste of
huts and dens/Where human nature seldom mends . . .'
Bernard Hale's sharp reply to an early question from the
judge must have been often quoted, perhaps uneasily. Mr
Hale had been asked why he supposed the Lord of the Manor
had brought the action if it had no substance. Mr Hale
answered that he had 'regarded it as another instance of (his)

. . . wish to create trouble . . .' His words could only have encouraged the factions . . .

The judgment in the case was challenged and in 1881 the matter went to appeal. The three judges sitting then did uphold the 1693 definition of litter taking as being 'by bite of mouth' but they agreed it had been proved by Mr Hale that litter had been cut and carried on his behalf and that of his predecessors for at least sixty years. However, that did not cover those claiming right of common over centuries past. Since they were no longer all poor men, the commoners instituted a cross-petition. They sought an injunction that would prevent the Lord of the Manor's interference with the commoners' day to day pursuit of what they knew to be their entitlement. His Lordship, they claimed, was ruining the grazing by developing stone quarries and the like. They also accused him, rather curiously as it seems, of allowing squatters to settle on the Forest. Perhaps this applied to workers in the business of stone digging? Gipsies were already a familiar problem.

This petition succeeded. Were there triumphal bonfires that night? There seems no record of any celebration, perhaps because there was still a long way to go. The setting up of the Board of Conservators, the registration of the Forest under the Commons Act of 1876 and the necessity for carefully drawn by-laws, kept everyone busy for several years. All this passed provisionally into law in 1885, to be confirmed and made positive within a reasonable time.

At last Ashdown was to be controlled democratically by Conservators voted into office and all of them commoners. It was certainly the dawn of a new age, though commoners of the lesser sort do seem to have reserved judgment, if quietly, on this new situation; perhaps they wondered who they would be able to grumble about in the future . . . The solution surely called for congratulation. It is to be hoped that William Augustus Raper, taking on the job of first Clerk to the Conservators, received all the applause he deserved.

Although Ashdown Forest was not to be 'safe for evermore' as has been claimed, it was on the way to an administration as democratic as any that could have been hoped for at the time.

CHAPTER FIVE

See How It Runs

The various offices concerned with the running of Ashdown Forest have persistently changed their titles over the centuries: Master of the Forest, Master of the King's Game, Steward of the Forest, Sheriff, Bailiff, Ranger, Looker, Forester, Walker, Reeve, Wood Reeve—they are shuffled and re-aligned constantly, leaving behind for today little more than Ranger and Forest Superintendent, the last combining a number of past high- flown titles. The one constant, the one thread never broken or frayed that ties the times, is the Commoner. From the beginning, the commoner has been far and away the most significant ingredient in the running of the Forest. From being the poorest they became, as has been witnessed, the most powerful. However challenged, whenever threatened, however whittled away, they have seen to it that the Right of Common remains—as it must always remain. The claim that but for the stubborn determination of the past commoners we should not have Ashdown Forest for our delight today is by no means an exaggeration. Their nagging and defiance, their often unruly attitudes and far from mild behaviour, have paid a dividend we can only rejoice in— though how things go on the Forest today would surprise many and appall more. Even many of today's third and fourth generations of Forest families may be heard complaining of restraints which they are convinced were never so bad in the bad old days. They are as much at odds, though in a calmer way, with the Board of Conservators as their forebears were with the Lord of the Manor, with the Sovereign. It cannot be said too often that contention here on Ashdown appears as an ingredient of the soil and if it were ever conquered it would be the end of far too much. As it is, any crisis brings about the knitting of old loyalties and the strength engendered then can be actively inspiring . . .

In the days when the Master Forester stood on a convenient height and sounded his horn to summon interested parties to discuss and deal with such matters as the taking of estovers and the allotment of other rights, the rates of remuneration to the various Forest servants were exceedingly modest. The whole place was divided into *walks* and *wards*— now more often called *chases*—and these divisions were over and above the boundaries of the parishes that stretched into the interior. A lot of policing was needed before enclosures snatched much commonable land away. Wages remained low for years, though they were supplemented by whatever came to hand—game, venison, wood; sometimes poached, sometimes taking the shape of rewards for services. It was implied at one point that such people as attended to the needs of the Forest did not even desire more than they received. It has been noted earlier that the top Forester often earned as little as 4d a day, his underlings 1d a day if they went about their work on foot—or *snudged*, to use a highly illustrative Sussex term. A man riding about his work earned 2d a day. Much later, Lookers were paid 12/- a week for their daily vigilance, and an extra £4.10 a year for attending woodmotes and the like. The rate paid for animals grazed by commoners varied according to their status, their form of tenantry. *Foreigners*, that is those outside the categories described later in this chapter, often sent their animals to commoners for grazing, the custom called *agistment*; presumably such commoners grazed less than their entitlement and the arrangement gave them some profit. At the time of Elizabeth I, the charge for grazing a horse was 1d; ½d per head of cattle—called in this context *Rother beasts*, since there was little care in their breeding and the term was rather mysteriously pejorative.

The commoner of those days was also allowed 'all the hogges which he may nourish', except of course during the fence month, those days on either side of Midsummer when the does are dropping their fawns. Pigs got their own back for this exclusion, for between Michaelmas and Martinmas, that is from the 29th September to the 11th November, no other beast might graze, that being the season of beech-mast and acorn, and the Forest then pure pig's paradise. Pigs were charged at 2d, 1d or a ½d, according to age. Any commoner putting ten pigs to pannage also paid to the Crown annually 'the third best hogge'—a custom that carries a ring of benevolence.

The various local courts that dealt with Forest affairs had been in existence from feudal times, long before the Royal Chace came into being. The annual Evesfald, or Aves Court, was held on the first Tuesday after All Saints'; next the Woodmote, three weeks later, concentrating on the tenants' grievances and misdemeanours. Finally, there were the Courts Baron, held regularly every three weeks to deal with property, leases and allied matters. A jury was sworn for these occasions and it could be difficult to get enough to sign on when the matters to be reviewed were all too often questions of principle and loudly expressed opinion. In 1381, when John of Gaunt was the Forest's Lord, feeling was running high against the new poll-tax—the Peasants' Revolt, under the legendary Wat Tyler. The Administration of the Forest suffered during these uneasy times, the holding of the customary courts was often prevented, even violently; this was where Sir Edward Dallingridge took a hand . . .

In later years, when magistrates' courts took over the hearing of local cases, examples of foresty misbehaviour quite frequently received sympathetic handling—which was gall to prosecutors who might easily be strangers to the neighbourhood. Then came that hardening of attitude to-wards labouring men, when sentences became much harsher. One man, a tanner by trade, who stole two oxen, was

sentenced to hanging, and there were cases of hard labour.
Nowadays, the occasional summons issued by the Conservators is heard, too, by local magistrates. The offences usually
concern instances of sheep chasing by dogs, riding without a
licence, litter dumping—and still fire-raising and still encroachment. This last flourishes as it has always done and is
as regularly condemned. There is always a reluctance to
prosecute, however, the mood now being one of tolerance
and a sincere intention to keep people happy while they are
about the Forest; there is almost certainly a warning or two
before action is taken. This last follows long precedent, for it
was at a very early Board Meeting that the policy of leniency
was formulated. At that meeting was passed the often-mocked
resolution already mentioned: 'It was UNANIMOUSLY resolved
that the Clerk be instructed that it shall be in his discretion
not to prosecute for a first offence if regret is expressed to him
or the Ranger and a promise not to repeat the offence is given
by the offender.' It is impossible not to relish the vision of a
commoner, cap in hand and tongue in cheek, promising to be
good . . .

It is the survey of 1273 that divides the tenants in and
around the Forest into three classes, so it is one of the most
ancient of the laws of the countryside. There are freehold
tenants, who hold directly from the King; inter-tenants,
answering to one or other of the neighbourhood manors; and
foreign tenants, alluded to a few pages back, who were more
or less the left-overs. The customary tenants, the commoners,
would belong to one or other of these classifications. They
were by no means always their own masters, but frequently
exercised common right on behalf of their landlord, working
for him at the same time as gaining the benefit of their own
copyhold entitlement, which was extremely modest. These
commoners numbered 208 in that early survey—today there
are 687, the result of splitting commonable holdings for
building purposes; very few exercise their right, which is a
fairly absurd situation. The rents paid by the 208 totalled

£1.19.½d. These were supplemented by gifts in kind to their overlords; 1 hen at Christmas, 216 eggs at Easter. Sometimes the 1 hen was replaced by 1d, or by a quantity of oats. In 1564, 64 foreign tenants paid 63 hens plus 10/6—surely a generous replacement for that missing 64th hen . . .? All classes of Forest tenant had right of pasture and herbage, but only freeholders and inter-tenants, having dwellings on land of their own, were able to take their estovers, or allowance of wood. From time to time one comes upon other benefits, as it were thrown in—such as that heather called *long heather* taken for thatching.

The administrative pattern was set for the Ashdown we know when, in 1887, the final settlement of the case between the Lord of the Manor and the Commoners led to the setting up of an officially recognised Board of Conservators, as related in an earlier chapter. The Board was there to 'protect the rights of the commoners', and since the early Conservators were themselves commoners the arrangement must have seemed a highly satisfactory one. The Board held its first properly ordered meeting on the 9th September in the year of its inception—the first was a brief, rather solemn, exploratory affair but matters were soon better in hand. A whole new order was in the making, and after the long years of struggle with authority there was a new spirit abroad.

At that September meeting it was resolved 'that the Clerk purchase a substantial book for keeping the Minutes in'. The Clerk, of course, was to be the admirable William Augustus Raper, whose dogged explorations were certainly responsible for the final success of the commoners' case. That first substantial book lasted until December 1897, ten years of increasing confidence though not, perhaps, of sensational progress. Voting on all matters dealt with by the Board was by acreage—one acre, one vote. The first Conservators were mostly property owners of some substance and there were ten of them, so they were well placed to get their way. It is many years before we find a more democratic set-up—one man, one vote was strenuously resisted and came into force only in the early 1970s, after an astonishing amount of wrangling.

The Board of Conservancy of Ashdown Forest, its title at the outset, then promulgated the Commoners' Annual General Meeting, which we know today. Then, as now, the commoners met essentially to elect members to the Board, the Constitution then requiring that four retire by rotation each year. At the first meeting of its kind, the commoners re-elected the Board *en bloc*; hardly a surprise, since they had barely had time to get themselves decently organised. The impression is gained that the bulk of the humbler commoners—if a humble commoner has ever existed—were mildly embarrassed by the whole business. Voting by show of hands is seldom easy. There seems then to have been some immediate trouble, for only a month later the Board was convened for a special meeting at Nutley Inn, which had become the customary venue, to deal with certain infringements of the by-laws.

Twenty-three admonitory by-laws had been drawn up; today we have thirty. No. 3 in the original collection has become today's No. 10: 'No unauthorised person shall shoot, chase, trap, snare or take any animal, bird, insect or fish, or any egg or nest of any bird upon any part of the Forest or shall have in his possession any gun or part of a gun, or any trap, snare net or any other instrument used for any of these purposes.' It should not be thought, however, that the first by-laws were drawn up in quite the same spirit as today's— their by-law No. 3 was merely to protect the sporting habits then prevailing; our No. 10 is in the interests of conservation.

No. 18 in the original forbids fighting, brawling and any nuisance contrary to public decency or propriety, any behaviour whatsoever 'of a disorderly or indecent kind'. This admonition has vanished, so presumably it is taken for granted that we are all much better behaved than we were. Forest users have not yet reverted to brawling, but there are lively goings-on at times among the bracken; the playing of

radios too loud, too long, appears as the only threat to
accepted good manners. As the *Ranger's Handbook* discreetly
advises—'Some people like to solve their own problems and
this should be borne in mind . . .'

The carefully collated Forest documents that take us back
so far are only a fraction more seductive than the Minute
Books that began with the substantial book, still resting on its
shelf in the Board Room cupboard at the Centre. It has
grown by now into a possibly daunting row of black-spined
volumes, each designed to cover a ten-year period, though
one runs a bit longer. Once they succumb to typewriting they
seem to have a shade less style, but that must surely be sheer
snobbery in the investigator; though it has to be remembered
that all minutes contrive to carry at least a faint stamp of their
recorder. This is very noticeable in certain circumstances.
There are meetings I recall as more than merely lively that can
read as smooth and boring affairs.

Like *The Raper Papers*, the minutes offer some engaging
item on practically every page. It seems best to keep things
within bounds by selecting the periods that cover a specific
event or crisis on the Forest and judge how the Board of
Conservators coped. Choice falls fairly obviously on the two
world wars, and on the parliamentary acts of 1937, 1949 and
1974. The war years are particularly interesting, partly
because they have left scars, partly because of the changed
attitudes that appear from one to the other. In 1914 the
business-as-usual stance is very much in evidence, at any rate
at the beginning. In 1939 there appears far less readiness to
accept without question what must happen to the Forest.
There is a clear awareness that this time there will be no
banishing of the conflict to the far side of the convenient
Channel. At both periods there is some reluctance, during the
run-up, to look the business in the face, for the assurance that
'it will all be over by Christmas' is there in the background at
both periods. Later, the truth is accepted in a good and sober

fashion.

In the minutes covering the 1914–18 war it is curious to find no positive mention of its outbreak or of its end. Outbreak and ending came between meetings and although the war is immediately present, it is so only in its impingement on Forest affairs. There seem to be no asides—or perhaps the clerk refuses to admit irrelevancies. The conflict, of course, was hardly unexpected and preparations were at least on paper. Camps were immediately set up under the *Defence of the Realm Act*. These were to cause endless headache and harassment for the Board. The War Department is so sweeping in its immediate demands, so authoritarian and ruthless that the Conservators are soon seen to be plunged into an interior war of their own. They can almost be seen to bridle their patriotism in the interests of good sense, in the interests, that is, of the Forest—which is still in their care, emergency or no. It is a delicate balance in a period of considerable jingoism. The Board, therefore, comes up with stipulations—when war terminates, the surface of the Forest is to be made good, manure from the horses to be left and spread, the ground re-seeded and the utmost precaution taken at all times against fire. And in the event of fire, the military to be responsible for its extinguishing. Such arrangements seem reasonable enough, but the trouble they led to at the end of the war dragged on for years. None of this can have been easy for some members of the Board which, in the nature of such bodies, included retired generals, brigadiers, admirals.

Camps were set up at King's Standing, Camp Hill, Kidbrooke Park, Pippingford, Forest Row, St John's Common, with other locations under review. The authority was really very stupid over some of these sites. One at Forest Row having been selected, it was then switched to a hillside full of springs that ran in winter into boggy ground. 'This,' the Board rebuked, 'indicates . . . some lack of both topographical knowledge and practical experience.' But the military from the start were careless and inconsiderate, putting up stables and latrines in inappropriate places, to the distress of property owners, polluting the rivers and ponds—there was, of course, no piped water supply at that time—and causing an enormous amount of mess. They also caused, it was firmly believed, a great many unnecessary fires.

The Army settled speedily into Pippingford, which they knew already from summer camps held there for some years. Quite early in the occupation there was a very big fire which caused a great deal of ill-feeling. The officer in command at Pippingford ordered out some sixty of his men to deal with the blaze—which the Conservators believed had been started by visitors to the camp, or by troops returning merrily from a canteen at Chelwood Gate. When it was all over, the officer wrote to the Board suggesting that a grant should be made for the services of his sixty stalwarts—since their uniforms had been damaged by smoke. The Board dealt with this pretty smartly. Discreet enquiry proved that only two or three uniforms had suffered the smallest damage, and the Board resolved as follows: '. . . that inasmuch as all the Military Authorities are fully occupied . . . the Clerk do not reply to the application of the Officer Commanding the R.E. camp . . . unless a further communication is received.' No more was heard.

With the ending of the war the Forest could surely breathe again and return to its own way of life. But as the war in Europe ended, the conflict for Ashdown Forest began in earnest. Communications thumped and barked from one side to the other, as nothing was done by the authorities to restore the *status quo*. There was a point at which the War Department denied that any arrangement for compensation and restitution had ever been formulated. 'Your reputed claim,' the Department calls the request, soon demand, by the Conservators that holes and trenches be filled in, asphalt tracks taken up, hutments removed, accumulations of rubbish and ammunition cleared, areas dug for vegetable cultivation duly restored. The nagging and the snorting continued for years and it says much for the determination of the Board that eventually there was a decent settlement and demands were met at last. Even the camp at Forest Row—a particular problem—was finally dismantled. In 1919 the East Grinstead Rural Council, as it was then, had thought it could be an excellent idea to keep the camp, converting it into 'a permanent hamlet'. There was, they claimed, a serious shortage of accommodation for local soldiers returning home. The reason for that, retorted the Chairman of Conservators, was that cottages and other dwellings were still being occupied by wives and relations of officers or men at the camp. The Protection of Commons Act was able to deal with the problem.

Between the wars, on into the 'thirties, the records make clear that the Forest is going through difficult times. In March 1936 a meeting of the General Purposes Committee looked squarely at a brutal financial situation. Income was about £500 annually—and expenditure was just about the same. It may have cost at that time a mere 1/7d a week to insure an employee, but the Forest rate was only 6d an acre—as it remained until 1974. As long ago as 1830 a levy had been proposed of 7d an acre and the subsequent revolt of the commoners was not forgotten. Some other means of fund-raising had to be considered. The general uncertainty about the situation was causing the commoners to behave in a most obstreperous way; rates unpaid, complaints about the rangers, all the usual rumpus. One commoner, having refused with great doggedness to pay his rate, offered to transfer it to a third party eager to acquire the right of common to which the rate attached. Impossible, replied the Conservators, correctly enough though no doubt gloomily, since they were inviting more trouble. It was not only the human element that was growing out of hand—the Forest itself was suffering and beginning to look wretchedly unkempt. For the first time, with grazing diminishing, the cutting of litter was positively encouraged and the time during which it could be taken was extended at either end.

Among all these worries, the characters emerge un-diminished and distracting. At this time the rangers—there were two of them by then—attended Board meetings and made each his report on work and events since the last meeting. There seems no declared explanation for the drop-ping of this practice, unless because it was inclined to become a bit long-winded. The custom might be restored with advantage, for the rangers in general know a good deal more about Forest matters than some Conservators will ever know. Since the Board meetings are open, this would be one opportunity for the rangers to make comments and give practical advice and feel that their combined voice is heard.

In the '30s, the first ranger was that necessary Mr Kirby who held the job for thirty-six years. His assistant was Ranger Hatchett, whose chief occupation, as it appears in the minutes, was the chasing of marauding gypsies. His reports suggest whole colonies of travelling people of one order or another, of whom he emerges as the willing scourge. He removes them with a firmness we can only imagine. 5 tents, 55 'vans, 19 carts and 9 trolleys, he reports on one occasion. On another, 36 'vans, 18 carts, 45 horses. Best of all, 6 'vans, 20 horses—and 5 boys' . . . One gypsy, brought to court at last, was fined 1/– for the trespass. *Gypsies on the Forest* is item 22 of a long Board meeting and it deserves to be quoted:

'Complaint was made that there was an increasing number of gypsies on the Forest, which it was alleged was due to the distribution of clothes etc. at The Convent, Ashdown Park. The Clerk was instructed to write to Mother Superior asking for her co-operation in the matter.'

Whoever made the complaint was possibly indulging a double grudge . . . Unfortunately, the Board being increasingly concerned with one crisis and another, there is no further report and we shall never know how Reverend Mother and the Clerk got on together. The gypsies, however, did not go away. Instead, finances became so tight that Ranger Hatchett was dismissed and Ranger Kirby once more had the place to himself and his bicycle—now a motorbike; Ranger Hatchett's bicycle was sold.

The '30s continued full of bother for the Conservators. Much of the neighbourhood was to have piped water for the first time, while electricity and telephone companies were moving in and making difficulties about the siting of posts and poles, the routing of cables. There were wrangles with the engineers about laying all cables underground. The companies were convinced they could not be forced into such a costly operation, but forced they were—though to this day there is certainly one overhead line on the actual Forest. Then came the dumping by some London firm of half a ton of wastepaper; almost worse, the selling of marsh gentians by the roadside by unscrupulous pickers. Finally the burden became so painful that the Conservators faced the necessity of reorganisation. In May 1936 a conference took place at *The Shelley Arms* in Nutley, which embraced the Board of Conservators and representatives of the various local councils.

At this gathering was drawn up the basis of a proposed Bill to be presented to Parliament, which would change the long-accepted form of administration of Ashdown Forest. It was proposed that future responsibility for the Forest should be shared by the Conservators with those councils whose communities used the Forest as an amenity. These were the East Sussex County Council and three Rural District Councils—East Grinstead, Uckfield and Cuckfield; all three now defunct and re-formed. The make-up of the Board would be drastically altered, with 5 members from East Sussex, 3 from Uckfield, 1 from East Grinstead, 1 from Cuckfield, 9 commoner members and 1 nominated by the Lord of the Manor. '. . . it was not expected that the total

expenditure would exceed £1000 per annum.' Then the
General Purposes Committee 'instructed the Clerk to proceed
with the preparation of a draft Bill.'

With very little difficulty on the way, or so the minutes lead
us to believe, the new Ashdown Forest Bill received the
Royal assent on the 1st July 1937.

While the Bill was speeding through Parliament, Forest
affairs had been proceeding as usual, unpaid rates being
pursued with a new vigour in contemplation, no doubt, of
changed circumstances. The Board had re-ordered its
authority and its energies, too, were re-charged. There was a
fresh problem to be tackled—the motorcar was multiplying.
Not only were visitors arriving and driving on to the Forest,
but commoners and other residents wanted to build themselves garages, to make up their rough tracks. This was a
difficult one to solve, since in many cases to build was
necessarily to encroach. The tale of the garage built a few feet
on to the Forest at one corner, and how its owners were
forced to move it back, has been told often enough, but it
proves a certain diligence. Other ploys must have been used
which were either permitted or escaped official notice, for
most houses about the Forest have their garages now.
Today's problem is that room for one car is no longer
sufficient and the rest get left outside where they certainly
should not be . . . There was considerable discussion, too, on
another point concerning cars—should Fairwarp Church be
allowed a 'draw-off' for worshippers on wheels? The unfortunate term *lay-by* was mercifully far ahead. Interesting to note
that at this date the Chairman of the Board declared the
Conservators powerless to compel motorists to park in any
given place. That was to come later, when the *draw-offs*
developed into properly managed parking areas; a lot of
people dislike them, but they work. They go some way to
concentrating the litter and make the task of clearance, at least
of picnic-type rubbish, a good deal easier.

The new constitution of Forest business was barely into

easy running order when the Munich crisis of 1938 broke in on everyday affairs. Not that this is mentioned in the records, directly or otherwise, but it signalled disasters ahead however soothing the official messages might appear. In the time between one September and the next, the Conservators as minuted appear somewhat tetchy and proscriptive. There were still plenty of recollections of what had happened to the Forest between 1914 and 1918, and there was nothing soothing about such memories. No doubt because of this mood local problems, naturally continuing, were dealt with far less sympathetically than usual. Perhaps some of this was due to the new regime, the presence of strangers, of non-commoners who might know far less of what they were called upon to handle. It is difficult to see, to quote a very suitable example, why a certain Mr Cottage, who asked permission to erect a stand for a dozen hives of bees, should be refused—what a sensible, admirable forest activity . . . And how about residents digging air-raid shelters? Somewhat surprisingly, these applications were dismissed with the resolution that 'no action be taken', though ARP training was well under way by then. At this unsuitable moment something near to a row broke out over the sanitary arrangements at Fairwarp School. They were emptying their lavatory buckets on to the Forest, to the scandal of a nearby resident. Since there was still no piped water there and the sanitation could only be primitive, this was indeed a poser. Letters flew back and forth until a skilful sanitary inspector defused the affair by assurances that apparently convinced the neighbours that the emptying practice could only be for the Forest's good . . . At such a moment it appeared tactless, on the part of Lord Cecil, to complain about litter in his area. Once again 'it was decided to take no action.'

As in 1914, war broke out between the July and October meetings of the Board and once again the actual occurrence is never referred to, though its results are immediately apparent. Petrol is rationed, which bears on Ranger Kirby's motorcycle and a supplementary ration has to be applied for and agreed to. He could certainly never have managed on the official five gallons for two months, for he covered two hundred miles a week on normal patrols. More prosaically, the owner of Lone Oak Hall at Chuck Hatch had settled an ice-cream van at his gate and was refusing to move it. And now there was a completely new problem to be dealt with. Water Farm, at Coleman's Hatch, put in an urgent application for a temporary water supply from a spring near the farm—where twenty-five evacuees were to be catered for. At the Vachery the demand was for temporary lavatories—fifty evacuees were expected there.

Then came a demand from the War Department for the use of the Forest as a training ground for 10,000 troops, with mechanised transport. That was the moment at which the 2nd World War began for Ashdown Forest.

Military occupation of whatever area is unlikely to be easy or enjoyable. It is impossible not to groan for the Conservators of Ashdown Forest over the next few years. Early responses are placatory, accommodating, almost genial. Yes, indeed, there have been as many as thirty-eight fires in the past month, but who can be blamed? Enemy action, perhaps—for now it was the summer of 1940 and the so-called *phoney war* was coming to its end. Soon there would be plenty of enemy activity to blame for disasters. At the end of the year the mood has changed again in the Boardroom and the clerk is reporting that 'differences have arisen in cases where the military had used the Forest and carried out exercises without notice.' Again memories of the last war bring anxieties about ultimate restitution and there is much troubled correspondence in which the usual delaying tactics of officialdom do nothing at all to assist the atmosphere. By this time the clerk was Mr Fovargue, the retired Raper's colleague, and his handling of awkward situations suggests a worthy successor, as resolute and clear-headed as his senior. Most residents appear after twelve months to have come to terms with such oddities as gun-emplacements, dug-outs on the Forest—at Gill's Lap to keep the mostly elderly members of the Home Guard moderately snug—slit trenches, tank traps, roads where never roads should be.

By 1941 a number of wartime schemes were being discussed. The wireless station at King's Standing is rumoured to hold mysterious secrets—nothing to do with the Romans—far more sinister but no one is prepared to speculate out loud. There is concern that the military have lowered the level of the ponds in Crowborough Warren—will there still be enough for cattle? Shall the Forest, or what is left unoccupied, be ploughed for cultivation—*Dig for Victory*! May pigs in some quantity be put out for pannage at Mudbrook? Bald statements abound which give the reader a bleak picture of attempts to keep control of events which gather speed alarmingly. The army has laid an underground water pipe . . . They are using the Forest at Greenwood Gate as a tank park . . . At St John's they are doing much the same only more so . . . They have put up a hut at Gill's Lap . . . As late as 1942 future compensation arrangements are nowhere near settled. Authority suggests 'that there was no reason why Ashdown Forest should not be requisitioned in the usual way'; this strikes a chill even now. Live ammunition has been used and insufficient warning given . . . The Board submits to an area selected for gas training; the fence is put up in the wrong place and must be removed and re-erected . . . Incendiaries fall . . . An RAF plane crashes as it limps home from a raid on Cologne and all on board are killed . . . Flying bombs, the cockney's *doodle-bugs*, were the last enemy device to hit the Forest, falling short on their programmed flight to London. The V2s, the far heavier rockets, missed Ashdown. Then silence . . .

The war with Germany ended officially on the 7th May 1945. At once the task was in hand to regain the Forest for its own people, the commoners and the Board of Conservators who were there for its protection. It was no easier than it had been in 1918. The military had no wish to leave. An assurance from the War Department that 'no part would be retained as a training ground longer than was necessary' was hardly comforting. Once again the correspondence passed ponderously to and fro; interested parties met, lawyers reported, discussed, prevaricated—and so slipped back almost to the beginning. 'The compensation claims,' it was explained, 'will be deferred until the release of the training area.' The Minister of Planning, at that time Lewis Silkin, who appeared sympathetic, none the less gave with one hand and clawed back with the other in the time-honoured Civil Service fashion. 'You may rest assured,' he wrote, 'that my views are that the land requisitioned should be returned intact to the Conservators and that my efforts will be directed to that end. In the meantime, I think that it would be better to leave the matter as it stands until the views of the responsible Departments are available.'

Just as well, then, that the old annoyances picked up splendidly to distract the Board slightly from a wretchedly worrying situation. There were still people putting up posts or making compost heaps where no such heap should be. Making 'bracken ricks' is mentioned, I think for the first and only time, and it has as suitable a foresty ring to it as Mr Cottage's beehive stand of several years previously. There was a vast amount of planting wrongly, cutting illegally—and it comes as a relief when Fairwarp Carnival Committee make a request for a November bonfire. At least one local tradition is obviously getting back into its stride, and although its derivation is exceedingly malign it appears in this carnival context as the merriest idea in the world . . . There was still, in the later '40s, Ranger Kirby's motorbike, but only just. It was at this time that he retired to the plaudits and gratitude of those who had employed him and relied on him for so many years—and now gave him a retainer of 10/– a week that his advice might be sought when it was needed.

The eventual settling of the military question—by no

means to the satisfaction of everyone concerned—necessitated a new Ashdown Forest Act; the Act of 1949. The Army had acquired the private Pippingford land it had known for so long, and is there today. They also retained the camp at St John's and claimed the use of the Forest for certain training exercises; subject to strict control in the matter of live ammunition, reparations and such like; these rights lapsed in later years. The public still had official access only to those clumps of Scots pine such as Camp Hill and the rest which had been designed to offer vantage points from which non-commoners might gaze upon what they could not possess. The Act received the Royal assent on the 30th July 1949.

This new Act, which should have controlled such faults, failed to prevent Army dumping of unwanted materials—50 sections of Nissen huts, old radio batteries, rolls of wire. Such infringements, along with great slackness over the filling-in of trenches and tank-traps, were being discussed as late as 1952. By then the commoners were back in the most splendid stubborn form. A good illustration is the case of 'Mr Moon of Nutley'. He was told by the Ranger to remove his stack of chestnut poles which constituted an encroachment and he responded by parking alongside a very large lorry containing a great many more chestnut poles . . .

Minute Book No. 7 is the thickest book of them all, not entirely because—I have no idea why—it holds twelve years' recording instead of the customary ten, but because everyone is so talkative about so many subjects. Already in this Book's later years attitudes were once more on the shift. The day of conservation had arrived. The forest floor, its vegetation, its animal life had acquired a new interest and importance. By the early 1950s the Forest was feeling its way to a course which is more or less what is followed today. But the link with William Augustus Raper was finally broken when his colleague and successor, Mr Fovargue, relinquished the clerkship in his turn. A new clerk, Peter Williams, a solicitor

of East Grinstead, took up the task of advising the Conservators and coping with all the time-honoured practices—of
common right, of evasion of rates, of encroachment and the
rest. At one time sheep were not commonable animals,
though there are so many stories of their being driven and
impounded—perhaps simply because they should not have
been there. Now they were admitted, by express permission
of the Lord of the Manor. Commoners were still putting out
a cow or two, sometimes wearing bells. A claim to pannage
in the '70s was sharply handled, but this could have been a
slightly manufactured mistake; it is difficult to discover any
proof that the rights of pigs were ever revoked.

It was during the late '60s that there began to build up a
new tide of dissent and dissatisfaction that gradually washed
through the Forest from end to end. Changes in the form of
local government in general had brought the necessity of
change in the composition of the Board. It would mean the
down-grading of commoner representation, for the remaining
councils, now Wealden District alongside East Sussex County
Council, would have a larger financial stake in Ashdown;
these appointed members would greatly outnumber the
elected commoners. All this, of course, meant the drafting of
a new Bill and the quarrelling that followed was extraordinary. A major issue was the voting system, which still
stood at one-acre, one-vote as it had done for the past eighty
or so years. Change in this matter was surely overdue, and it
became a key issue in the quarrelling that followed. As is
usual in such conflicts, the opposition was based on a core of
twenty or so dissatisfied commoners, sensible and right
thinking enough, give or take a fanatic or two. Looking back
on those times it is not easy to chart the exact course of the
revolt as it became increasingly well organised. By this time
another clerk had retired after substantial service and the new
Clerk-cum-Forest Superintendent was an ex-Navy man, Lt.
Comdr. Peter Angell. He was not a solicitor with other
interests to distract him but lived on the Forest and soon

knew it by heart. He was only the fourth Clerk to the Board of Conservators in a hundred years and he had arrived at a very difficult moment. Whereas in the past the commoners had been stubborn and stolid, the new issue were extremely vocal, sometimes vituperative and even strident. As I became involved myself I feel safe in making this comment.

The reorganisation of the rural councils round about and the setting up of the wider-embracing Wealden District Council inevitably upset Forest finances. It was at once necessary to think of considerable re-structuring. With the publication and discussion of the proposed new Bill, a Commoners' Committee came into being, to form a bulwark, as they believed, against over-weening authority. Uckfield had apparently been ready to oppose the Bill as drafted, but their own local arrangements were also on the point of change and the opposition was withdrawn. This left, as the relevant minutes sharply announce, 'the dissident commoners' entirely on their own. In the face of all this, the Board Chairman's remarks at the conclusion of one meeting are worth quoting. All parties concerned, he said, had in fact the same objective, which was the good of Ashdown Forest. 'Probably all must shoulder some blame . . . but good can yet come out of this common purpose.' Admirable tolerance, for he had been badly mauled already and knew well that the business was not nearly over . . . Incidentally, the minutes at this time were well and sharply written and frequently offer excellent examples of personal reaction which evades positive comment: 'Miss Y. and Mr X.,' the secretary writes, 'delivered a lecture on Parliamentary procedure.' Both were *dissident commoners.*

Besides the uproar about the voting system, the Commoners' Committee was concerned for the actual make-up of the future Board. If one vote per acre were to remain in force, authority could remain in the same hands for ever; if there were too few elected commoner Conservators, then the Forest might rest in the hands of virtual strangers, changing with the

local elections and offering little continuity. This was a
reasonable attitude. Some objections raised by the Committee
appear as routine and niggling—whatever was effected must
be challenged and at times the challenge could be silly enough
for good ground to be lost. An example of this turns on the
gift by the Friends of Ashdown Forest of two shot guns and
two humane killers for the use of the Rangers, who were
obliged all too often to put down deer injured on the roads.
Why in the world should any member of the Committee find
this valuable gesture objectionable?

A more useful move came with a letter signed by twenty
commoners requesting a special meeting with the Board, at
which only commoners or Conservators would be allowed to
speak. At the next Commoners' AGM, on the 11th
December 1973, the following resolution was carried by 41
votes to 12: 'That this Meeting ask the Board of Conservators
to withdraw their support for the Bill, and try to persuade the
East Sussex County Council to withdraw the Bill.' The East
Sussex County Council, however, had made up its cumulative
mind and continued to shove the Bill on its course, ignoring
yet another public meeting that 'deplored the action of the
East Sussex County Council in re-submitting the Ashdown
Forest Bill to Parliament and call(ing) on them to exercise
their right to withdraw the Bill forthwith.'

During these times, the lovely medieval word *misfeasance*
was bandied about the Forest as though it were nothing but
slang. I recall all this as being extremely absorbing, at times
positively exciting, once or twice downright melodramatic.
But when I read the minutes taken at meetings during those
uneasy days, I warm to the unfortunate Chairman and Clerk
who bore the brunt of the anarchy. And were all those past
troubles really so determinedly malicious as now they appear?
Meeting the Clerk/Superintendent out on Camp Hill during
this time, when I was walking the dogs, I said in the way one
does that it was a lovely day. It might be, he replied, but for
me and my friends. I was startled at the time and have never

forgotten the shock and the sting of the rebuke. Reading the records of what went on fifteen or so years ago, I can see his point.

For all the coming and the going, the strife and the strain, The Ashdown Forest Act 1974 was passed by Parliament and received the Royal Assent without much more delay. One man, one vote was achieved at last, for which the Commoners' Committee might well feel able to take much credit. The make-up of the Board, all the same, was disappointing, leaving the commoners with only five elected representatives. It seemed too few then and it seems far too few today. There would be eight ESCC appointed members, two from Wealden and one to represent the Lord of the Manor. The first Board of the new regime had five elected members who were all either members of the Commoners' Committee or else their candidate. I was one of those and so became a member of the Board in 1975 and stayed ten years, when I stood down as a matter of what seemed common sense. I was eventually the surviving member of the contentious '70s and perhaps I was there by slight *misfeasance*, but it was during those unregretted years that the Forest finally settled into my blood stream and there remains.

Compared with the complicated administration that attached to the Forest of the past, today's organisation must appear a model of simple planning; simple in this case does not mean easy. The Master of the Forest, in all his guises and manifestations, has become the Superintendent, which is a good deal more prosaic; he is no longer required to stand on some draughty height and summon his underlings by blast of horn. He doubles, as did the last Superintendent, as Clerk to the Conservators, with a Personal Assistant, five rangers and a tractor-driver on the payroll—while the whole structure is supported by a number of Volunteers, devotedly earning nothing but enormous respect and gratitude.

Before the opening of the Ashdown Forest Centre at Broadstone on the Ridge road—that is the road from Wych

Cross to Coleman's Hatch, an immensely ancient track—the offices of the Board were over the Village Hall in Forest Row. The fact that the lease was running out at the same time as the Rangers' Depot at Broadstone was falling apart, spurred on the effort to establish permanent headquarters allied to a depot and also to some sort of information service. There were the usual neighbourhood cries at the mere suggestion of change—the Conservators would be building on the Forest, outraging their own dictates as well as breaking by-laws and practically flaunting Parliament. The site chosen was not Forest ground but a part of the enclosure which was Broadstone Warren, owned by the Manor Charitable Trust. An Ashdown Forest Trust was then promulgated, the land was leased, three ancient barns discovered, purchased, re-erected, thatched—and with heather in the true local tradition. 'Asking for fire,' came the comment from the opposition . . .

That was in 1983. By now the fact that the office is no longer conveniently near to butcher, baker, chemist, post office has been more or less accepted. Enquiries, certainly, cannot be made by merely popping upstairs after a jumble sale in the hall below, or a visit to the branch library in the same building—nor can complaints. It is just possible that a telephone call or a drive of a mile or two may take the edge off some simple grievance, though life in the office does not appear to be quieter or easier than it was in other days.

Above the Information Barn, the Clerk/Superintendent sits in his office, with his Personal Assistant next door in a room twice as big. There, the telephone bell rings constantly, the radio-link with the Rangers talks away in its corner and there are computer noises, typewriter noises, photocopying noises. Fortunately for the nerves of those who work there, tea-and-coffee-making devices are also present, adding a more comfortable note.

The day begins something like this:

By eight o'clock in the morning the Superintendent is out

on the Forest, walking the dog, certainly, but initially taking
a look at the state of the ground. Is it in a fit state for riding,
or is this one of those days when the forest floor is so clogged
and over-trampled that some restriction will have to be
imposed? In extreme cases this can mean a complete ban;
Riding Suspended goes up on the big main road notice boards
where, at licensing time, we are reminded that riding is by
permit only. It can happen that a semi-stricture is all that
seems necessary, such as *Walking Only*. This is difficult to
enforce. Riders are instructed to call the office ansaphone to
discover in doubtful weather what they may or may not
do—but of course it is easier not to know. All the same, one
appallingly wet winter when walking was the order of the
day, practically all riders appeared to comply. These riding
bans are imposed with great reluctance, whatever the riders
themselves may think—and sometimes they roar into the
office demanding money back on their restricted licenses. The
other side of the horse business is the annoyance of walkers
who find their favourite ways running thick mud; they, too,
telephone the office to object . . .

Having made the day's outdoor decisions, the Superintendent arrives at the Centre by 8.20 or so, probably just
ahead of the Rangers, who are due at 8.30. The day's work is
discussed and allocated with as little hanging about as
possible. Each Ranger has his own area—the *chase* already
mentioned as taking the place of *walks* and *wards*. He is
responsible for everything within his allocation, and this
works well as, with any luck, people get to know their
Ranger and look to him for help in any foresty problem.

The Rangers on their way, the office day begins at 9
o'clock, when the Superintendent and his assistant open the
post. The mail may be one of those carrying letters of rebuke,
sharp or plaintive, of enquiry from new residents, of
information about birds sighted, of neighbouring encroachments and so on. There may also be a pile of applications of
one sort or another, that need to be dealt with as soon as

possible, perhaps about school visits or about charity events. There are requests for the go-ahead to re-make a bit of licensed track, to install an underground telephone line, to put a new sign at the gate—all too often because the name is to be changed—, or to cut down some intrusive tree. This last can be a difficult one, as the tree that offends one is sure to be the delight of another. There can seldom be a letter arriving at the Centre that needs no reply. And throughout the day the impingement of commoners and residents on the office routine is likely to continue—and indeed that is as it should be; such matters as they present are the essence of the Board's excuse for existing. For this it was brought into being a hundred years ago, as it was for more direct contacts, for visitors who come with queries—or opinions. Some need to be dealt with by the Superintendent, others perhaps less controversially knotty can be dealt with very effectively by his PA-cum-Secretary in the outer office. Both these permanent officers wear a good many more than two hats and are constantly changing one for another. What with inside work, outside work, talking, planning, typing and re-typing, drawing up agendas, duplicating minutes of various meetings, dealing with riding permits, collecting the forest rate and fees for wayleaves and rights of way, not to mention the preparation of estimates and accounts, there is not a lot of time for dallying.

On Mondays the Superintendent presides over a Rangers' meeting at which the coming week's work is discussed and plotted. In winter this will include felling, cutting and planting. Conservation measures agreed and declared in the Management Plan call for cutting of heather and bracken and dealing with old tired gorse which is no longer anything much more than an eyesore. There can be problems here since gorse, even dead gorse—and gorse everywhere has taken a terrible beating from fierce winds over several years—still gives cover for small animals and some birds, of which the office will certainly be reminded. Very little goes entirely unnoticed and when some planting of conifers was made in order to give shade to a newly aligned car park, there was a good deal of muttering. The management, however, are certainly not into the conifer-planting market. They are constantly destroying seedlings which, like birch, root quickly among valuable heather. And they must, of course, maintain in good repair those high-sited clumps which by tradition are of Scots Pine—the clumps that were planted, it will be recalled, to provide the thankful public with a viewpoint. Another necessary chore, constantly renewed, is the repair of crossing places where riders and walkers have both contributed to the breakdown of the surface into unmanageable mud. Wood chippings have been used to deal with this problem but a layer of sandstone has recently proved more effective . . . There is almost more outdoor work in winter than in summer and shorter days for its accomplishment. Over the past several years the Rangers have been helped by a team of 12, plus a supervisor, from the Manpower Services Commission. The number fluctuates and has been as low as 7.

Each Ranger now having his own chase has specific seasonal jobs in that area. Once a year he will walk his bounds, his eye on encroachments, trees needing surgery, overgrown tracks. Rangers are on call for long periods and are likely to be called out, mostly in spring, for fire-fighting; or for the humane killing of deer too badly injured on the road to be allowed to survive—this may well mean turning out in the middle of the night. Besides all this more obvious work, the Rangers are committed to certain information aspects concerning the Forest, and based on the work of the Information Barn—discussed in the chapter covering Barn activities. Inch by inch, the Forest is Ranger territory and they always know what they are looking at. If that seems a bold claim, I still believe it to be a true one.

At weekends the Volunteer Rangers turn up and do their stint, visiting car parks and casting an eye over visitors who may have some problem that needs solving. Sometimes

visitors put up tents which they take down very grumpily
when challenged; and sometimes they have unruly dogs,
whose delight in freedom impels them to dash after horses—
the present lack of sheep is a blessing for dog owners. A
number of Volunteer Rangers find plenty to occupy them.
Their work, too, must be planned at office level according to
seasonal requirements, and this is another occasion for
bombardment by telephone. All Rangers are in radio communication, and their reports and queries may also involve
the office.

When the Superintendent changes his hat to become Clerk
to the Board of Conservators, today's successor to William
Augustus Raper, he has a completely different set of problems
to deal with as well as the impingement of one lot on the
other—a sort of three-bank file in which one factor may well
quarrel with another. There are five annual Board Meetings,
and the same number for each of four committees—Finance
& General Purposes, Roadways, Conservation, Riding.
Twenty-five meetings in a year is a fair muster for a small
concern. Committee meetings call for a good deal of consultation on the way—Roadways, for instance, will include
site meetings and often long and delicate discussion with
residents or commoners wanting, say, to change some
alignment to do with their property or make an entry where
none ever entered before.

When it comes to the sixth annual meeting pertaining to
Forest affairs, the Clerk takes little part save to declare it in
being and retire—unless specifically invited to remain. This is
the Commoners' Annual General Meeting, now past its
centenary. It is held in March in one or other of the relevant
village halls, fairly obviously in rotation. It meets to discuss
commoner problems, to cast a probably critical eye over the
past year's doings by the Board, and to elect its own
Conservator in place of whoever is retiring. These members,
it has already been said, are elected for a term of five years,
and may be re-elected, as far as can be seen, any number of

times. Thirty years and a bit more when I was first entitled to
attend the Commoners' AGM, such gatherings were small
and seemed to make little more than a formal gesture. A few
years more and they had become very lively indeed. Lively is
perhaps too meek a word, though rowdy would be too
strong—say forceful. They were, it seems to me now, the last
upsurge of feeling inherited from older and far tougher days.
There were still 'real' commoners to rise up and complain of
conditions—far better than those their forebears had known
but clouded with unwelcome change to what had seemed
immutable. Things are not what they were, was the general
theme. True foresty men saw only that change—not to be
confused with progress—was taking away for ever something
unique that quite probably they would not have cared to
name—a way of life tied hand and foot to a wild and
contentious ground. They saw it being teased out and
weakened, with ever fewer commoners concerned about
grazing and the rest, and strangers settled in places that did
not always suit them, or they the place. Commoners of the
'50s and '60s may not have traced the elements of their
resistance any further into the past than to their grandparents
but they were unprepared for acceptance of the unavoidable
shifts of time.

These were the men who could always be relied on,
increasingly as they found sympathy and support, as happened in the '70s, to speed up a quiet meeting into an
unorganised but powerful protest. They have almost all gone.
Commoners' Meetings have become well-organised, efficient,
often with good discussion. Old so-and-so is no longer there
to spark off some ancient argument and the result, though
business-like, can be vaguely disheartening. In the '80s came a
threat far graver than anything else to date, a possible change
of ownership that could be more drastic than any since the
law suit of 1693 upheld the enclosures and halved the amount
of commonable land. Or since that other great case of the
1880s created the quite false impression that, thanks to the

tenacity of the commoners, the Forest would be preserved as itself in perpetuity. Perhaps it can never be safe, never unthreatened. It must be watched over always, closely and jealously.

CHAPTER SIX

Bird, Beast and Blossom

Britain as a whole is so sparsely supplied with large wild animals that the deer is bound to command respect and delight. Unless, that is, some handsome young buck finds the garden gate open and with his fellow males comes tripping in silently but eagerly, as if by gracious invitation. The females are every bit as inquisitive, if a shade less confident. None thinks of concealing the visit, leaving behind generous scatterings as if in fee. They will delicately remove the heads from rows of precious plants, and they are devils for roses. Their propensity for holly has already been noted, and they are relishers of yew, poison to common cattle; a well clipped yew hedge, therefore, is a bad recipe for keeping deer at a distance, though they might be wary of ornamental hollies, familiar garden store in these days of shrub planting. My protection is the height of the garden hedge, and they only came into the garden once, when the gate was left open on a mild and moony night. A dog must have barked, for there was no damage but a slot or two, deep printed, as though they had taken off at speed; and of course the distinctive droppings, called *fewmets*.

The Ashdown deer today are fallow deer, though in the past there were red deer, too. It was written of the Five Hundred Acre Wood that 'Deer, red and fallow, are to be seen in every direction; and with sheep, Welsh and Scotch cattle scattered about, the landscape is perfect.' The red deer traces a very ancient lineage in Britain, back to the ending of the last ice age, according to those who must know; but the fallow deer, we are told, was a Norman implant. It was introduced to France from the east, by some observant crusader, perhaps . . . The name *fallow* comes from the ancient word *fealou*, meaning simply pale brown—or, indeed, *fawn*. Unlike the fox, deer offer more than mere sport. For centuries the species was essential to the economy and they can justifiably lay claim to being the cause of Ashdown's dedication as a Royal Chace. In the early tradition, the red deer is called a beast of the Forest, the fallow a beast of the chase. They may be said to have changed places and it is fitting that a fallow deer should stand as the emblem of Ashdown Forest, much employed on official notices and such useful artefacts as notebooks and the like, on sale at the Information Barn.

With the setting up of the pale, the deer obviously became more regimented. Since they could leap in but not out, their numbers must have increased rapidly; they were numbered in thousands until the bad days of decay and collapse, when the broken pale gave them exit to a wider countryside. It is clear that the early care afforded the herds had decayed along with the pale. Whereas commoners had always been warned off grazing their animals during the fence month, this rule was increasingly evaded, so that the pasture planned for unshared enjoyment by does and their young was no longer theirs alone during those important weeks. It is a little surprising to learn that when the game was properly preserved, and the does and their fawns protected for that Midsummer month, it was from Midsummer Day until the 14th September that the males, red stags, fallow bucks, were held to be in prime condition for killing. They were, it was said, *in grease.* They were also coming up to the October rutting season, which was why they were in such competitive fettle. To pick off the males at such a moment appears a curious way of increasing stock—it is also, of course, a reasonable means of culling. The females appear little better treated, for from that same 14th September—that is Holy Rood Day, called also the Feast of the Exaltation of the Holy Cross—hinds and does became fair game and remained so right round to Candlemas, the 2nd February. The females feed their young for six months, so there must in consequence have been many orphan fawns still less than self-sufficient. Maternity benefits for these animals appear somewhat spare.

Venison remained a courtly gift for centuries—many such awards and presentations appear in the Forest annals. In Henry III's day they salted six carcasses of each sex to supply a feast day which, one concludes, must have fallen during the close season. Not at all—the feast in question was the celebration of the Nativity of the Blessed Virgin, the 8th September, when the male animal is still *in grease*. Salted venison for that particular occasion must have been by preference or custom.

Foresters, too, had official benefit of venison; that is, the top echelons, who could claim one hart and one hind, or one buck and one doe. More modest was that custom of a haunch of venison in payment of winter haying of the deer.

All that happened legally to the deer herds, red or fallow, at whatever period, was of course compounded by poaching. Poachers were not all sly chaps slinking through the undergrowth in dirty doublets and torn hose. John of Gaunt's own dean, John de Wolleston, was one such culprit—brought to book, or we should not know of the affair. On a distinctly lower rung was a commoner of the poor sort, William Burgess, who became renowned for the excellence of his venison pasties. In the various court findings there is constant reference to the poaching of deer, which at some levels was clearly as much a sport as any huntsman enjoyed. However, sport was incidental, the main purpose of poaching was the meat it offered, and the more one pries into the economy of the Forest, the more obvious it becomes that many forest dwellers were desperately poor. One of the cruelties of early law-makers in this field was the choice they offered to men considering the support of themselves and their families—

starve or hang.

The Rev. Edward Turner claims to have been present at
the killing of the last Ashdown Forest deer by the Hartfield
& Withyham harriers, in 1808. 'I was there,' he tells us. That
was a time when there were few deer of any sort, and that last
deer is sometimes qualified as the last *red* deer. However it
went, the red vanished utterly while the fallow crept back and
here they remain. The fact that deer are no longer hunted
here and that there is so little grazing, robs the creatures of
one ancient advantage—we have no fence month now for the
does to give birth in peace. The midsummer young are no
longer to be disturbed by commoners' animals, but they can
suffer from dogs. Fawns are easily damaged, even killed, by
dogs coming upon them without warning—it happened in
my slice of the Forest a summer or two ago. The visiting
public is not sufficiently aware of this hazard, for they seldom
see deer about and can hadly be expected to know all their
ways. Sometimes, well-meaning humans, finding among the
bracken what seems to them a deserted fawn, with misplaced
kindness try to rescue it. This is a terrible error pretty well
bound to end in disaster—as the Rangers know who are often
handed such supposed victims. And victims, in fact, they are.
Fawns are left while their mothers seek their own food, and
however deep-seated the kindness that imagines them
neglected and must help, it is often quite impossible to
re-introduce such an animal to the wild. Though once, years
ago when the Forest was still very isolated and little visited,
before I ever thought of coming to live here, I saw a yearling
apparently composed and content, wearing a collar with a bell
that sounded strangely in the quiet of an end-of-summer
afternoon.

There can be no knowing what became of that particular
animal, but a Ranger's wife could tell a different tale. A
supposedly rescued fawn was brought to her and she did her
best for it. Deer on occasion may get into a nervous frenzy
which can kill them so this one was most tenderly treated and

did well enough for a captive. But it was a male, which made things difficult, for it would surely escape during the rutting season in its second year—and what welcome was it likely to receive? Eventually it had to be handed on to a wildlife zoo, where it may or may not have flourished . . . Gilbert White tells of a doe brought up from infancy with cows. It settled, apparently, easily enough, moving as they moved at milking time, grazing quietly where the cows were turned out. Clearly it was a herd she needed to replace her own sort; but what became of her maternal impulses we are not told.

Like any other kind of their species, the male and female fallow deer separate into individual herds once the rutting season is over. The does, and fawns of both sexes, stay together for six months, when the young males join their fellows to begin the progression to fully antlered maturity. There are six stages in the development of a full *head,* and at every yearly stage the antlers are cast, to recommence their growth immediately to whatever size and shape fits their years; and all in a matter of months. The new antlers are coated with a furry substance called *velvet,* all of which is gradually rubbed away in the process known as *fraying;* evidence of this appears on tree trunks. The fallow deer's antler is individual in this country, reaching eventually the fine palmate formation worn by the mature buck; worn arrogantly, a frightening weapon. In the rutting season, when the bucks round up and select their ladies, comes the classic 'clash of antlers', as a couple fight over the doe they have both rashly selected. The ground is trampled into a recognisable ring where they have stamped and battled and bayed in victory. That sound may not so often be heard, but the bucks also make a noise known as *groaning* when they are in an emotional state . . . Only the true patient watcher, the dedicated nature man, is likely to witness the conflict of the bucks, with the does standing self-consciously at a discreet distance. Most of us can only know the scene from our television screens, where it seems impressive enough. In the

92

half-light, deer-light as it has been called, the scents and
sounds and the half-baleful magic of the Forest's depths must
add a hundredfold.

The Ashdown deer are considered rather poor specimens
since there is no breeding programme but nature's, and no
culling save what the motorist achieves. The hunting horn is
no longer heard over this forest, unless in the feebler version
accompanying fox-hunting, of which there is less than might
be expected. The deer by now should have hardly an enemy.
Unfortunately, poaching may still take place, and the
lamented reappearance of the cross-bow, in even nastier form
than the original, is bound to be a threat. Also, deer-farming
is with us, with its easy luring of animals on to private
ground, its advertisements in newspaper columns: *Live red
deer for sale. Hinds and stags. £350 each* . . . The fact that in this
particular example *deer* was spelt *dear* made the item no
pleasanter. For all that, it would be hypocritical to pretend
that venison is anything but a wonderful meat.

The great threat to the deer of most forests is the motorcar.
Unnumbered deer have been slaughtered on the Ashdown
roads and many others, injured, have limped away into the
Forest to die. In spite of warning notices, the cars tear on
their way and the deer cross when they choose. The speed at
which cars are now travelling can batter an animal to death;
any damage to the car, and it can be considerable, must
appear as just retribution. Of course true accidents happen to
careful innocent drivers, and distressing scenes attend the
occasion, particularly if there are child passengers. The siting
of reflectors on low posts along the verges does seem to
check the animals in some cases. The posts are a bit unsightly
but must be endured. Unless an idea mooted in a recent letter
to the press were taken up. This suggested that tufts of
human hair, strategically placed, send deer flying away in
disgust. Rabbits are the same, so long as the tufts are placed
at rabbit height. Supplies might be difficult, though—and
how long does a tuft of human hair, subjected to wind and

weather, retain its repellant powers . . .?

Here, as on other main roads cutting through forest, the Highway authority declines a speed limit, partly, no doubt, because the police do not relish the added chore of enforcement. The Forest roads, with the exception of the main A22, which jabs a way through Ashdown's vitals, still carry right of common and animals in law therefore take precedence over humans, most of whom unfortunately cannot bring themselves to accept the fact. The early morning and the evening traffic whizzes and swoops and slams. The reason there have been few grazing sheep for the past year or two is entirely due to the indifference of drivers bent only on getting there. Breakfast television, one might suggest, has not helped at all, with its delaying tactics for workers inclined to start late for the office. Drivers have been observed using their shavers as they speed.

The commoner who put out the largest number of sheep until recently, abandoned the practice because he lost so many animals. It is not easy to forget his story of a lamb, following its mother across the road not far from Duddleswell, being hit so violently that its head was severed. There is far less excuse for daytime slaughter of sheep than for the running down of deer at night, or in the half light of dawn or dusk, but the sheep always get the blame. And sometimes otherwise charming and sensible newcomers, walking their dogs on the Forest for the first time, can be highly indignant that grazing requires dogs under control and that damage can lead to prosecution. Once I owned a sheep-chasing dog and that was a wretched time, of ruined walks, of anger and anxiety. In these cases, too, it can never be right to blame the sheep, infuriating as they are when they come plunging without warning from dense bracken, and cannot decide, in their alarm at what they find, which way to run. Enough to rouse the mildest dog to wild excitement. Sheep have no means of self-defence, they have never got themselves accustomed to modern life; they still, ideally, need a shepherd. But who is

TF—H

bred now to such a lonely life . . .

What other creatures live and breed on Ashdown? There are no ponies, as on Dartmoor, as in the New Forest, no otters as on Exmoor. Once the hare abounded but has now vanished—thanks, perhaps, to the eccentric Mr Fuller of Lavertye. Time and again in Forest reporting of the 19th century come tales of this volatile character. Cast in the mould of such as Squire Weston, Fuller must have dreamt of hares, been nourished by hare jugged or roast; his tempting of the locals to hare seeking and betraying makes extraordinary reading. He seems never quite matched by rival neighbours, retired generals and the like, who none the less eagerly supported him—the owner of Twyford Lodge, for instance. There was some protest from authority but not a great deal; they were all sportsmen, all country gentlemen together . . . Centuries earlier the hare had become so scarce that certain hunting practices were made illegal—hunting them in the snow was one. The question of sporting rights on the Forest remained a touchy subject, so it is surprising that Fuller and his friends enjoyed themselves so much . . .

Rabbits play a really important and historical part in the animal history of Ashdown. Some say they were introduced into England by the Normans, others that the Plantagenets saw to it. As the animals were most carefully cultivated they soon became no mere delicacy but a very welcome and important item of diet. It is sad to consider that plenty led to their loss of status and at one point their classification as vermin. Though they came to be called poor man's meat, it was long before they were restricted to the poor man's table—if in fact they ever were or will be. There was a good deal of quiet snaring when I first came to live on the Forest. Snares are a beastly menace; we lost a cat that way. Sometimes black rabbits are seen on the Forest; they are said to be descendants of tame rabbits kept by Army families during the war, and released when peace crept back and the military went away. There were black rabbits, it is said, in

Essex long ago. Perhaps after all they are a breed on their own, returning from time to time as sports of the common coney. After the myxomatosis business in the 1950s rabbits vanished from the Forest as elsewhere, and the habitat changed accordingly, the heather growing long and stringy without them, the fox population in bewilderment taking to the raiding of village dustbins. Perhaps because there are dogs, there have never been rabbits in this garden, though besides abutting on the Forest itself it is neighbour to a useful paddock.

In the early days of the royal chace, warrening of coneys became a flourishing business. There are records of production, of sales and of gifts. Earliest of all, these were offered for the recipient's table, and later, live, as contributions to private warrens. On Ashdown today the remains of several warrens can be seen when the bracken is down—in Old Lodge Bottom, short of the estate boundary, and fairly obviously at Broadstone, at Hindleap and other places that commemorate the trade by name. The coneys were still used for meat, but in the month of November they were killed for their pelts. In the 1660s it was said that the coneys had quit the Forest through the broken-down pale, though that seems a slightly tall story. At that time, though they had been kept in enclosures which had also come to decay, the acres of forest land would surely have offered enough of a living to prevent desertion. Perhaps some earlier rabbit plague took its toll at that time, as did myxomatosis three centures later.

In the 18th century, warrening became popular all over England. These later, farmed animals were not penned so close by their *burreys* or *berries* and when they roamed beyond the old pale into the manorial waste, they became the perquisites of the Lord of the Manor, or Lord of the Soil, as he is called in one particular writ, 'to take and destroy to his own use.' The late C. F. Tebbutt did a good deal of work on warrening and warrens of the sort called *pillow mounds*. He was a spotter by instinct and intellect; a man born, someone said enviously, 'with a flint arrowhead in his pocket.'

The breeding and preservation of game birds has already been mentioned with regard to common and sporting rights. The enquiring Rev. Edward Turner, with something to say about everything, declared that you could not walk a yard on Ashdown without putting up blackcock. Today we have plenty of pheasant, some partridge and the occasional snipe and woodcock. One of the Rangers has listed ninety-six kinds of bird that should be seen on Ashdown Forest, and of these there are only thirteen he has not actually sighted himself. The list was made to refute the claim that the Forest birds are far scarcer than they were. It is a melancholy plaint to which I am bound to contribute and it seems reasonable enough when one considers the enormous growth in the number of visitors. The Rangers are fortunate in seeing the Forest at morning and evening, before and after the cars come into the parks and unload; no doubt that is when the birds discreetly withdraw to more distant groves. Many visitors, of course, remain near their cars, often picnicking at the wooden tables that are mostly at hand—and mostly commemorative of some Forest lover, which is pleasant. But large numbers ply further and fare better.

The Information Barn offers various leaflets that prescribe chosen walks. This could be a mistake. Come and look! cries the Conservationist—and off they trip, trampling on the way what may be equally important ecologically, ten of them at a time. Of the ten, how many see with the right kind of eye? Many are plain bored and might have kept their feet to themselves. When it comes to parties of schoolchildren the damage could be greater—but if only two of such a party are imaginatively captured, then the exercise is more than worthwhile, it is a triumph.

These walks have indeed taken some toll. Remote tracks have become widened and they lie like arrows pointing the way to places that, ideally, should never be visited. There, until now, the true denizens of the Forest have been safe from intrusion, the deer moving noiselessly, the birds nesting, water-voles busy in the banks of the small waterways, many of them minute tributaries of the Medway, that criss-cross the territory. Those creatures should be there still, secure in places altogether their own. It is of course inviting criticism to say these things, since it will appear that an exclusive right is being claimed. Not a personal right, but a right for the ground. This place needs its privacy.

At one time the birds were all about as one walked. At the height of summer the small sort were forever flitting over the heads of the bracken. Once I came on a reed warbler caught by one leg in a tall bracken frond whose neat sections had acted as louvres. There the bird hung, head down, madly fluttering. It could be said that if more people in those years walked that particular track, the warbler need not have waited long for rescue; now I see no warbler, happy or distressed, but I trust the Ranger who tells me they are still about . . . That particular little path, incidentally, has quite vanished.

The increase in raptors has certainly affected those birds who come into the garden. They are too bold in such bird-table places. Wicked-eyed rooks and jackdaws, comic magpies, evilly beautiful jays now save themselves too much searching after food and instead sit yawning and waiting for the next supply to appear. On the open Forest they have taken over the car parks as officiously as any warden. Before those open places were tidied up they were much favoured by larks and pippits. Below the Friends' Car Park, along Old Lodge Bottom, for many years curlew nested; they seem to have moved on into secluded places, probably the enclosed parts of the Forest denied to the public. As a neighbour pointed out recently, those hated enclosures, the bane of past commoners, may well be the salvation of the Forest birds and beasts.

The open Forest is good ground for various sorts of hawk, as it was in those distant days when they were preserved for training as mews birds. Hobbies, buzzards come and go. On a blowy day, white clouds, blue sky, hen harriers are

particularly apt, for their undulating, questing glide is
perfectly suited to long banks declining into reedy bottoms. I
remember seeing kestrel parents once, at the exactly right
time, for they were instructing five nervous young. Sparrow
hawks I have not seen for some while, but they are still about,
probably in that very area in which they were sought years
ago. Once, unfortunately drowned and floating in an enormous puddle, I came upon a kite. The bird is not on that list
of Forest species, so I daresay it was an import by a resident
who has sometimes introduced large birds. The buzzards are
often his and their sociability startles newcomers who feel that
eagles are abroad and they had better hide the baby.

Night birds have suffered, like hedgehogs, from too much
late movement on road and tracks, and the intrusion of
headlights. Poor summers have perhaps sent off the nightingales. Nightjars, too, enjoy warm evenings. Noises of the
dark, like theirs, are among the best of country
sounds—frogs, grasshoppers, crickets close to the ground,
grasshopper-warblers, the frantic crying of vixen and fox
intent on mating or hunting. Such unchanging sounds are
one of the neatest devices on offer as ties with the past.

There are certainly plenty of foxes about. They use the
garden as a short cut to a neighbour's hen-run. Out with the
dogs in the early morning the way is ripe with the
unmistakeable stench. And there are increasing numbers of
badgers contributing in their own way to the forest floor and
the garden grass. Armies of squirrels make excellent use of
the plentiful hazel nuts. They, too, suffer from the self-assured
crows and their fellows. It is quite distressing, having
watched a squirrel cleverly patting down a few chosen nuts
into the turf, to be obliged to watch a jay just as cleverly
unearthing them. Best to accept the eternal contradictions
philosophically, no doubt, rather than bang on the window.
How lovely to see a heron by the pond—how beastly for the
fish . . . One of the best garden-bird days began with a heron
and concluded neatly with a goldcrest . . .

Like any other wild place with good ground cover, Ashdown has its measure of snakes. Grass snakes suffer cruelly from the lingering satanic image; they are, of course, perfectly harmless, though they do enjoy goldfish in conveniently adjacent gardens, and frogs, of course, are their prey. The grass snake is big and beautiful, never to be confused with the smaller, slicker adder. Grass snakes are not interested in the human kind. Adders have a different outlook, but they are nervous, too. Leave them alone and they will do the same for you; the number of people bitten by adders is minute, one death in nine years, it is claimed. Not that one invites such disaster, and trouble can come with running or questing dogs. A dog that steps on an adder may be badly bitten, though happily a quick rush to the vet will almost certainly put things right. A cat living here was once bitten, but though there was some swelling it was soon cured. Cats like to play with slow-worms and lizards so they are understandably likely to try the same thing with larger snakes. Cats who live at the Forest's side roam mysteriously and must encounter far more than the voles and fieldmice that they could as well find in the garden—stoats, for one. How fine a life for any cat, in such a place; how fine for any dog, for any child, for any fortunate human . . .

In spite of that inevitable plaint that there are fewer of all flying things than there used to be, and none to blame but Man, there is plenty of insect life on the Forest. Over the pond at the foot of the long track mounting to Camp Hill, the dragonflies accumulate. The bee-noise as the heather comes into flower can be quite extraordinary. Butterflies more than any other insect, or so it seems to the layman, are affected by the weather, and in some recent years the count has been very disappointing. The white admiral, however, has increased over the past year or two, and there is the silver-spotted blue butterfly, very much an Ashdown speciality—but you must keep your eyes open. There are not the same clouds of butterflies that must once have frequented the Forest. They have not, like the masses of butterflies that crowded the Downs, suffered from the ploughing of turf that was full of thyme and clover, bugloss and camomile. Pesticides are not used on the Forest but all the same the wild flowers needed to sustain butterflies are inevitably reduced by increased trampling of the ground. Without the sheep, too, the forest floor is changing, though one advantage of no-grazing has been the welcome spread of marsh gentian, Ashdown's most cherished plant.

There has often been a cry for the controlled burning of heather, as on moors in the north. Certainly left to itself the heather can grow high and leggy. In the past, commoners burnt to improve grazing and it has often seemed an excellent idea. But it is a touchy issue to anyone unfamiliar with the practice, and too many of us have groaned over the devastation of fires accidental or malicious. This is the last protected heathland in the south-east and it deserves care. It has been possible to improve large areas by planned cutting and the uprooting of birch and pine from good heather stands. The result seems worth the effort, even if that effort has undoubtedly somewhat outstripped nature. To control but not to tame calls for a very fine balance and judgment and can easily go too far.

Increased use of the Forest has obviously changed it a great deal in many ways. Many rides have been cut to accommodate horses; it is said there are about eighty miles of these and they alone have given the place a new look, originally ploughed as fire breaks they are now much widened. Horses and their riders have been a problem ever since a system of licensing was introduced at the time of the Act of 1974. Strictly speaking, before that only commoners were at liberty to ride, but over the years defiant horsemen accumulated and the Board eventually decided to issue riding permits. The fact that this is a recent concession has been forgotten—more recent permit-holders probably have never known of it—and it is a sad fact that horsemen can be very arrogant and unsympathetic when challenged. As always, there are the good and the bad, the good so thoughtful and sympathetic, the bad often rather awful. Antagonism between riders and walkers will probably never end, and no one can doubt that the horse in this particular situation is in some ways an enemy. They have their own useful way of repaying hospitality and their generosity may be said to assist the soil; except that it falls too often in the wrong place and cannot be employed thriftily, as in gardens. There is no denying that hooves are terrible, demolishing weapons, though they are not the sole destroyers about the Forest. Forest users fall into factions, riders, walkers, dog-walkers—and the dogs can be tiresome, too. It is true, also, that disturbed plant life often contrives to retreat to some less invaded spot. A fine stretch of wood-anemone seems to have picked itself up bodily and re-settled on safer ground. This give-and-take remains for comfort. There was a hollow full of foxgloves that was gradually wiped out as improvements were made to the nearby track—but a useful small pool has appeared to redress the balance.

If the marsh gentian takes precedence here, the orchids of one type and another are close rivals. They always seem more influenced by lack or supply of sunshine than any other Forest flower, appearing pale and fragile from lack of light and warmth, even though they grow in open places, and colouring up in a matter of hours as sunshine increases. They arrive almost without warning and vanish just as mysteriously; that is a casual impression—a botanist would know better.

The Forest lacks primroses but is increasingly a bluebell place, with a few wild daffodils. Sometimes these will increase, with a bit of protective nurturing by friends, but they seem unable to carry on for long against changing times. Bog asphodel, sundew—the list is as long as the list of Forest birds. Whatever else may happen to them, wild flowers no longer receive the treatment they once suffered—when on summer weekends, rows of merry cyclists rode home with great bunches of bluebells hanging captive on their saddles and handlebars, and families on spring picnics gathered vast bunches of primroses. Of course there is a reverse side to this happy conclusion—fewer people know much about their own countryside's wild flowers.

CHAPTER SEVEN

Hammering the Forest

If anyone knows anything about Ashdown Forest other than its qualifications as a place for walking, riding, botanising and plain picnicking, it is that the Wealden iron industry flourished here. Interest has increased enormously over the past years and the members of the Wealden Iron Research Group could be forgiven for regarding themselves with satisfaction. Their approach, however, has acquired the humility of the true seeker, and their hard-working enterprises have resulted in a considerable amount of discovery and analysis which has been suitably recorded. WIRG as they now call it, in the current fashion, is a source for congratulation and inspiration.

Acronyms hang about the Forest like flies. It has long carried the tag of *A.O.N.B.*, or *Area of Outstanding Natural Beauty*. It can also claim *S.S.S.L.*, standing for *Site of Special Scientific Interest*. There is an echo here of recurring historical situations; now, as in the past, these magic charms hold little force when it comes to any over-riding governmental decision. The conflict between utilisation and conservation is as keen today as in Tudor times, when there were petitions against over felling, which was seen as a threat to shipbuilding, to shore defences and the like. The Forest, as we know, is a prime target for the oil men, professionals moving in where once amateurs were discovered prospecting and were sent packing. It could be argued, of course it *is* so argued, that the place having been once industrialised might as well be exploited again. Time heals all—the national

interest—employment—the catchphrases spin like plates in
the air. Time indeed has healed that ugly blackened expanse
that Cobbett writes of in such disgust. The image he presents
is one we know well for we see it after big fires in the early
months of the year. But when hundreds of acres have been
seared, how speedily they are papered over by sheets of green
bracken springing from the ashes. Can it really have been as
bad as Cobbett declares, 'verily the most villainously ugly
spot I ever saw in England'? Probably yes, for reasons to be
argued, though it should be remembered that Cobbett was
riding through on his way to Lewes on a January day and he
was always inclined to see the worst side. Perhaps this 'forest
without trees' was not even then quite so disgusting as it
appeared to 'eyes crazy with agriculture', as one authority has
called William Cobbett's often dismissive and unaesthetic
gaze. However that may be, he has left a sad slur on
Ashdown, called by him *Ashurst*, which, oddly enough at this
distance, is still often quoted. Though the iron industry as a
whole trailed on throughout the weald into the 19th century,
it vanished from Ashdown many years earlier. Coal took over
from charcoal as the favoured fuel, and trade shifted to
different locations, to the Forest of Dean and on into the
Shropshire countryside.

When the iron industry pulled out of Ashdown Forest the
timber must indeed have been in poor supply. Though there
is plenty to learn from the records of wood awarded, wood
illegally taken, there is little in the accounts of Forest
economy to suggest planned re-planting. The roasting of fuel
to feed the furnaces was only one part of the problem. There
was also that careful choice of the best oaks for ship-building
and the rest. Wood fed fires to produce iron to make
guns—but if there was no wood left for the ships, what was
the use of the guns? Had the iron industry not moved
elsewhere, then indeed there might have been no single tree
left on Ashdown. Even as the ironmasters withdrew to
woodier areas, or coal bearing areas, their day was on the

wane, the industrial revolution loomed. Ashburnham, in the east of the county, was the last Sussex furnace blowing—a little short of that year when Cobbett was riding disapprovingly on his way.

The early 19th century was in any case a troubled time for Ashdown, though whether more troubled than any other time is probably questionable. It was the period of Arabella Diana's game reserves, the fuss over holly, the beginning of a long build-up towards change. It could be said that industry had brought it to this pitch and industry must never again be allowed to threaten. Present-day industrialists, the rich oil men with their speculative glance, are subtle planners who with smiling confidence assure us of the best will in the world. It is their world, so they really mean what they say and shake sad heads when any disagree. Modern methods, modern attitudes, the awareness of conservation as an uncomfortably hot issue, mean of course that the Forest need not be ravished. It would be invaded, though, with six-wheelers rumbling. It could become another place altogether.

How perverse, then, to stand at the bottom of Kidd's Hill, where the little stone bridge spans the memory of bustling Newbridge ironworks, and feel entitled to recall it all. Again and again Newbridge is named in the archives of the Forest, back into the late 15th century, when the Wars of the Roses were moving to a close. Its fortunes sometimes gushed, sometimes ebbed—once into ruin. There are scatterings of slag in the stream and along its banks, and sometimes ancient charcoal thrown up casually by moles working alongside. But a pond nearby, recently restored, is not the furnace pond. Newbridge is often claimed as the first wealden ironworks to produce cast iron by the new process of blasting, but Buxted is its rival. 'This year,' wrote Holinshed of 1543, 'the first cast pieces of iron that ever were made in England were made in Buckstede in Sussex.' Cast iron was in production on the Continent at a much earlier date and when the new process took hold in England, French experts were enlisted. One,

known as 'Graunt Pierre', described as an *yernefounder* of
Hartfield, had connections with several sites in the neighbourhood. Newbridge is within Hartfield parish. There would
presumably have been some interchange between neighbour
ironmasters. At Buxted the master was Ralph Hogge, who
became famous by royal warrant as 'the Queen's gunstonemaker'. The jingle about Master Huggett—that is, Hogge—
and his man, John, and how 'They did make the first
can-non' is an anthem for researchers into the industry. That
first cannon was, of course, the first cast in one piece and then
bored. Hogge should have made a fortune but there was so
much quarrelling over the rights and wrongs of the trade that
he died almost a poor man. His house still stands at Buxted,
adorned with the rebus of 'a hog' and lived in now by the
gunstonemaker's biographer, Edmund Teasdale. In his book,
called *The Queen's Gunstonemaker*, the author has much to tell
of the Henslowe family and their connection, both by
business and marriage, with Ralph Hogge. Hogge married
Margaret, Edmund Henslowe's daughter, while Edmund
himself is locally affiliated by reason of his having been
appointed Master of the Forest. He held the position for
many years and had the usual skirmishes with the commoners.
Edmund's son, Philip, takes us to Shakespeare's London, to
Richard Burbage and Ben Jonson and the theatres, *The Rose,
The Fortune* and others less well remembered, which Philip
owned and managed. To carry the linkage still further,
Edward Alleyn, man of the theatre and the founder of
Dulwich College, married Philip's daughter. 'My dear sweet
Mouse,' he calls her in his letters . . .

The problems raised by the iron industry were hotly
disputed over a long period. Pleas and plaints about the
destruction of forests proliferate, while writers famous in
their day and famous still, pontificate on the problem, often
differing sharply. Camden, dealing with iron mills in his
Britannia in 1586, is sceptical: 'Whether the nation is in any
way advantaged by them, is a doubt which the next age will

be better able to resolve.' Michael Drayton has his forests
bewailing their impoverishment—' . . . we, poor woeful
woods to ruin lastly sold', and describes how 'the hammer's
dreadful sound Even rent the hollow woods and shook the
queachy ground.' *Queachy* I take to be a word allied to Sussex
stoachy . . . One Andrew Yarrenton in 1677 takes a bland view
that leaves the modern reader gasping—for he is convinced
that 'ironworks are so far from the destroying of woods and
Timber that they are the occasion of the increase thereof.'
And blithely he denies that charcoal is made from wood but
is some quite other substance; hardly a reliable witness. But
he is not alone in dismissing the problem. Daniel Defoe finds
warnings that soon there will be no wood left for ship
building almost flippant—'perfectly groundless'; for the
whole of the south is 'one inexhaustible Store-house of
Timber never to be destroyed.'

These varying opinions are quoted by Ernest Straker in his
Wealden Iron. He is too modest a writer to overbear any of
them, but he does seem to wince a little when he mentions
John Evelyn's reckless statement that the best fuel for
charing, or charking, is good oak.

Visions of a forest bright with birdsong are very much
interrupted by the tales of industrial clamour. Quite apart
from the noise of the hammers, which weighed as much as
1500 pounds, the furnaces *blew* for several weeks at a time.
These periods, called *foundays*, must have produced terrific
clamour and clang. Accounts suggest that men worked day
and night at such times, there was no such thing as shift
work. When it was over, when the furnaces cooled and
activities ceased, the workers would surely have fallen
exhausted to the ground. It seems unlikely that foundays from
one working to the next coincided, so that as the clamour
ended on one site it would have been taken up by another,
and another . . . At the industry's height it stretched all over
the south-east, from beyond the Rother at Biddenden,
Tenterden, Tonbridge, back along the Medway to Cowden

and Hartfield and Buxted, on by the county boundary as far as Linchmere, and up into Surrey to Shere and Abinger Hammer. Along the south the industry was contained by the downs, the best-found having access to river transport and so to the Channel—a stretch of the Ouse below Newick is called *The Iron River*. These are sites covering a period of five hundred or so years, not all in use at the same time, so the hammering and beating lessened in one place to increase in some newer working. How bright the skies would have been on those nights when the furnaces were blowing.

The Wealden iron industry is recognised these days as a subject of immense scientific and archaeological importance. For years the authorities were Ernest Straker, with his *Wealden Iron*, published in 1931, and a work with far wider scope, *The Story of the British Iron & Steel Industry* by H. R. Schubert, which came out in the same year. These two works had a forerunner, *The Historical Geography of the Wealden Iron Industry*, described by Straker as 'the admirable brochure of Miss C. M. Delaney', already long out of print when he was writing. If there can be two bibles to any one faith, then Schubert and Straker are their authors and held that position for many years. It was not until 1985 that they were followed by the immensely informative *The Iron Industry of the Weald* by Henry Cleere and David Crossley which brings the subject up to date.

Schubert covers iron in Britain from 450 B.C. to 1775 A.D. Schubert is a scientist, Straker a more homely figure, and his explorations over the area concerned are painstaking and affectionate. 'I have endeavoured', he says modestly in the Preface to his book, 'to compile a connected statement.' He follows after the Sussex historian, Mark Antony Lower, a Lewes man of 1813 to 1875, founder of the Sussex Archeological Society. Straker pays tribute to Lower, expressing his admiration for work done at a time when, he says, there were but meagre means of transport and few large-scale maps. But we are many years after Straker and think with sympathy of

William Augustus Raper. The Man Ashdown Must Remember

Pippingford: Days of Glory

From the Terrace of Pippingford Park

The Pageant: The Stars

The Pageant: The Players

Pageant of . . . Ashdown Forest

Kidbrooke Park, Forest Row, Sussex.

Time Table and Order of Scenes
July 16th, 17th, 18th & 20th, 1929

1.30 p.m.—GROUNDS OPEN TO THE PUBLIC.

2 to 3 p.m. and 5.15 to 7 p.m. } Grand Bazaars, etc. Private Grounds open at additional fee of 1/-.

Band of 1st Bn. Royal Sussex Regt.
(By kind permission of Lt.-Col. C. C. Harman, D.S.O., and Officers.)

3 p.m. & 7 p.m.—THE PAGEANT.

Torchlight Tattoo c. 9.30 p.m. (Saturday night only).

Special Trains to London and Tunbridge Wells and Intermediate Stations, 10.30 p.m.

[N.B.—Names of Representatives of Characters are liable to occasional change.]

PROLOGUE.
REPRESENTED BY NUTLEY, EAST GRINSTEAD AND FOREST ROW.

Principal characters:—

Anderida	HON. MRS. TATHAM.
Elves, Gnomes and Fairies	CHILDREN OF FOREST ROW.
Aella (King of Sussex)	SIR FRED. GREEN.
Queen of Sussex	LADY GREEN.
Earl Godwin	MR. S. DENISON.
Count Robert of Mortain	MR. J. HARLEY.
Gilbert de Aquila	MR. R. WILSON.
Count Peter of Savoy	MR. F. GIBBONS.
Eleanor of Provence	MRS. READ.
Edward II.	MR. HARWOOD.
John of Gaunt	MR. READ.
John Wyclif	DR. CARLING.
Jack Cade	MR. RAYSON.
Lord Dacre	MR. FESSAS.
Queen Elizabeth	HON. MRS. H. GODLEY.
Anne Clifford (3rd Countess of Dorset)	MRS. DASHWOOD.
Lady Compton	MRS. SELSDON.
Cromwell	MR. GOLDING.
Edward Gibbon	MR. JOHNSON.
Lady Hamilton	MISS HENRIQUES.
Wellington	MR. T. WALL.
Florence Montgomery	MRS. MCLACHLAN.
"Misunderstood" Boys	D. SPINDLER and DAPHNE MCLACHLAN.

(Full description of Prologue on page 9 Main Book.)

how he might have had difficulty in finding access to out of
the way sites. Today's workers in this field have easier
transport but probably even more difficult access. But both
Straker and today's archeologists share the struggle to be
ahead of modern development.

To make a good job of describing the iron industry as it
affected Ashdown Forest one needs to be geologist–archeo-
logist–historian. A potted impression is all that can be
attempted here, but the experts are easily accessible: Schubert
for width with technicality, Straker for the intimacies of
personal exploration, Cleere and Crossley for an impressive
summing-up. The partnership of Henry Cleere and David
Crossley led to the formation in 1968 of the *Wealden
Iron Research Group*—WIRG—and their book contains an
impressive recording of a successful enterprise. They had
intended to set up working parties all over the weald, but in
the event the society became based on the Buxted group.
There was great enthusiasm in those early days and membership increased rapidly. No doubt this may be the experience
of any such enterprise in its keen infancy, but WIRG retains
its momentum. Members are agreeably close to their quarry
and from the beginning it was easy for even simple-minded
enthusiasts to rush about the Forest, picking up fragments
from suitable banks and streams, and seeing immense possibilities in every land formation. 'Look, look!' an eager member
might cry, 'What's that? That! Just ahead, look!' It was
probably some quite ordinary little hillock but in those days
excitement was considerable. It is all much more solid and
established now. Members know what they are doing, they
have reliable experience to draw upon. WIRG is now very
well set up, skilfully organised, fraternising with the Sussex
Archeological Society and producing valuable bulletins that
cover its researches and make good reading.

Those early Buxted days as I remember them owed an
enormous debt to the steady influence and enthusiasm of two
men—Joseph Pettit, a schoolmaster ready not only to teach

but to learn, and of course C. F. Tebbutt. Pettit's profession
led to his moving away from the district, but Tebbutt put in
a great deal of work before his death . . . A small
furnace was set up on ground belonging to the Tebbutts,
organised by a WIRG member, Roger Adams, assisted by a
team of members. The experiment was described by Margaret
Tebbutt in the *Ashdown Forest News*:

'The purpose of the exercise,' she wrote, 'was to try to make
iron under conditions as similar as possible to those experienced by workers in the Romano–British period, using
materials that would have been available to them. The vital
ingredients are iron ore and charcoal, and clay is needed to
build the furnace. The ore and clay were both dug locally, the
clay actually on site. Charcoal, of course, has to be made from
wood, and the traditional method in a clamp needs constant
attention over a long period. This was not a practical
proposition for the weekend iron workers of WIRG, so a
different method was devised. The locally cut wood was put
into a pit in which a fire was already burning strongly, and
the whole then sealed with turves and soil. (The use of a
corrugated iron sheet to improve the seal was admittedly a
non-authentic touch.) By the following weekend charcoal
could be taken from the pit and after sieving could be used in
the smelt. All this involved a good deal of hard physical
work, as did the preparation of the ore, which had to be dug,
roasted and then broken into walnut-sized pieces before it
could be smelted. We realised that a supply of water was
surely another important requirement on the site; it would
have been needed for drinking as well as for mixing clay from
which the shaft-type furnaces were built . . . Each smelt lasted
for several hours, during which time one or sometimes two
sets of bellows were operated to maintain the necessary
temperature inside the furnace . . . Romano–British bellows
would presumably have been made from animal skin . . . we
had to make do with plastic . . . The end product of all this

activity was the bloom of iron formed inside the furnace, which had to be partially broken down in order to remove it. Before being forged into tools or weapons it would have to be re-heated and then hammered in order to remove bits of charcoal and other impurities.'

The products of the bloomery were tools and weapons, and no doubt domestic things like cooking-pots. A license was granted in 1502 for a six-acre site which was to produce iron plate for harness, before that there were nails and arrowheads in production.

When the blast furnace came into being in England the day of the bloomery was done, though records quoted by Straker and others show that a few lingered. The blast furnace was far less laborious, inasmuch as the process was a great deal faster; the iron cast by the new process formed into a *sow*, later to be broken into bars and finally forged as required. In 1496 when Henry VII moved to prevent a Scottish invasion, he granted a commission to Henry Fyner for the supply of arms, which he would make at Newbridge. He was given funds to pay workers, called by then *founders*, and ordered to erect whatever buildings were needed. H. R. Schubert finds for Newbridge as the first blast furnace of the area, considering that the one reference to Buxted is 'much too vague to justify the conclusion that a blast furnace was in existence in this country in 1490.'

I have complained of a lack of women protagonists in the affairs of the Forest, in spite of early regal ownership. Not to be forgotten, however, is Denise Bowyer. Her husband John supplied shot and 'bambardys' to Henry VIII and the Bowyers were based at Parrock. Once John had died, Denise was persecuted by her landlords, who tried to drive her from her holding and take over the iron. A large force descended on Parrock 'with swords, bucklers, staves and other war-like weapons', attacked the workers and broke up the mill. A battle raged between the two forces, in which Denise was

carried away bodily. All this resulted in a hearing in the Star
Chamber, but as Straker reports 'it is not on record how the
case was decided.'

In spite of suffering its own industrial revolution, the
Forest continued with its usual concerns and quarrels—still
the trespassing, still the encroachments, still the arguments
over the cutting of litter. It was in the early days of the new
process that there came an influx of foreign workers, mostly
from France, who were already familiar with these matters.
They produce some finely mangled names for the records.
Graunt Piere we know already—but what of Clay Harms,
Pauncelett Symart, Peter Baude, Isambart Pynyon; and a
sub-tenant of Newbridge, Simon Forneres . . .? What a
curious invasion for those commoners of Ashdown whose
names so often remained the same generation by generation.
Did they come to social accommodations? Did the families
mingle, inter-marry. The local name Divall—thirty-odd in
today's telephone book—derives from Duval, and there have
been Pinyouns not many miles away.

Even in its early days, the blast furnace produced about
seven times as much iron in twenty-four hours as the
bloomery had contrived. As the industry enlarged its scope, it
was bound to cover more ground—forges, ponds, necessary
buildings covered acres. Fortunes rose with war, declined to
the point of ruin in some cases during times of uneconomic
peace. Even famous Newbridge was broken down and
deserted in the 1550s. For the wider wealden area the peak
came in the 1570s, when there were fifty-two furnaces
working steadily.

It took them a good two hundred years to fall into total
disuse . . .

Iron was not the sole industry pursued on Ashdown
Forest. Stone digging and carting, brickmaking with its
diggings of clay, marl for manuring, turf cutting, peat
cutting. There are photographs taken at the turn of our own
century which look little better than Cobbett's description of

the place. I think, too, of my own early times here, when the forest floor spread black after so many silly fires; for weeks until the bracken sprang the desolation was miserable, particularly as at that time a great deal of household rubbish was emptied on the Forest, and there were blackened tins and bottles, scraps of glass from broken jam-jars—perhaps the very jars which had held the fatal candle and paraffin of the skilled fire raiser.

Besides stone, ore was still dug on the Forest until near the end of the 18th century. A good many fines for theft resulted, fines also for not filling in the pits after use. William Levett, presumably of the Buxted connection, was fined 6d in 1545, the parson of the parish was in trouble for the same offence the following year, while the last recorded case was in 1774.

Nor were locals the only ones granted stone quarrying concessions; the demand was considerable and the grants prodigal, perhaps because the Commonwealth, at the time of those very particular surveys, had decreed that commoners should be permitted to take stone for their own use. At times, denying such favours, the Lord of the Manor took 1/– a load for stone and later it rose to 3/–, but few appear to have paid their dues in this respect. On one occasion recorded by Raper, the Lord is reputed to have said that 'he had nothing to do with the Forest beyond being Lord of the Manor', but what his expectations were in that regard does not appear; they must have been considerable. He could have lost a lot by the action of the gentry alone—consider how Sir Spencer Maryon-Wilson built his big house, Searles, of all that purloined stone, not to mention Lord Colchester's brave doings at Kidbrooke Park. Sir Spencer was eventually brought to book, but the case was settled out of court. Lord Colchester appears to have been left in peace.

In Raper's interviews with chosen commoners, the local brickyards are often mentioned. At that time the industry was clearly long established. The brick was made from the dust of the ironstone, it was light in colour, though with a flush of

subdued red from the mineral. Sad to say, there is none to
point to since stone remained the cheaper material for
building locally. Sir Edward Dallingridge built in brick, and
Bolebroke at Hartfield is said to be the earliest brick-built
house in the county; later he carried the practice to Bodiam
Castle. There was more than one brickfield at Nutley, south
of the Stonehill (Crowborough) Road not far from the
Marlpits, while another at Horney Common was just outside
the pale.

Then there were gravel diggings to add to the ravishing of
the ground, small sites often running out of easy supply. The
soil was thus broken and trampled in a destructive cycle. And
there was for long years the digging of marl, broken down
chalky soil in a good state of decay, used for manuring,
mostly freshly cleared, or *assart*, land. The practice had been
going on for centuries. Again according to Raper's informants, the use of marl was dwindling by the 19th century, its
value to the ground coming into question with the arrival of
more advanced methods. Arthur Young, ever the expert, was
one who doubted the efficacy of marling. At Nutley, besides
the *Great Pit*, there was *Sweet Mine Pit*, its nearby house still
carrying the name, the area always alluded to as *The Marlpits*.

Water mills, corn grinding, appear in the Ashdown Forest
accounts by the 16th century, but J. K. Irons, whose thesis on
the Forest is a miracle of order and information, considers
that Nutley mill, on the mill brook, may have been in
existence even in the 13th century. Newbridge had its mill as
well as its *yernemylle*, and that has a long history of its own.
Again quoting Irons' researches, it seems there was a *furze-
crushing* mill, used in the preparation of cattle-food, while at
Boringwheel Mill in Cackle Street the mill remains still
stand.

Hop growing may not be quite an industry in the strict
sense, but it is best to note that there were at least a couple of
such enterprises, one in the Nutley area. A very old man, now
long gone, told me of an incident he claimed to have

witnessed as he worked with his mother in the hopfield. The story is of a young village girl with a baby born out of wedlock. She walked through the hopfield with the baby in her arms, and no one glanced at her except my informant, who was then about eight years old. She moved slowly towards the nearby pond, which was deep. She stepped into the water and waded deeper and deeper. At last she vanished and the baby with her. 'There was no hand raised to save her.' That would have been in the last years of the last century and may sound far-fetched, but this is a curious corner of Sussex with manners of its own even now, and this is not the only haunting tale told of Forest behaviour.

CHAPTER EIGHT

The Gentry in Residence

Architecturally, of course, the Forest should be a non-starter—none may build on that ground. But there was necessary building, administrative, dependant on such as the ironworks, throughout a very long past, while within the designated enclosures there can fairly obviously be building still. The entire story of Ashdown Forest could be said to find its original inspiration in that lost royal hunting lodge, that vanished palace built six hundred-odd years ago to furnish accommodation for the sporting proclivities at the least of King Edward II. Such places, according to ancient opinion, were 'the sanctuary and special delight of kings, where, laying aside their cares, they withdraw to refresh themselves with a little hunting; there, away from the turmoils inherent in a court, they breathe the pleasures of natural freedom.' Such a residence was bound to have had its attendant buildings, one certain to be a chapel; there is one recorded often enough as the *free chapel* of Nutley. Though it is known to have been in ruins by the mid-16th century, at the time of the Reformation, there are often references to its having stood until the 18th century; quite a span, surely, for a modest ruin. Traditionally it stood in the Chelwood Gate neighbourhood and that seems extremely reasonable, since *Chelwood* is said to be a contraction of *chapel wood,* and sure enough it is in Chapel Wood that some evidence came to light. But in John Kelton's map of 1714, a suitable date for the varying suppositions, there is a *Nutley chapel* set a mile or two nearer the village. It is easy to say we shall never know, but the past so often appears out of the ground that there can be no certainty on the subject.

What is claimed as the font from the vanished chapel is now in Maresfield parish church. According to the busily investigative Rev. Edward Turner, it was discovered two feet underground—in Chapel Wood. It was then carelessly mislaid, but turned up again in use as pig-trough at a nearby farm. When this presumed font found its way eventually to Maresfield, it joined other church furniture, chalices and vestments and suchlike ceremonial necessities, deposited when the chapel went out of its original use—when, in fact, it became free.

That is not the end of local chapels. There is St Dudeney's, marked on some early ordnance map as standing by Duddleswell—Dudeney's Well—crossroads. That is near the spot which hearsay claims as the site of a Roman posting station. Whoever it was who presumed during the wartime excavations that such a building had left its mark, could have been looking at remains many hundred years younger. Thanks to present day developments there it is highly unlikely that any more will be heard of either speculation. When the BBC, with the World and Diplomatic Services settled in, the station grew a very large listening audience in the surrounding countryside. At the outset there was some jangling of frequencies. Telephone talk might be interrupted by sweet music, or passing car radios pick up snippets of erudition. Once, when a church concert in Fairwarp called for amplifiers mounted on pillars, the mixed musical effect that poured from them cannot be forgotten. Like all remnants of devoted amateurism in a set-up utterly professional, these manifestations resulted in a possessive affection towards the service. When the BBC pulled out and the pylons came down—they were almost missed. At a later date, earth-shovelling with monster machines created a score of scarey rumours. We watched glumly and were informed that the place was to be 'a possible administrative centre in time of emergency.' What could be more reassuring . . . ?

A problem for anyone attempting to trace domestic sites on
the Forest is that buildings constructed of the local stone react
sharply to neglect. The stone crumbles, falls and is soon
dispersed, either by stealthy quarrying at the hands of thrifty
foresters, when it is quietly carted away, or through the
trampling of animals, the nature of the soil. The royal lodge,
the free chapel are not the only known buildings to have
vanished. On the Stonehill road, near Londonderry Farm,
there was Leap's End Farm, the name clearly marked on the
award map of 1887. Nothing remains. There was a cottage
here, a cottage there, one is told; but they are gone. Even
over the past forty years, the remnants of such a dwelling
have silently disappeared. For a long while the footings made
a neat architect's drawing; then everything vanished but a
battered picket fence round the property. All that now
survives of what the estate agents would call, even today
when property descriptions are increasingly absurd, a 'desirable character residence with uninterrupted views to the south
downs,' is a pear tree. All around the Forest one is likely to
trip over what the dialect knows as a *shatter* of stones, far
from quarrying and often shaped enough to suggest use. It is
as well we have that letter 'from the Palace at Notlye' or the
King's hunting lodge might seem a mere invention. Owners
of houses built and re-built within the enclosures will readily
boast that their particular dwelling is all that remains of 'John
of Gaunt's hunting lodge.' Never a popular man, how
surprised he would be.

And then there were the administrative buildings, dwellings of the various masters, the court houses for woodmote
and the rest; the Old Courthouse at Duddleswell; the
Chamberlain's house, called White Lodge, of which
Whitehouse Farm is an echo. There are small farms, some in
the area of Nutley and Fairwarp, some of which are old at
heart but have been altered, enlarged. In at least two cases,
growing prosperity added a Georgian wing and frontage, the
ancient thick-walled originals demoted to mere kitchen

quarters. One at least of these houses has particularly interesting windows, the panes measuring two of the usual length for the period.

Those substantial gentlemen's residences built through the 18th and 19th centuries mostly cluster on the edges of the Forest, sometimes risking encroachment. Houses built within the enclosures granted by the Decree of 1693 mostly belong to a later period, from the beginning to the second half of the 19th century. One of these is Ashdown Park, on the way to Coleman's Hatch from Wych Cross. It has a curious history which is recorded by C. F. Tebbutt and may be found in the Sussex Archeological Collections. Differently presented, the tale is also told in a brochure issued by the present owners, Barclay's Bank.

The first house built within what was immediately called Ashdown Park is not recorded any earlier than 1822. It was then owned and occupied by Admiral—or Rear-Admiral, a difference of opinion here—Jacob Henniker. He was probably the second occupier, the first having been Thomas Bradford Esq.—or was he the builder, even the architect? Admiral Henniker came to Ashdown Park on his retirement from the Navy; he died in 1843. Ashdown Park was then in the hands of Henniker's son, Edward; he also owned Old Lodge, where his mother lived in her widowhood until she died in 1860. But it was with the arrival of Thomas Charles Thompson from Durham in 1867 that Ashdown Park gathered some importance. Within ten years the new owner pulled down the original house and built another, slightly smaller. Victorian Gothic executed in stone then took over and remains today. Mr Thompson was a wealthy man of immense philanthropic impulse.No doubt our more cynical age would call him a *do-gooder,* a word as grudging in sound as in its interpretation. His contemporaries were more graceful when it came to writing his obituary in 1892. 'His life,' says the correspondent of the Durham Trade Directory, his home journal, 'was passed in the enjoyments which are at the command of those who have culture enough to appreciate leisure.' As graceful a conclusion as any man could come to.

Mr Thompson was a considerable employer. His house and park called for large numbers of workers, and a prospering farm added to the demands of the estate. Dwellings were provided for employees, a school for their children; what emerged was almost a self-contained village. Since Mr Thompson was naturally a considerable churchgoer, it worried him that his employees had to walk four miles to worship at the parish church in Hartfield. He built them a church in his own Park.

The church was unexpectedly large, a copy, it is said, of a church in his native Durham; the architect, rather curiously, is unknown. This imposing private place of worship was dedicated to St Richard de Wych, Bishop of Chichester in 1244—fairly obviously because of its proximity to Wych Cross. This may have been a little unsuitable; the word *wych* is frequently spelt *witch* in early maps and records, suggesting some stake-through-the-heart burial place. The church also commemorated the Thompsons' two sons, one dead at eighteen, the other in infancy. A curate was employed to minister at the church. Thompson's daughter, Penelope, married the Vicar of Forest Row, the Rev. George Fisher and they lived in a house at Wych Cross that belonged to the estate. This was later, according to one authority, to become *The Roebuck Hotel.* According to two others, what is now *The Roebuck* was originally an ale-house. This is supported by the recorded remark that Mr Thompson purchased *The Roebuck*— that is, the ale-house—because his wife would send the butler along to collect supplies. Probably the original *Roebuck* was an earlier building that later vanished, leaving the house where the Fishers had lived to become first a public-house, then an hotel, under the old name.

The estate passed to Thompson's grandson, the immediate heirs having died long ago. He was C. K. T. Fisher, said to have been a considerable water-colourist. He was killed in the

1914–18 war and the Thompson tie was then sadly broken for ever. Capt. Fisher had left Ashdown Park to be used as a convalescent home for Belgian officers—and so its days were completely changed, the sounds that echoed about the big house were altered in volume and key, the very language being changed into a mingling of two tongues. The Belgian connection led, in 1920, to the purchase of the estate by a religious order, the Sisters of Notre Dame de Namur; it was to be occupied by a teaching section of the Order, who took over the school as it stood. The nuns declined the church, however, feeling a need of their own chapel closer at hand. In due course this was achieved and with the building, also, of a church at Coleman's Hatch, St Richard's grew neglected and gradually derelict. It became the prey of vandals and was demolished in the 1970s; the stone was sold to a nearby firm of quarriers. The house itself continued a distinctly varied career. The nuns having departed, it became a branch of the International University of California. This gave an intellectual lift to the neighbourhood as it was possible to attend lectures there, but the occupation was brief.

Today, Ashdown Park is run by Barclay's Bank as a staff training centre. The nuns' chapel has become a conference hall but the adaptation has been discreet. Much glass remains, while the sculpted Stations of the Cross along the walls have been carefully panelled away to save them from damage.

A footnote to the fate of St Richard de Wych is supplied by a neighbour who went to look at the church after it had been vandalised. 'Graffiti everywhere—litter—all disgusting—windows smashed . . . ' He had a particular interest. His father had worked for some years at Ashdown Park Farm, where the grandparents were tenants; all the family regularly attended the church, though the children were still small when they moved to Nutley. Many years later my neighbour, needing stone for his garden, went to a local stone merchant to see what he could find. In fact it was the firm which had carted away the broken fabric of St Richard de Wych and there, still in evidence, were fragments worked in an ecclesiastic fashion. 'And what's that?' asked the prospective buyer, pointing to a useful looking stone trough. 'Oh that—that's the font from the old church.' A curious moment. 'I'd like it,' my neighbour said. 'I was baptised in that font and so was my sister.'

An extensive survey of the Forest in 1564 names Kidbrooke Gate by Forest Row—more or less at the bottom of Priory Road, where, too, the Medway runs very small and narrow. The house named for the gate, Kidbrooke Park, was not built until a couple of hundred or so years later. Pevsner in the Sussex volume of his *Buildings of England*, says that too little architectural history of Kidbrooke can be discovered; the name of the architect is not recorded. According to an earlier writer, Thomas Walker Horsfield—*The History, Antiquities and Topography of the County of Sussex*—'This mansion was built under the superintendance of Mr Mylne, the well-known architect of Blackfriars Bridge.' Horsfield has often been taken up rather sharply for unverified statements, and Pevsner doubts this one—though he does agree that Mylne was about Kidbrooke in 1805, but admitting him only as one who 'worked on the house.' It must obviously have had great elegance and its setting was superb. 'It is simple but elegant in its architecture,' says Horsfield—and he praises its *scite*. Kidbrooke was originally owned by the 42nd Baron Abergavenny, but he moved away to Eridge, selling the house, with its gardens and park, to the Rt. Hon. Charles Abbott, Speaker of the House of Commons. He has already been encountered as Lord Colchester, making away with cartloads of forest stone for his building activities, notably those cascades in his grounds. 'The park is not large'— Horsfield again—'but many improvements were made in it by the late lamented nobleman, under the direction of Mr Repton, the celebrated landscape gardener.' Kidbrooke had a notable stable block and a library with an ornamented plaster ceiling. The *long room* seems to have been a showpiece, as

Pevsner records. It is 'decorated with Pompeian taste, with much dainty painting, also, of the chimney-piece.' In the 1970s the house and much of the ground became a part of the Michael Hall School complex. The rest was used for a very large housing estate. Somewhere in those hundreds of small gardens must linger a remnant of Repton planting—or perhaps the place may be visited by his frustrated ghost . . .

It is to be noted that Horsfield contributes his own conclusions to the saga of the royal hunting lodge, when he is writing about Forest Row. 'Tradition tells us that this little vill was built for the accommodation of the nobility and their retinue, who in former times came to hunt in Ashdown Forest.' This would be applauded and underlined by the owners of a house a few miles north of Forest Row, who make no bones of their certainty that they inhabit the disputed site of the royal hunting lodge. Some prospecting enterprise, even the dreaded oil, might just make payment by re-discovering what has been so long lost.

Accustomed conundrums are offered, also, by Chelwood Vachery—or Vechery—or Vaccary. It stands just off what was once the turnpike road from East Grinstead, now the A22 from London to the coast. For long years the London road diverged across the Forest from Wych Cross by Chelwood Gate to Nutley and so on. Of a number of coaching roads, or tracks, that once carried travellers across the alarming Forest, this is one that has certainly been upgraded for today's use, important still in its own right as it leaves Chelwood Gate and rushes on by Danehill to Sheffield Park and beyond. The stretch of the A22 between Wych Cross and Nutley is still spoken of as *the toll,* with Toll Farm confirming its history; since the word for the high clumps of Scots pine is also *toll* this can be confusing. The Vachery is a little back from this length of the main road and is invisible to passers-by, who are in any case most often rushing in their cars from one point to the next. Here, too, as has been noted already, the ghost of the palace, the spirit of that hunting

lodge rises to feed conjecture. Was The Vachery the farm that
supplied the royal residence? Certainly one reference ties it,
not unexpectedly, to the matter of cows, but there is possibly
a confusion here—by ancient entitlement the Prior of
Michelham grazed a fair amount of cattle in this area.

I have mentioned the investigative clergyman, writing in
1902, who states that the ruin of what he calls 'the castle' was
still to be seen in Vachery wood. This part of the Forest has
always seemed exactly right for a building of the kind looked
for—high, open, space for dependant dwellings, outhouses, a
farm. The present Vachery is only a stone's throw away and
Chapel Wood not very much farther. It is more than
tempting, it is extremely enjoyable to speculate, whatever the
experts say—and perhaps it was just about here, during the
hasty clearing and preparation for the war-time landing
ground, that there might have been discoveries which the
urgency of the moment would have put out of bounds to
hopeful archeologists. Archeology, anyway, had not moved
anything like so far into popular awareness as it has today.

Today's Vachery is dedicated to more mundane affairs than
hunting the deer or grazing priory cattle. Disputed ante-
cedents have been shrugged away, the place flourishes as a
Group Management Centre of BAT. The difference is fairly
sensational, but in other such estates, existing rather secretly
in the old enclosures, various slightly alien enterprises have
their being. The actual house called Chelwood Vachery was
built within its enclosure in 1906 by Sir Stuart Samuel. By
some adjacent standards this mansion could be called modest.
None the less, it is fairly huge, imposing, dominating
enormous views of the downs, and with a crowd of rather
dotty gables, derivative chimneys and crenellated central
tower. Wealth rather than taste is inevitably displayed and it
is difficult not to hark back rather wistfully to the positive
austerity of Kidbrooke and such turn-of-the-century
mansions.

In 1925, house and grounds were purchased by Mr F. J.

Nettlefold, a necessarily wealthy business man, who cared with great scruple for the estate. He was a considerable benefactor of Nutley village, a couple of miles down the road, building a cricket pavilion on the Green and sponsoring the resultant club. Even today, there is an annual cricket match between Nutley and a Vachery eleven. Mr Nettlefold also made himself responsible for a village hall, now in dilapidation and superceded by the much larger hall at the other end of the village. It is not a beautiful building and one cannot forget the row of high elms that came down to accommodate it—but maybe they would have fallen, anyway, to the sad destruction of Dutch elm disease.

Mr Nettlefold's great achievement was to rescue a decaying wealden hall house called *Trimmer's Pond,* dating back to the 13th century and standing in Forest Row more or less on the banks of the young Medway. The river's perpetual overflowing no doubt accounts for *Pond,* as also for the fact that the building was fast deteriorating by the time Mr Nettlefold decided to take it home. A house that stands near the original site of the ancient building was called, *in memoriam* presumably, *Trimmers End.*

Trimmers was rescued with the greatest care and attention, the move supervised by the *Sussex Archeological Society* in the person of Ian Hannah, an architect expert in such matters. The building was dismantled, transported and re-erected by the Forest Row family firm of H. & E. Waters; 'Mr Waters,' writes Ian Hannah, in his booklet on the enterprise, 'is one of our members and a keen antiquary.' The house now stands in the grounds of Chelwood Vachery, cared for in a fashion that may disturb its ghosts, so clean it is, so neat. It does seem rather a mistake to have made it so very black and white. A suggestion of original cow-pat would be comforting; I think of Ightham Mote in Kent, of Woodcock Farm which is a forest neighbour, and of Goat Farm—the colour of the original plaster has been maintained in all these with great effect. Trimmers now supplies club premises for BAT

TF—J

employees and trainees, and is always alluded to as *Trimmers Club*.

Best seen in spring, the Vachery gardens are excellently maintained—but better still is the reserve set up by the company's *Bird Watching and Preservation Society,* which came into being in 1967. In this wild area, the remnants of grand design show waterfalls and what would have been cunningly planted glades. Here again, in a decay far from melancholy because of what it now harbours, is that memory of a lavish time. Then, no doubt, guests would be taken to wander on summer evenings through gentle woodland, along paths planned to do the least damage to ladies' fragile evening shoes. I like to recall *The Country House,* that novel of John Galsworthy's that epitomises the wealthy sociabilities as they are performed in the village he chooses to name *Worsted Skeynes* . . .

More or less across the road from The Vachery is another of those enclosures that came into being under the Decree of 1693—called then Pippinford, or Pypynford, or Pippingworth and eventually Pippingford Park, which it has remained. The enclosure in this case had been made some thirty years ahead of the Decree, before the return of Charles Stuart to the throne of England, with his free-handed gifts of Ashdown land to one faithful follower and another. In a general forest survey of 1658, which covered other forests than this one, Pippinford is named as the home of John Franke, gent., who held office as keeper and warden in that part of the Forest. His 'capitall messuage dwelling house or lodge' is said to consist of 'a brew house, kitchen, parlor, larder and butrie below staires', with a 'stable, Ox stall and barne, w'ch said stable, Ox stall and barne are out of repair.' What may be above stairs is not mentioned. The land attached is described as 21 acres, one feature being 'a gardine'. This spelling is used in other records and maps for what we now call Garden Hill, in Hartfield parish. Besides the 21 acres, there is also 'comon waste ground', which is described in detail. The survey speaks of water running through the gill below the dwelling place and dropping into the Stele Forge river—for the land connects finally with the Newbridge iron working land. Various clumps of woodland are described as being 'little worth but for fiering'; they are valued at £40, a moderately substantial sum at the time, it might be thought, and one which gives some impression of how wood in prime condition would have been valued.

Two years after this survey, as meticulous, as scrupulous and detailed as any other Commonwealth survey, the enclosure was purchased, along with Old Lodge and its dependant land, a total of 5,000 acres, by a William Newnham. There is some irony here when it is recalled that commoner John Newnham was to be a star performer in the case leading eventually to the 1693 solution—which would have confirmed William Newnham in one of those very enclosures against which John Newnham and his fellows would be fighting. Much later in the history of Pippingford, in the early part of the 19th century, another duplicated name appears, when the estate is bought by William Bradford— Thomas Bradford having already appeared as concerned, round about 1815, with Ashdown House. William Bradford of Pippingford set about building himself a new house but his debts overwhelmed him and he made the property over to his lawyers.

In the 1830s Pippingford was purchased by a gentleman of substance, Henry Shirley Esq, and immediately shifted nearer to its more extraordinary aspects. For in 1836, in the course of a wedding reception, the house caught fire—tradition tells of an overturned oil lamp, a drunken butler . . . Most unfortunately, all this happened on the 5th November, and those afar off who saw the smoke and flames, concluded that Mr Shirley and his friends were enjoying a Guy Fawkes celebration. According to a newspaper cutting of that time, the house was 'nobly furnished' and all it contained was lost except for plate and linen and some of the paintings. 'A loss,' the report tells soberly, 'of £30,000, no part having been ensured.'

In 1840, Pippingford was in the market once more, described in the *Sussex Advertiser* on the 18th May as a 'very valuable and compact freehold estate of about 851 acres.' Among its charms could be counted 'a noble Terrace walk, upward of 800 feet in length, commanding most extensive views.' As the specifications expand into eulogy one gains a good picture of the place as it was then, for if one knows it now its charms can be recognised—the lake, the stream stocked with trout, the stone quarry, the pasture and the woodland. Whatever else time changes of the landscape, water and contour remain to tie past and present images neatly together.

A wealthy Mr Mortimer was Pippingford's new owner, a gentleman of flamboyant taste, as very soon appeared. For having decided that a new owner rated a new mansion—and indeed the charred remnant of the old house must have been a wretched sight—he engaged as architect the Frenchman, Hector Horeau, then at the height of his fame. Building began in 1857 and the completion was certainly achieved by 1859, since the original drawing made by the architect was exhibited in London in that year, with the caption: *Castle recently erected in Sussex*. A castle it most certainly was, though since it had a French creator and French architectural style it simply must be called a *château*. There it stood, rearing up over the treetops, with turrets, with pinnacles, with great ornamented windows and a main doorway that shouts aloud for portcullis, drawbridge and lily-filled moat. Its high tower, capped by a funny little viewing platform that completely stripped it of dignity, could only have given a view that would have rated far more than the estate agent's 'extensive'. Southward it stretched over forest to the downs and so to the sea; northward it must surely have reached London, while the east gave it Kent and the west added the rest of Sussex and possibly something of Hampshire; in this it must have far outstripped its neighbour, Chelwood Vachery. How many rooms? How many servants, indoor and out? How immensely grand a life must have been lived here to fit such a setting. Carriages would have come spanking from London, with the county aristocracy converging from east and west for balls and receptions, banquets and shooting parties. Though *le week-end* came fully into fashion rather later—Worsted Skeynes parties, it may be remembered, were taking place at the start of the 20th century—surely the sociability must have had its beginnings in such a setting as this one . . . ?

Over the years, with changing owners, this near-folly has been discreetly scaled down. First that little platform went, then the spire it had topped. At one point the surviving stouter part of the tower took on a slightly Norman appearance. The walls became creeper-covered, the windows more like ordinary people's windows. Exoticism was gradually reduced, the place became as it were Anglicised, much like a good, if grandiose, Victorian invention. Obviously it was by then far more manageable, an acceptable country house, if you were into that sort of thing, with gardens still large and elegant and still cared for by a sizeable outside staff.

Captain Banbury, of the Royal Engineers, became squire of Pippingford during the first years of this century. He frequently invited his military colleagues to conduct summer exercises over his land and it was partly because of this that the Army moved in quickly to already familiar territory in 1914. When, after the considerable occupation of those war years, the Forest returned as it were to civilian life, the connection remained, and still remains. The occupation by the army of many acres of Pippingford ground has long reached acceptance. Times have changed, anyway. During both wars the Forest suffered bitterly, but those in the know will tell you that the Army have become reliable conservationists.

When Captain Banbury left, the house was sold to a Mr Anderson. He paid £74,000 for the estate, but relinquished it very soon. In 1919 it was sold to Haley Eustace Morriss for £12,000. As his son, the present owner, points out, land values had been declining almost since the repeal of the Corn Laws and reached their lowest ebb after the First World War, coming back to a boom period in the first flush of E.E.C. tactics.

Pippingford is the site of more than one iron-working, but a story softer than iron tells of that part of the Forest called Three Wards, which touches Pippingford, where sparrow-hawks have had a favourite breeding ground. From here, it is said, King Charles II took his sparrow hawks for sporting, and many—too many by today's thinking—must have found themselves fast in some royal mews. A forester protecting a pair might earn a reward of 2/- in Gaunt's time.

Probably the best known of Forest houses is Old Lodge, which can be eyed across that shallow valley known as Old Lodge Bottom that runs below the Stonehill, or Crowborough, road. The original house was always alluded to as *The* Old Lodge, as distinct from *The* New Lodge, both being points of Forest administration. The Old Lodge was in total disrepair when Sir Henry Compton was Ashdown's Steward—but that was a time of ruin over the whole Forest, before the enclosures of Charles II brought the place back into order of a sort. Being within range of both Pippingford and Ashdown Park, Old Lodge has had links with both.

The most extraordinary thing about the present house is that no one, least of all the present owners, the Castle Stewarts who have been in occupation since the 1920s, knows anything about when it was built, or who by, or who for. Whatever its original dates and style, it had an entirely new facade clapped on to it by one of the De La Warr dowagers about the turn of the century. It appears today as a Tudor manor house and the lay-out of the whole estate reinforces the impression—farm, dependant cottages, wide acres with grazing and in earlier times some tillage and cropping. Today, there are also managed conifer plantations.

Among the cottages is one dating back, it has been judged, at least to Tudor times. It could be that this building holds what is left of that original Old Lodge from which the Forest was administered by its defaulting steward.

This house, too, knew that Forest society which one imagines as being bound up with tennis and garden parties, following on such occasions as have been imagined for Pippingford and Chelwood Vachery. Here there was also a cricket pitch, and once it would have been possible to gaze across Old Lodge Bottom and catch sight of white-clad figures, and on fine summer days declining to evening hear the clonk of the ball on wood and the shout of the umpire. And if it all sounds too impossibly idyllic, there has been tragedy, too, in war time. Also the nightingales, it seems, flew huffily away from coniferous woodlands which do not appeal to their kind . . .

Ashdown House, originally called Lavertye, is a little way out of Forest Row on the Hartfield road. It is one of two houses in the neighbourhood whose architect was Benjamin Latrobe; they may be the only surviving examples of his work in England. The second is Hammerwood House, which cannot claim to be of the Forest, though its affiliations with the iron industry seem to allow it a non-voting membership. Latrobe emigrated to America in 1795, where he came to great prominence, being the designer of such as The Capitol and Baltimore Cathedral. Pevsner agrees that these two Sussex mansions were built in the years immediately before Latrobe left for the States. The present owners of Ashdown House, which has been a school for many years, give 1788 as its date. The house was originally built for Lord Heathfield, whose title, Baron of Gibralter, is commemorated by the Gibralter Tower in Heathfield Park; the Tower was erected by an admiring later owner of the Park at a cost of £3,000—a stiffish sum for an 18th century folly. Lord Heathfield died in 1790 and he seems never to have lived in the Latrobe house, an extremely beautiful example of its date, described most

conclusively by Pevsner as 'very perfect indeed.' Lord
Heathfield's daughter, Anne, certainly lived in the house
when it was still Lavertye. She married John Trayton Fuller
and we know already that the eccentric Elliott Augustus Fuller
lived there while it was still Lavertye—he was the one who
kept his own pack of hounds to aid his great obsession, the
hunting of the hare.

Later still, in the summer of 1843, Ashdown House was
re-named Connaught House and opened as a boarding school
for boys; according to the records, it numbered at one time a
startling 340 pupils. The school there today has a rather
dazzling reputation. Pupils, girls as well as boys by now,
make up 120 places, which must be a great deal pleasanter.

CHAPTER NINE

Points to View

Apart from the large houses still flourishing on Ashdown
Forest, there are several lesser sites that must be added to the
Forest's curious miscellany. Any visitor to the place almost
certainly comes upon the name *King's Standing*. There was a
building there once, so it rates inclusion in this chapter.
King's Standing is a pleasantly dramatic name, instantly
attaching itself to activities long past. It is not the only place
of the same name, but it is immensely important in the overall
picture of Ashdown as a place of history and tradition. The
name remains easily in the memory—for some, no doubt,
because the adjacent car park is named for it, and for visiting
children because an ice-cream van is admitted there. It is also
a plantation, or *toll*, like those at Camp Hill, at Greenwood
Gate and the rest. There is a difference, though. Instead of
featuring a round enclosure, or what was once an enclosure,
King's Standing bank and ditch are square. The site has
suffered a good deal over the years, as C. F. Tebbutt
discovered when he began looking over its possibilities. Not
only the basic ravages of time had to be considered, the
further results of two world wars, but also a sad blunder
mysteriously perpetrated in the '70s. For some reason best
forgotten, the bank was bulldozed and the spoil flung into the
ditch, more or less obliterating that as well. It can only seem
very strange, now that so much archeological and historical
information about Ashdown has come to light, that such an
exercise should ever have been considered, let alone actually
carried out. But mistakes often lead to further discoveries and

this one, too, offered compensations. Tebbutt alerted other
experts, among them Ivan D. Margary, whose *Roman Roads in
Britain* and *Roman Ways in the Weald* have become classics of
their subject. He had used aerial photography to great effect.
The work that followed revealed evidence not only of Roman
occupation but of prehistoric. Pottery and tiles came to light,
some medieval, some 17th and 18th century.

Over the years there has been much speculation, indeed
much pontificating, over the significance of King's Standing,
which is mentioned time and again in the records of the
Forest. It is the later periods of its existence that have in fact
caused the most enquiry, the centuries since the Forest was
enclosed; that it turns out to have ancient affiliations, too,
may seem less to the particular point. The first I was ever told
about the place was that it was where the King stood to
watch his herds of deer driven and counted. The second
explanation was that the King stood and the deer were driven
to be shot at. This sorted better with its period than the first,
since destruction in the days of those kings was more popular
than conservation.

In a magnificent book called *The Master of the Game*, either
written or sponsored by the 2nd Duke of York in 1406, there
is much about what is called 'the King's standing' in any
Royal Chace. Rules are laid down for its management. It was
to be prepared in advance of the King's visit, by the Master
Forester—sometimes called the *Parker*—who would then
'remain there without noise' until the King's arrival, by
which time he should be able to report what game was about.
There would be dog-handlers with leashed greyhounds to set
on when needed; these men were called *fewterers*. The Master
Forester was also required to supervise the making of shelters
for the Queen and attendant ladies—and for the greyhounds,
too, a nice touch, to shield them from the weather. The
shelters are described as 'fair lodges of green boughs'. These
long-gone shooting parties must have been exhilarating
affairs, but one cannot but hope that the participants were

often clumsy with their bows, and that the deer were fleeter and more cunning than on any other day in the year . . . The medieval picture is almost tiresomely attractive, familiar from tapestries and illuminations, the 'fair lodges' filled with twittering ladies in rich gowns and blowing veils.

In later years, King's Standing on Ashdown Forest became Queen's Standing in honour of the reigning monarch; a few years later it became King James Stand, and was so called as late as 1813. It is suggested that in the reign of James I the banks and enclosures were replaced, or augmented, by a solid hunting tower. So there must have been, over the years, a good deal of building and demolishing and re-building.

When romantic-historical connections attach to such places as King's Standing, they invariably work their way round to Henry VIII; Ashdown can hardly hope to escape him. For here, it is sometimes claimed, the monarch met Anne Boleyn for the first time, and the whole business began that led not only to the block but to the Virgin Queen. It is not by any means an impossibility, for Anne's father, Sir Thomas, was at that time Master of the Forest; but at Hever Castle they tell a different tale. There was the Boleyn home, not many miles away—near enough, probably, for the royal party to ride on there for lodging and feasting after a day's sport . . .

A more positive landmark than any plantation, even of Scots pine, is Nutley Windmill. Cars must be parked at Friends' Clump. Turn left down the wide riding track and the mill is immediately spotted over the trees ahead. The mill can also be reached on foot from the main road, by way of an extraordinarily long track which actually ties the north side of the Old Lodge estate to Cackle Street south of Nutley. It is sadly broken here and there, but it can be followed with a bit of a struggle. When walking towards the windmill from the main road one passes the house called Sweet Minepits, much altered lately. Then comes the restored mill with Mill Cottage opposite.

The story of the windmill is a romantic one and is dealt

with very thoroughly and entertainingly in an excellent history-cum-guide written by two specialists, Simon Wright and Frank Gregory. It seems unlikely that there was a windmill on Ashdown before the present one was established in 1836 up on its height north of the Stonehill road. A suggestion that there could have been an earlier cornmill, that is in the late 17th, early 18th centuries, has never been authenticated. There were, of course, the watermills—as witness Millbrook running down in the bottom below the present windmill. John Norden's *Description of Sussex*, appearing in 1595, claims two watermills for Ashdown. There is mention of a mill at Nutley in the reign of Henry VIII, which was rated at 18/– a year. At the time this is noted in the Forest records, that mill had decayed and the new one constructed in its place was defaulting on rent. In the Crowborough Warren area the Old Mill and the New Mill are still marked on the map, but they need not be the two mentioned by Norden, or even the two in confusion about their dues in the 16th century. The Old Mill has long fallen away and the New Mill—said to have milled the flour for Queen Victoria's wedding cake—was dismantled and its stone sold. That was not so many years ago, for a neighbour bought a load and then needed only half of it; the rest is in this garden.

The Nutley Windmill that stands so proudly today is said to have come originally from Goudhurst in Kent—one writer tells of its having vanished from Goudhurst in the mid-18th century. It was not unusual for windmills to be dismantled and carted elsewhere. So the Goudhurst mill could indeed have sojourned for a time in Crowborough—as is claimed by a local who says that it was his grandfather who brought it at last to Nutley. However it may have gone, the Nutley mill fell into sad disrepair and was rescued in the nick of time. It belonged to the Castle Stewarts of Old Lodge, who willingly agreed to repair work being done on the structure. The prime mover in the enterprise was a Nutley man, Tony Turner, who had known the mill all his life. He had a family connection with Mr Stevenson, a brickmaker who had built Windmill Cottage nearby. Stevenson and the actual mill owner, whose name was Taylor and who lived in Nutley village, had a useful partnership—Stevenson was responsible for turning the mill into the wind when its true master was absent.

Thanks to the enormous amount of interest aroused, the mill was triumphantly restored and is a monument to the skills and enthusiasm of a band of keen amateurs under the advice of experts. I have given the merest snippets of information from the enormous amount gathered into the official guide, published by *The Uckfield & District Preservation Society* and on sale locally. Among its contents is a three-verse poem by J. B. Paddon, written long before the windmill was restored, when it stood 'Forlorn and frail . . . On Ashdown's heights.'

Although a camp can hardly be called *architectural*, it is bound to have temporary building of some kind, and this seems the best place to write of that big camp set up on the Forest in the summer of 1793. War with France was still in its earlier stages and as usual was going to take far longer to dispose of than anyone had supposed. In the summer of this year a great recruiting drive was under way, and there were camps in many other parts of the country. The one on Ashdown Forest appears to have been forgotten in the neighbourhood and details eventually came to light more or less by accident. Aerial photography over the Forest in the '20s had attracted attention to what had long been taken for granted—a number of curious grass-covered mounds in the area between Duddleswell and the marlpits at Nutley. The camera naturally picked these up and they were then labelled *tumuli*; not the only example on the Forest. It was many years later, in 1964, that an East Grinstead member of the Sussex Archeological Society who was making a study of early Sussex maps, came upon one in the Public Records Office of *The Camp on Ashdown Forest in 1793*. Keen investigation then began.

In an article in Volume 103 of the *Sussex Archeological Collections*, Ivan D. Margary tells what happened then. The map showed rows of the 'mystery mounds' in relation to the encampments, and it came to light through consultation with military authority that they were in fact the remains of field kitchens. A fascinating story unfolded. Records showed that the encampment had held a force of 7000 under the command of the Duke of Richmond and that its main object—apart from the obvious one of recruitment—had been to try out a new system of drill recently being introduced. The lay-out of the camp is shown remarkably clearly in the map reproduced in the *Collections*. It covered ground, as expected, from Duddleswell to Nutley, with lines of tents, the kitchens, the trenches dug for the exercises, and various administrative sections. The camp had first been set up some miles away at Broadwater but was struck on 4th August, when the force marched with drums and colours to Ashdown. The camp had been organised in advance of their arrival by a detachment of Sappers. The military stayed a week, then no doubt with a similar display of regimental music, proceeded to Brighton, where they 'drilled for a fortnight', producing some 'grand military displays in the presence of the Prince of Wales.' Such visits by the military to one suitable district or another were accompanied by various sociabilities. An old print—again produced in the *Collections* from the original in the National Army Museum—shows much activity around such a camp, with strolling visitors, itinerant vendors, and even a fat man walking his dog. There would have been much activity, too, in the Nutley neighbourhood in August 1793, with carriages plying and guests, most likely, to be catered for in convenient cottages. There is a row of cottages in Nutley called *The Barracks*; it would be good to know if there were any possible connection. There is also, in the Worthing Museum, a lady's fan commemorative of three 1793 camps, one being Ashdown, with a stylised plan of each by way of decoration.

It is called below its border *The New Camp Fan*, which suggests that such fans were a feature of this kind of semi-sociable military exercise, presented, perhaps, by gallant officers to lady visitors. Did Jane Austen's Lydia Bennett receive such a gift when, with her friends, Colonel and Mrs Forster, she was among the visitors to the camp held in Brighton only two or three years later . . .? Further frivolous speculation might be forgiven—did the young ladies of the day actually collect such mementoes—were they, even, dubbed *fans* themselves?

When the mystery mounds were opened they were found to contain indeed the kitchen refuse and other detritus left behind all those years ago. It was the custom, it seems, to bury all the rubbish and make good the site after such an exercise, but for reasons never likely to be known, it did not happen quite like that on Ashdown Forest in August 1793. As Margary says, it is pretty extraordinary that 'no recollection of this military incursion seems to have survived locally.' There is, of course, Camp Hill, positively in the required vicinity, but the name is far older and appears much earlier. It might be, perhaps, that the name actually suggested the site.

The 1793 exercises may have been totally forgotten, but camps on the Forest still exist. It is a wonderful locality for such activities as scouting. The *Isle of Thorns*, by Chelwood Gate, enclosed at some time or other, was purchased in 1928 by a merchant banker of philanthropic intent called Alfred R. Wragg, to be a holiday camp for boys. The area covers 100 acres and was generously planned for its purpose, with open air pool, sports facilities and all to be expected of its date. It was created, so its Manifesto declares, 'in order that the health and happiness of an open-air holiday may be for ever available to those who need one.' According to age, payment was at the rate of 12/–, 15/– and £1 a week.

It could not, of course, be 'for ever', as its founder hoped; the Isle of Thorns is now a part of the University of Sussex.

But the Forest is still host to projects whose aims are the same, all under the aegis of the Manor Charitable Trust founded by Wragg. I say the Forest is host because, although the camps are permanencies within enclosures, activity depends on the fact that these places are enriched by their surrounding. One of the camps, at Broadstone Warren, is run by the *East Sussex County Scout Council*. It covers about 400 acres and has its swimming pool, as expected, but also grass ski slopes and accommodation for archery as well as more familiar sports. There are the usual necessary hutments, shop and so on. The whole thing is carried on with remarkable self-containment, and although you may sometimes meet a party of scouts about some such ploy as orienteering, they seem on the whole to be largely invisible.

More or less across the road, but just as secluded, is Hindleap Warren. This is run, again under the Trust, by the *London Federation of Boys' Clubs*. It is more modern and seemingly richer than its neighbour. It began life in 1974, though its parent body is celebrating a centenary. 'Among the main disciplines taught at Hindleap,' says its brochure, 'are canoeing, climbing, sailing and caving.' They have *abseil* platforms and a climbing wall. Hindleap's simple pleasures are obviously part of an elegant and sophisticated programme.

Though there are many ancient inns within easy reach of the Forest, none are on Forest ground. *The Goat* changed its function many years ago and *The Foresters* at Fairwarp, though incorporating old buildings, has no very long history as an inn. *The Hatch Inn* is the one with secrets to confide—and so it certainly appears, hugged into the landscape, low, rather dark; full of legendary promise, surely a smugglers' haunt. It was originally a row of three cottages, said to date back to 1430; which means they were there before Newbridge furnaces were 'blowing', so they might well in due course have housed their workers. It was not until the early 18th century that the cottages became an inn, called at

that time *The Cock*. Or was *chark* the word used and then
corrupted by time—for the present landlord tells of its use by
charcoal burners, who came toiling up the long hill for
refreshment. A good deal later the name was changed to *The
Hatch*, for the simple commemoration of the original coal-
men's gate on to the Forest—that is, Colemans Hatch—in the
days of Newbridge's fame. The inn is indeed claimed as the
expected smugglers' haunt—rum was the speciality. Captain
Kidd, it is said, was in charge of the racket, but there seems
some confusion here. The Rev. C. N. Sutton, in his *Historical
Notes of Withyham, Hartfield & Ashdown Forest*, writes of how
the farmhouse called Snows Hole became the site of a
mansion named Hartfield Grove, built and occupied by a
Captain Kidd—and this gave us the name Kidds Hill. *The
Hatch* must have many other mysterious connections but at
present it is busy about its own concerns. Appropriately in
this particular setting, it is a Free House.

The *Nutley Inn*, so often quoted in the records of the Forest
as the scene of meetings, successful or combative, in earlier
times, has long vanished. The name *Nutlin* carries its memory
into today. When the London road ran via Chelwood Gate,
The Shelley Arms at the Nutley crossing catered for coaches—
which it still does, of course, in a somewhat different context.
At the further end of the village *The King William IV*, always
called *The William*, is a pleasant pub of no great age but
considerable popularity. The Nutley place-name *Horse &
Corner* may suggest an inn, but in fact it commemorates the
field, just off the old Drift Road, where mares were brought
to the stallion, walked from village to village by its owner.

Although it is perfectly obvious that Ashdown Forest
would have been an ideal place for smugglers' storage
arrangements or going to ground, there is not an enormous
amount of information about this particular activity. There
are certainly some known smugglers' tracks and one accepted
hiding place at Beggars' Bush a little west of the High Road
at Duddleswell; round about here, too, was Howlers (or

Owlers) Oak. There were others at Nutley and Fairwarp, but whether in suitable barns and outbuildings supplied by conspiring farmers or whether just in holes in the ground is not known. There is that track already mentioned that entered the Forest by Twyford and led on up to *The Goat*; and there is another very suggestive path running from Cackle Street along by Spring Garden Farm—but that is speculation.

So much has been written about smuggling in Sussex as a county that it is tantalising to be unable to pin more on the Forest itself, and to offer only a couple of positive locations. Two writers on Sussex smuggling tell one Ashdown tale— how Gabriel Tomkins, member of the notorious Mayfield gang, spotted at Burwash and pursued all the way to Ashdown, was cornered 'in a lane at Nutley'. So he was about halfway between two possible sanctuaries, for *The Goat* and *The Cock*, as it was in his day, were both within a mile or two. The Rev. Mr Sutton knew men with memories of smuggling grandfathers. One told him of an exciseman done out of what had seemed a certain arrest; Mr Sutton also speaks of 'an old woman living in a house on the Forest which was formerly an inn and a meeting place of smugglers.' Her uncle had been a smuggler and she described how she saw him go riding on his grey horse, with his brandy kegs slung about him and an excise officer hard on his tail. But he put his horse at the forest gate and was over and away before the poorer horse could rise to the occasion . . . Could she have been Susannah Rice, seventy-eight years old when interviewed by Raper in the early '80s of the last century? She, it may be remembered, lived at *The Goat*.

The parishes which extend into the Forest have their churches in each case several miles away. Nutley, Fairwarp, Coleman's Hatch and Forest Row have 19th century churches, of which Fairwarp has considerable individuality.

The Ashdown Forest Centre, by Broadstone Warren, was opened in 1983, the ceremony performed by the late Lord of the Manor of Duddleswell, Earl De La Warr. It had taken just two years and three months to construct, often in an atmosphere of not-so-muted public disapproval. The whole business was a complete triumph of energy, enthusiasm and self-help. Local contractors gave their time to clearing the site and constructing its road; the *Manpower Services Commission*, in the shape of the *County Enterprise Programme* supplied a site foreman, a joiner and two labourers, and the *Youth Opportunities Programme* provided ten lads to swell the labour force. Technical advice was given by Steve Comber, of Comber & Sons; the quantity surveyor was Arthur Wells. This comprehensive force was under the general organisation of Ranger Pedder and the remarkable fact is that except in two cases no outside help had to be enlisted.

The Centre is based on three old barns, which had to be sought out, then bargained for, then taken down, then transported, then re-erected. Only one is a true Sussex barn, but the others are more or less neighbours—one from Kent, the farthest from Essex. The work of bringing them to the cleared site fell to Durtnells of Brasted, and their task must have been fairly daunting. The dismantling of such buildings, with the necessary numbering of every piece and its jig-saw-like re-forming calls for an enormous amount of patient skill. And when all was done, the framework up, the plastering finished—this was one of two jobs that needed outside help, for time was running out—the thatch went on. Wherever possible local materials had been used—where original beams needed repair second-hand forest oak was used; and as is pointed out in the Centre's leaflet on the building, even the weathervane on the biggest barn was made from scrap collected off the Forest. But the thatch was surely the biggest triumph of all. For one thing it was to be made of heather, in the traditional fashion for these parts. Each cut and carried bundle of heather weighed 40 lbs, and even the smallest of the three buildings took 3000-odd bundles, with 75 bundles of hazel poles. The metal hooks that held the thatch, 500 or so, were made on site. Jim and John Kenward of Edenbridge spent twelve months on that amazing thatched roof that crowned the Centre with considerable distinction. Perhaps some among those young lads who worked along with the experts, the master thatchers, may have been left with a useful interest in the craft.

The barn of barns is indeed the Sussex barn, brought here from Hassocks. Its actual physical shape is outstanding. The great oak beams rear and span, and the best feature of all, perhaps, is the gallery. Windows along the north wall open onto a staggeringly fine view. This is the exhibition barn, the core of the Centre; already, in one aspect, the core of today's Forest. Well managed displays present the history of Ashdown, no aspect ignored. There are excellent photographs, many by one or other of the staff. The place is run by volunteers, often extremely busy—though on some winter Sunday with the rain teeming over a deserted Forest, they may perhaps wonder if their devotion to the job is a bit extreme. They are there to answer questions, to direct and advise. More and more school parties apply for visits with a talk, or a video, to be followed by a walk. All this, of course, has to be organised from those two offices on the floor above, where the Superintendent and his assistant cope with an increasing mass of work, and where the Rangers pick up their briefing—Rangering has become an exceedingly varied job.

One activity here that has gained in importance during the past year or two, is the use of the gallery for small exhibitions. These may be a display on a theme chosen by experts, or an exhibition of painting by some local artist, or photographs connected with the Forest. These are possibly outnumbered by school projects on the countryside or some allied subject—frequently extremely heartening.

The Anderida Barn is open to visitors through the summer until September, each day from two o'clock until after four; on Sundays and public holidays it is open from 11 a.m. There is winter opening on Sundays and holidays from 11 to 4.30. It is true enough that when this project was first mooted it caused very mixed reactions; they were mostly unwelcoming. The place would be a *honey-pot*, it was said. There would be crowds and silly merchandise. There are crowds but so far not unmanageable—and we are not yet into T-shirts or tea-towels . . .

It seems a little curious that there is so much to tell of actual Forest habitation when, officially, there should be none. It is also rather extraordinary that so much can go on in such seclusion that casual visitors are unaware of anything much more than open space and its pleasures. There are many other houses on the perimeter whose owners and tenants in the past made use of grazing and the rest. To write of them would be to add another whole chapter, but such as Marshall's Manor, Masketts, both very old in foundation, Oldlands Hall which is named for its ground that the Romans mined, Holly Hill and Legsheath and enormous Wych Cross Place, all influence the impression of times and manners hereabouts.

CHAPTER TEN

War and Peace

To settle anywhere is to settle among prejudice, ancient or modern; to settle among country prejudice offers a regime more demanding; to settle with forest prejudice is toughest of all—it is probably the same in any forest you care to name, since men root in such places as positively as the trees that make the bulk of their background. The friend who warned against quitting downland for forest proved, in a way, to know what he was talking about. Downland, open and airy, invites confidence; forest, be it woodland or open heath, has a depth of its own and seems to call for a guide. Feelings on Ashdown run high that in other parts have shifted discreetly underground. There is a foresty eccentricity about long established local families that is worth respectful cherishing even while it is driving the well-meaning amateur forester almost to distraction. Such families are instinctively on their guard against a power they have forgotten, which no longer properly exists but to which they never have and never will surrender. They are also so closely intertwined that they sometimes give the impression of having come out the other side of conventional ties and are now well able to consider their various branches with dispassionate assessment—until some issue concerning the Forest arises. Then passions are roused with as much bitter fervour as ever they were under the Plantagenets, the Tudors, the defaulting Stuarts and the rest. At once there is union; the struggles of the past, the blurred memory of long gone commoners are asserted to defy whatever the local power seems to pose. Take the matter of the Rangers, descendants or at any rate heirs, to an oppressive presence. They are almost always cast as villains, foreign wastrels lolling away their time for extravagant sums of money. 'What happens to my money?' demands a local of long years' standing, when asked to contribute to a fund vital for the maintenance of the Forest. 'You won't find me paying the Rangers' wages.' And there is sometimes an amazing aggression when it comes to payment of the Forest rate, yearly confirmation of that common right fought for with such turbulent bitterness—in many cases by the protesters' own grandfathers and great-grandfathers. 'If they want it, let them come and get it.'

Thirty-odd years ago, when I came to know Ashdown Forest as my home, the place was far freer in many of its aspects than it is today. It is now caught up, as any similar place in the south-east, probably in all England, in the toils of the motorcar, the endless chains of traffic that twist and trip and manacle. A great many visitors come to the Forest now, at any weekend, on Bank Holidays, during the summer holidays—indeed on any fine day there are people arriving and departing, many of them retired, pensioners, with time and a car of their own. It is after all the first good breathing place on the way out of London—though sometimes during a hot summer it is by-passed in the rush to the sea. All this has led to the many car-parks that some find offensive. At weekends they are often alarmingly full, not helped by the sanctioning of ice-cream vans—these, however, do produce a bit of useful revenue as, by recent decisions the parks themselves may do. Stone-built collecting boxes, of the sort favoured by the National Trust, are being installed into which offerings may safely be dropped. Many people who visit the Forest frequently will be glad to make some contribution to the upkeep of the place. No doubt there will be a clash of opinion over this development, as in the first place about the car parks themselves. It is true that when these were first laid out they looked pretty raw, but they have mellowed. The bank-and-ditch arrangement has thrown up some pleasant side effects—heather has settled along many of the banks, and in one place where the bank catches a phenomenal amount of sun, there was one summer a sensational display of butter-cups. People who have lived here a good deal longer than I have see all this as the ultimate in interference with a natural order. Yet these confining areas are also a buffer, for many casual visitors stay near their cars and so leave endless spaces for the walking sort. It is true that I have sometimes looked rather gloomily across managed areas, seeing beyond them rides cut through bracken, and wondered if wild Ashdown is beginning to look a shade like Richmond Park, where even the deer stand to be admired.

How are the pressures of today's mobility to be resisted, unless by some tactful shepherding? Best to recall that but for that law suit that dragged through the 1880s the whole Forest might be fenced and forbidden to all but its Lord. It is still a surprise to realise that this was pevented in an age in thrall to riches and rank. Astonishingly few people who know and enjoy the Forest have paused to discover its origins and many are victims of the fallacy that *common* means belonging to all. Even those who live near enough to watch the place daily and claim to love it are casual in this respect. Many who were born here and have never had any desire to live elsewhere in the world, give the impression of knowing for certain that the Board of Conservators is nothing less than a close-knit band of despoilers. I have already spoken of that forest-born man who accused the Conservators of driving away all the wild life—the one who had such fun with his mates and his gun in boyhood. Others will tell you that the Conservators have put up notices everywhere, forbidding this, excluding that. In fact there are no such restrictions; horse riders are *asked* to keep to recognised tracks, sometimes marked with a post and a horse's head—but that carries no authority beyond good manners and the recommendations put forward in the very brief Riding Code. A ban on litter and sporting weapons can hardly be looked on as needlessly restrictive, while the ban on picnic stoves at the danger seasons must be best for all. Sometimes when a stretch of track has become eroded, one is asked to *Keep Off Re-seeded Areas Please*, and there are the by-laws pasted up, as legally they must be, at various points.

You can't do this, they won't let you do that, comes the cry. But the right of common remains, although too little exploited, and no one can stop a commoner grazing his allotted number of beasts or of claiming his wood and litter quota at the approved time. Four-footed beasts still take precedence, remember, over roads never released from their inherited right. What has to be faced is the fact that just as seven centuries ago the forests were being thrust back to satisfy the demands of population, so now the countryside in general is being filched, eroded, tamed. There is little such bodies as the Conservators of Ashdown Forest, or the Verderers of the New Forest, or of Dean or Epping or any other forest, are able to do about it save adjust as best they may, stand firm and keep a constant vigil.

When I write this, I write it, of course, for my own comfort more than in sweet reason. In every such place as this there must appear mistakes on the ground which it will be hard to correct. The invasive bracken is being increasingly cut back, and needs it, since it is no longer claimed for litter. After a few cuttings, the grass returns as it has always returned for the benefit of grazing. But there are many swathes cut that do indeed suggest very strongly the pattern of parkland—and though this place was once called Lancaster Great Park it was not quite in the sense of the word we use today. I think of London commons grazed by sheep well within living memory, of sheep, too, in Hyde Park—and I realise that what sound like grumbles and complaints are often anxiety. Conservation has come, strangely enough, as an opposing force and it is not always possible to love what conservation brings. It is an advised practice to cut the heather in due season and the results have been magnificent.

But this will drive many into tantrums. Yes, of course they cut the heathers in their own gardens, but the Forest was never meant to be a garden, was it now . . .? And of course this is basically, logically correct.

It has become fashionable in these direct times to dismiss recollection as nostalgia. This does seem folly, for remembrance is full of spice and I recall with great warmth and pleasure the Forest as it was when I first began to learn of it. That was in the '50s, before the reunions and recoveries of war's ending had lost their flavour, before speed was a science, before little deserted Gatwick became a London airport. Then, the majority of the dwellings round about, many of them heirs of aged holdings, were occupied by the people for whom they were intended, proper foresters, members of families who had been in these parts for ever, who knew their rights and enjoyed them and accepted what else was to hand with confidence. These were people who certainly never bothered about London, for whom a trip to Brighton or Eastbourne involved a good deal of effort—a long walk to the bus, and a long walk home carrying whatever spoils had been the object of the outing. On the grass clearings around such dwellings the washing blew on lines long established on proper poles; 6d a year was charged at one time. Children's toys lay about and cats sunned themselves in a good, comfortable, customary way, ignoring any other domestic clutter, such as a picking hen or two, a strutting cockerel. The children walked across the Forest to the village schools and back in the dim winter evenings unafraid. They crossed little rivers on their way and toiled up the steep banks they would race down on the way home . . . And if this sounds somewhat idyllic, I have not forgotten the days of soaking rain when they arrived at school bedraggled and probably never properly warmed up till they were home again. At one time, on two adjacent farms, young families were growing and the mothers often set out together on summer afternoons to shop in the village, each with a child in a pushchair; you could hear them chattering as they came, or the babies in some quick-shrieking protest being rebuked or encouraged. Successors would find it hard to shove a pushchair down that track now, for it is rutted and ruined and narrowed. There seemed to be few perils then. Children roamed the place and their mothers knew no qualms. Where's young so-and-so? Oh—somewhere about the Forest . . .

These children have long grown up. Because of the change in schooling routines, they progressed to schools in the nearby towns and their prospect widened. When they set about getting married, as they mostly did at that time, they were already conditioned to the easier living of friends whose homes were equipped with washing-machines and the like. They moved away, settling in less inconvenient places, even if that meant nothing more foreign than housing estates in the villages. Then, for one reason and another—retirement, failing health, a desire to be nearer their grandchildren—the parents, too, were moving away in their turn. They sold at a welcome profit to strangers seeking *second homes*, whatever the expression really means. So the neatening began, the cottages enlarged, the so-called firebreaks round the properties mysteriously widened; unsanctioned, indeed illegal, plantings were made beyond the bounds of the property, even on the far side of the accommodation track, hedges grubbed up and replaced often with little suitability. The irony is that these Forest dwellings now possess the comforts that earlier had to be sought elsewhere—but they have lost their true heirs.

Though many of the oldest Forest names have endured, far more have been lost. Lavertye seems a more distinguished name than Ashdown House, Snows Hole more characterful than Hartfield Grove; though the newer names no doubt appeared in their day more gentlemanly. Lately, newcomers are inclined to change the name of their house almost as a matter of course. This is murder for local historians teasing out clues and references. As an example, the word *fern* incorporated into a house name becomes unsuitable to the locality, since bracken is rarely alluded to as fern in these parts. 'Fern,' it says somewhere in the records, 'or, in English, brakes.' It is difficult not to mourn the loss of Workhouse Farm as well as Streeters, already mentioned. A changed spelling can banish the name of an ancient family recorded as owning adjacent property for centuries. And when *The Crows Nest* becomes *The Doves Nest* anything can happen. Perhaps newcomers to the Forest could be visited in time and wheedled into accepting the historical importance of their property, however modest—a kind of counselling, in the modern style.

Local councils, too, can be offenders here. A spate of nameplates has appeared on roads and lanes in the last few years, which can only be welcome for motorists, as somehow it always appears that nowadays there is no one about to ask the way. But Chelwood Gate has only one beacon—and it was one that flared for the Armada—yet the road appears as Beaconsfield Road, merely, one supposes, because it is a more familiar word. Crowborough has done better by its beacon, and the nearest road is correctly spelled. Pronunciations, too, changing with time and usage can equally confuse and conceal. The soft *G* used for Gill's Lap has already been mentioned here, but Rystwood, now with a long *Y*, is more often written in the records as Ristwood; since phonetic spelling obtained for so long this, too, poses a problem.

Names in these parts can in any case be eccentric. It is a place for nicknames which after a few years very often cannot be explained. In earlier days such fancies included Fashion Nairn and Champion Young, while City Bannister has already made an appearance. And what about Mouse Williams, sub-forester from 1377–1384 . . .?

When it comes to recreation on the Forest, shooting and fishing have, literally, gone by the board. That leaves riding as the mainstay, with a certain amount of hunting. There is some flying of model aircraft, a pastime that came into being

between the wars, when the models were a good deal gentler
than they are today. Even so, an East Grinstead club came to
grief in those early days, when it was accused of 'inconveniencing the members of the Ladies' Golf Club.' The golf
club has done some inconveniencing of its own from time to
time. When the model aeroplane craze started up again in
earnest there was some discussion as to the advisability of
allowing it at all, for a number of similar areas had ruled
against it—the New Forest was one. But since it had been
allowed on Ashdown so many years previously, it was
considered difficult to refuse the licence. Today, all fliers of
model aircraft are required to be club members and flying is
restricted to certain hours in certain spots. The model that is
radio controlled can seem rather threatening, and there must
surely come a day when one goes out of control and lands
under the nose of some nervous horse. It must be admitted
that the noise of these artefacts can be very spoiling of
simpler delights—on some still sunny morning in summer for
instance. It is a long time, as far as one has heard, since there
have been complaints, so it is fair to conclude that model
aeroplanes and their sometimes over-kitted operatives have
been absorbed along with much else. Sometimes the layman
can understand the fascination of the little planes, but no one
can deny the charm of real kites lovingly flown by the young.
So utterly quiet, sailing and swooping and beautiful.

In these days of charitable sponsoring, the forest floor is
pounded in many ways. There are walks, there are runs, there
are rides. Large sums of money are collected for excellent
causes and there is always a grateful cut for the upkeep of the
Forest. These activities, too, somewhat surprisingly, can raise
questions: 'Why is it allowed?' is too often heard. Certainly
for visitors who have driven some way to walk and picnic
quietly it may well be disconcerting to find the place hung
about with competitors, their support transport and their
urgers-on. Those of us who have constant opportunity to
enjoy the Forest find such events pretty unobtrusive—which

may be cried down as mere privilege. Blessings should be counted—once upon a time the So-and-So Harriers would leave a trail of paper clues behind. Barring an occasional marker-pennant missed in the clearing up, there is little to show the day after the event but an inevitable trampling; with luck and good weather it quickly repairs itself.

There are also the dog days, when the training clubs visit and the creatures, certainly great and small, go through their exercises, tracking, working through an intimidating programme of canine skills. These visitors are probably the best behaved of any. If less ambitious dog owners find their favourite walk denied them for a day, there is plenty of space a little further on. Dogs, of course, are high up in the total of Forest users.

As soon as the season opens, there is regular hunting on Ashdown. *The Old Surrey & Burstow, The Southdown & Eridge* packs appear, swarm about a bit, annoy some—though not by any discourteous behaviour for they are clearly well briefed in subtleties—fill others with admiration, and set all the usual arguments going once again. What and how often they find is not much spoken of. It is quite a time since there was evidence of digging or other traditional exercise, though that does not necessarily mean there is never a kill. The hunting question may never find an answer satisfactory to a majority, for even patently anti members of the local population will prevaricate. One cannot quite reject the excitement, another is a respecter of tradition. And it is hard not to feel some sort of stir at the sight of the pink coats, the sound of the silly little horn, those waving hound-tails. As they pour down steep slopes to some bushy bottom the fox knows well, the sight can only be admired for its pictorial excellence. And very often, when they have all gone straggling home, a fox crosses the track with an air of tired self-satisfaction, to come snuffling through the garden as usual when it is night. Those are the macho foxes still in their prime. After a long day streaking through gorse and bracken, older animals may not quite make it across the main road, and in these speedy, pitiless days he may lie there till his last bone is ground to dust, his last hair vanishes. He represents the reverse side of a coin never tossed quite far enough for a real challenge; there must be many among the rushing drivers, flattening him hourly, who would speak out loudly against fox hunting.

The foot followers, who are really wheel followers and shift their cars from park to park, wearing extraordinary expressions, familiar faces quite changed, shoving past, unseeing in their eagerness to spot some horrid climax—these are distinctly unlovable. As for the rampant *saboteur* I cannot tell, for the only ones I ever saw went past the gate once, looking tired and disheartened. They were the unhairy type—a young father wearing an expression compounded of determination and pain, his ethnically-clad wife, and two little sons, eager but a bit pale and worn out. Not very threatening.

Once, in a situation that shall remain for ever without identification, the fox was a welcome guest in a forest dwelling. There, so the tale went—and the teller was reliable—the young gambolled peacefully while the pretty vixen sat on the sofa, not so much watching over them tenderly as mopping up the offerings made by her admiring friends, the owners of the house. It must have been as enchanting as that novel of the '30s by David Garnett—*Lady into Fox*. That is a tale upsurpassed even by *Beauty & the Beast*. Both these tales, however, belong to other forests than our own.

Once there was talk of centenary celebrations for the setting up of the Board; there should be a pageant. How this would have been greeted it is now rather hard to imagine. It was being discussed, very wisely, several years in advance of its date and at that time it seemed an exciting idea. It seems doubtful, now, if it could have succeeded. The matter did not, in the long run, have to be decided, as the project some-how dribbled away and was lost. Sometimes I stand on the slopes where the audience would have been sited and remember our optimistic vision of riding Romans and dashing cavaliers streaming along Old Lodge Bottom. It strikes me now as a pretty frivolous idea.

There had in fact been a *Pageant of Ashdown Forest* long ago, in 1929. The venue was Kidbrooke Park. The pageant's author was Lord Edward Gleichen and he headed an enterprise lavishly decked out in titles of all sizes. The programme tells a tale of immense organisation and alarming expenditure. The physical production seems to have been rather more impressive than the script, judging by the synopses of scenes in the programme, and the evidence of photographs. The pageant must have played for hours and hours. It was produced by the most distinguished pageant-maker of the day, Gwen Lally, and opened with verses specially written by the châtelaine of Sissinghurt, the author V. Sackville-West, whose family connection called for her participation. Guy Warrack, a well known musical director of that time, took care of the orchestra and A. A. Milne wrote a piece for the programme. The cast ranged from Lord Howard de Walden to Master Christopher Robin Milne (afternoons only) by way of best-selling author Ernest Raymond, who lived at Haywards Heath. All the cast are given their titles—Lord, Lady, Sir, the Hon., Rev., Mr, Mrs, Mesdames, Messieurs, Miss and Master. Such formality may be forgiven in such circumstances; the programme indeed was printed as once a theatre programme would have been—and that not so long before the programme of Ashdown's pageant.

The various episodes, eight of them, were presented each by a different nearby town or village group. The action was set stirringly in motion by *Anderida, the Spirit of the Forest*—the Hon. Mrs Tatham, riding a white horse—who proclaimed the Prologue, concluding with the inspiring lines—

> Nor shall you think them figures in a dream
> But very men and women that in truth
> Toil'd, hunted, rode, loved, laughed and sometimes wept
> In this same Forest when these trees were young . . .

'After this, she rides away into the wood, whither her procession has by now preceded her.'

This rich and gracious bit of play-making at the end of the lively '20s can be thought of as a swansong for Kidbrooke Park as it once was. Everything about the pageant appears as a model of organisation. The costumes were supplied, as costumes should be, by the long established firms of Nathan and Clarkson, with wigs—at any rate those of the stars—made by London's top wigmaker, always called plain *Bert*. Everything was kindly supplied that could possibly have been asked for, right down to the insect repellant, *Flit*, contributed by the Anglo-American Oil Company. The pageant played from the 16th to the 20th July. How welcome the *Flit* must have been for an audience sitting in the evening in that great garden with its lake and waterfalls—the 'cascades' that Lord Colchester made when he owned the place, employing all those loads of purloined stone.

Although another ten years were to pass before war once again threw the country into confusion and misery, that pageant in Kidbrooke Park was in its way a signing-off, an unexplicit *envoi* to a way of life which, never entirely recovering after 1918, yet had a comfortable affluence for those warmly settled round about. The mansions of the early 19th century were followed by many more in a slightly less grandiose style; Victorian family houses where carriage-folk dwelt gracefully, and daughters were given marquee'd wedding receptions in grounds tended by several gardeners. The appearance of so many substantial properties at that time may have been caused partly by railway expectations which materialised only in part, since the Forest villages were left to their own devices, with the exception of Forest Row—whose perfect little country station is still missed. But the Victorian householders left behind coach houses which were easily converted into garages for their later owners. Although life has become a good deal more demanding than in the days when twelve gardeners were claimed for The Vachery with as

many and more, no doubt, at such as Oldlands Place and
Wych Cross Place, the flush of leisurely living is almost
visible today, a nearly perceived nimbus round those big, self-
confident dwellings built a century or so ago for the
comfortably-off. Somehow the whole atmosphere of those
pre-war times, of tennis parties, garden parties, summer
dinner parties, is meshed into the established well-cut hedges,
the specimen trees, the conservatories; even the occasional
glimpse of a blue-bottomed swimming pool fails to destroy
the older picture.

These well-built, settled houses have kept their character
far better than the smaller dwellings, the traditional foresters'
cottages whose original owners sadly moved away. A country
cottage, when such things became fashionable in the days of
the Rosettis and William Morris and their brethen, was most
likely to be rustically dark within, dark paint, dark curtains—
even electric light, where used, might be of deliberately low
candle-power to maintain the illusion—as at Standen near
East Grinstead, though that can hardly be called a cottage.
From the '50s on, that gloom was banished, light paint took
over, as technology took over in the '60s and made living a
good deal more comfortable. A large percentage of the small
houses about the Forest have by now been drastically altered,
enlarged, centrally heated, double-glazed and freezer-bound.
Does this mean they are spoilt? There can be no answer to
such a query, for we live as our times and circumstances
allow—to do otherwise, of choice, would surely be condemned as eccentricity. Many of these properties have right of
common, others have lost it—and no doubt with no open fire
and no sheep to graze it must have seemed good sense to stop
bothering when in 1965 re-registration of all common lands
called for a bit of effort. But once lost, the right is gone for
ever and there are many now, concerned for the Forest and
anxious for its future, who would dearly like to regain the
privilege of being a commoner . . . There is just one
recorded occasion when the matter went the other way, when

the owner of a property discovered that her acre carried, after all, no common right. She claimed her money back; she had paid her rate willingly for sixteen years. The Conservators agreed without quibble and sent back by return the 8/- to which her 6d rate had by then amounted. It is best to add that the lady was herself a lawyer . . .

Garth Christian writing in 1967 of the triumphant commoners of the 1880s, quoted the cry that the Forest was now 'safe for ever more.' This was a sadly over-optimistic cry. Within a span of years the Forest was threatened by the quest for oil—that threat is dealt with in the following chapter, along with its connection with the author, A. A. Milne. There is on the Forest a rather well managed memorial to A. A. Milne, his illustrator, E. H. Shepard, and the characters they invented between them—the curious bear, Winnie the Pooh, with his attendant boy, Christopher Robin, and other followers. It overlooks Cotchford Farm, where the Milnes lived for some years and the view it offers is spectacular. It is strange to recall that the first requests for some sort of memorial to Milne and his creations were confined to the planting of a plaque-bearing tree. This was resisted; the much bolder enterprise went through. Certainly it carries the query: if one memorial, why not others, and how long, then, before the place would begin to look like a rather straggling garden of remembrance? Those picnic seats donated in memory of one or another Forest lover, neatly inscribed and useful, seem to cover all needs. One memorial stone of a personal sort can be found on the Forest, and there are of course commemorative clumps of trees. One celebrates the visit of President Kennedy to Birch Grove, the home of the then Prime Minister, Harold Macmillan; another is for Macmillan himself. This last was dedicated on a day of torrential rain and gusting wind, which in no way deterred the principal characters—Macmillan, by then a very old man, and the Chairman of the Board, Bridadier Tim Scott, in much the same bracket. There they stood, bareheaded until the ceremony was completed, sparse white hair lifted by the wind, flattened by the rain.

Such clumps, or *tolls*, are easily based on those far older, Camp Hill and the rest, where first the public set foot on Forest ground. The precedent in one case may seem to have proved a little unfortunate. In 1973 we were all planting trees. It was *Tree Year*, or *The Year of the Tree*—I forget which. *Plant a Tree in '73*, ran the slogan and the Friends of Ashdown Forest decided to honour the challenge. Time, thought, money all went to the creation of *Friends' Clump*, which has alas, in many more opinions than one, become an eyesore on a prominent skyline. Dense, black, growing beautifully, it can only seem to threaten. It dominates Old Lodge Bottom like some wicked great bat, and seen from the house itself it gives an even more painful impression. When tempest scoured the Forest, Friends' Clump stayed undisturbed—so perhaps on that night it justified itself by offering shelter to deer and other threatened creatures. Cobbett can be quoted again here, though in respect of a different setting: 'What he can plant *fir* for, God only knows.'

The Forest has one memorial which most people know about, which appears on maps and in various country books that feature walks here or there. It is known as *The Airman's Grave*, It is of course no true grave but a very touching monument to the pilot and crew of the Wellington bomber that limped home from a raid on Cologne in 1944. The plane, off course, crashed; all on board were killed. The so-called grave contains personal belongings which were scattered around, then gathered up by the families of the dead men and buried. There are men still living in these parts who remember not only the incident but the messages radioed by the pilot, his anxiety lest he came down on actual dwellings.

The mothers of the men who died met at the site and decided to make some kind of memorial to their sons. The Rangers reported to the Board in 1945 that a wooden cross had been erected on the spot, with about twelve feet of ground fenced to protect it and the flowers they had planted

round it. It had not occurred to them, of course, that there
would be any difficulty over this infringement of by-laws. In
any case, the Board could hardly feel anything but sympathetic. The pilot's mother, Mrs Sutton, was contacted and
eventually a wall of local stone was built round the grave.
Mrs Sutton looked after the place for years, given lifts in the
Land Rover by one or other of the Rangers as time went on
and the walk became too difficult for her. When she had to
give up, the Conservators took over. At one time the grave
was cared for by Air Force Cadets; at another it was
vandalised, which caused great scandal. A custom grew up
within the Riding Association of laying a wreath on Remembrance Sunday, and then the Conservators joined in. People
walking paused to look at the wreaths and many then added
the poppies they were wearing for the day. So gradually it
became a place of modest pilgrimage where the dedication
was read, perhaps with a little awe. Besides the conventional
words inscribed on the stone, there was another of admonition, of sombre warning: *To the boys who would destroy—
Around this spot is spilt the blood of six heroes. This spot is sacred.
They died that you may live.*

One day at the beginning of a November, I was walking
along that wide track that leads eventually to the two
Misbournes when I saw a woman coming to ward me. She
was carrying a plastic bag from some supermarket and I
stopped to speak to her. I asked her what shopping she had
been doing at what secret store—what treasure she had
found. She laughed and said she had been to the Airman's
Grave. The bag held fork and trowel. She had been weeding
the plot in preparation for Remembrance Sunday. 'The pilot
was my brother,' she said. So we stood some time on that
sunny calm day, talking about our brothers; for mine, too,
had died in a bomber crash on home ground, though not in
this Forest. She told me she would be unable to get to the
Sunday Ceremony , so I said I would go in her place. I have
missed only one year since.

This is truly an occasion unlike any other. It takes place on one of the loveliest parts of the Forest, the contour to every quarter graceful and generous, the long line of the downs containing the horizon. Lately the numbers who arrive at the grave have swelled and a very brief, unsentimental celebration is organised by Bill Hulme, honorary secretary of the Friends of Ashdown Forest. The sight of a small portable radio on my first visit raised my eyebrows and sank my heart a bit. But it is needed. The familiar Whitehall sounds are thinned and lightened by the width and breadth of the setting and there is something dream-like in the effect.

Those who will attend the ceremony leave their transport at *The Hollies* car park. Most are elderly and have left time to proceed slowly. Many are alone. As we take our way along the wide and generally muddy track to the assembly point, we are inclined not to overtake, not to call greetings. Many of us take the opportunity to walk the dogs, possibly wishing to give the impression that this is a day like any other, and maybe we shall stop off for a moment, and maybe not. Representatives of the Board, various Rangers, volunteer or regular, are congregated when we later comers arrive. We hang about in the sun, the various dogs a bit at a loss, though one or two have been regular attendants for some years. As we stand waiting our numbers increase by ones or twos—twenty-two, twenty-five . . . Then the riders appear—over the brow to the north, up the steep bank from the south. There is a hazy sunshine, enough mist for the riders to appear as from behind effective gauzes. They group as casually as we of the humbler sort are grouped. Then it is time to begin and the London sounds promote silence and attention.

Sometimes walkers in the autumn weather pause, take in what is going on and decide to stay. Others cast glances at once incredulous and embarrassed and hurry on. No one so far has either continued talking or burst into giggles. The chimes of Big Ben, the Last Post, the Silence; then the usual few familiar lines, spoken here and hardly heard in the vast openness but known too well for that to matter. Reveille brings us back to life. The wreaths are laid, the poppies tossed over the wall. We turn for home, to the enormous relief of the dogs; neighbour now greets neighbour . . . It becomes after all just a Sunday in November on which, briefly, we have discovered that the Forest and the Airman's Grave are sheer holy magic when it comes to remembering.

CHAPTER ELEVEN

Disaster Year

1987 was a year of overlapping crises for Ashdown Forest. Possibly it had never been quite so beset and beleagured, even in its furious years. The declared salvation of a century was torn apart by succeeding threats. As that New Year moved into its place the word MURDER appeared on police notices across the road from the gates of Pippingford. The whole matter was totally unconnected with the Forest as such, but the word set the key for the months that followed, to future troubles which were already sounding. Only a couple of months later, British Petroleum announced its opinion that Ashdown should be the next south-eastern beauty spot to be explored for oil.

This was, as we know well, by no means the first time such a threat had loomed. In this case it seemed the more alarming for being one of a long list of explorations proposed or executed within a few miles of each other by one or other of the oil companies. The company's prospectors had selected, with an unwelcome flair, a site fractionally off the Forest—a farm that none the less nudged the line of the original pale. The Forest, claimed the company, would barely be affected, its inhabitants and its visitors would scarcely be aware of what was going on as BP carefully set up the exploratory bore hole—just off Kidd's Hill. Yes indeed, they agreed, it would of course need many lorry-loads of suitable stone for basic construction, the local kind being too soft—it was a little as if we were being rebuked, as if we had only ourselves to blame in that respect. Naturally the lorries would have to travel across the Forest, and there were several ways this might be done—ending of course with a trip up or down Kidd's Hill, one of the show bits of Ashdown—and they would certainly have to return empty. But it would be for only a limited time, and the restoration of all that had been disturbed during the purely exploratory operation would be so skilfully handled that no one would know thereafter that anything unusual or untoward had ever taken place in that delightful spot.

Curiously, quite a lot of people were perfectly satisfied with these assurances. They thought no further, partly, I daresay, because all the BP representatives were such pleasant people, one wanted almost to help them on their way to achieving their ambitions. It was truly surprising to find so many people ready to be persuaded, never considering what could happen next, what the consequences might be of a successful strike. BP put on a nice little show at the Coleman's Hatch Village Hall, with photographs of quality to prove their past expertise. The public turned up to look round and rightly admired the exposition of what was indeed impressive—sites that had been explored really did look as if nothing much had happened there. If challenged on the results of a successful strike the BP men would reply reassuringly that they had already failed to get any positive result from at least fifteen carefully chosen locations. And the sixteenth . . .?

Then there were arguments about 'the national good'. This concept appeared to hang entirely on the over-ruling need for industrial development, whatever the consequences. And never mind that part of the nation concerned to protect and preserve a wide and beautiful area where each year several million people find rest from turmoil, enjoying recreation of the simplest and most fundamental kind—and even an accepted allowance of aesthetic uplift . . . Again some voices were heard proclaiming benefit to the locality from the employment of neighbourhood workers. Quite apart from the fact that the oil companies bring their own men with them, jobs in the south-east were outnumbering those who were prepared to take them. The only local benefit, surely, would be to the pubs, the ancient *Hatch Inn* or the bigger, brasher hostelry at the far end of the same road, where for many years a stag's head sign proclaimed *The Roebuck*.

The East Sussex County Council turned down BP's application, but Parliament may all too easily over-rule silly locals who somehow never know what is good for them and seldom appear to recognise their duty to the nation . . .

The campaign against the oil men gave rise to some off-beat publicity which was enormously useful. If the exploratory borehole proved successful, if there was a strike, then that might happen to Ashdown that had already happened to Wych Farm in Dorset. There would be a development of alarming proportions. Pipelines would be laid under one of the Forest's best known spots—Gill's (Ghylls) Lap. This lovely place, with its high sightings on all sides, was one part of the Forest which had inspired stories now internationally known. A. A. Milne, when he was living below at Cotchford, had renamed it Galleon's Lap, and it was an important location in his children's books about Christopher Robin, Winnie the Pooh and the rest. For the next weeks and months the animal symbol for Ashdown Forest, the deer, retreated into the shades, while Pooh stamped his old grounds in its place, was interviewed as it were *in absentia* by countless journalists brushing up their childhood recollections, and came to stand for victory over industrialisation. Really dedicated Pooh-fans, by now mostly rather elderly, rose in anger and anguish at the hint of sacrilege; letters appeared in national newspapers; voices were raised in fury, horror, in Australia and the United States. . .

What price those others—the kings, the lords, the customary tenants? What of Sir Edward Dallingridge, John of Gaunt, Arabella Diana . . .? And what, indeed, of William Augustus Raper, accustomed to arguing all cases closely and rationally through the personal experience of tenants and the inalienability of their rights—what in the world would he have made of this small, stumping symbol, this imaginary animal who lived on while the living great were long forgotten . . .? The bear did seem to some a rather quaint, a somewhat embarrassing symbol for what was to them a great cause. I doubt if many were bold or ungenerous enough to say so, for the resultant publicity was invaluable. 'Winnie the *what?*' demands a family of big, rough, *real* bears, in a cartoon that came this way at the time of the next Ashdown crisis.

Two crises were actually running concurrently. Before ever the first was dealt with, at least temporarily, the second was rearing its head. The Lord of the Manor was proposing to sell Ashdown Forest—to the East Sussex County Council if they would buy it, otherwise probably piecemeal on the open market.

Any reader who has reached this point will know that the Sackville family first became Lords of the Manor of Duddleswell, therefore of Ashdown, in the reign of James I. Thomas Sackville, Earl of Dorset, was granted the manor in 1605, but an ancestor had been Master of the Game in the very earliest days of the royal chace. To recapitulate— Thomas was followed in 1609 by his son, Robert, who apparently kept rather quiet during the days of the Commonwealth, but in the 1660s the restoration of the monarchy led to a more relaxed lordship under Robert's son, Richard. He, it will be remembered, was tied up with the law suit of 1693, when the enclosures were sanctioned and the commonable land reduced. Earls of Dorset became Dukes of Dorset but they held the manor until the 19th century, when the succession was broken by the death of an heir and the early widowing of his mother—that Arabella Diana who continued to call herself 'of Dorset' even after her re-marriage. On her death the lordship moved as it were sideways and into the female line through Arabella Diana's daughters—De La Warrs took over the Forest freehold and the present Earl now wished to be rid of it.

Perhaps we were all so accustomed to the *status quo* that it had seemed unalterable. The sense of shock was very great. The Earl had offered the Forest directly to the Council, but the news did not break for the Conservators until later. It was by no means certain that the Council would be able to accept.

The spectre of partition brought back a memory of a man, whose name I forget, who stood once looking out over the Forest and reflecting aloud that what it really needed was a bit of light industry. Some, in present circumstances might very well have agreed; others certainly had dreams through those months of uncertainty—not all as moderately acceptable as the vision of a profitable trout farm.

When the news broke of the threat to Ashdown Forest intensive action had at once to be planned. The Policy and Resources Committee of the ESCC passed a resolution at their October meeting approving Council participation, suggesting a promise of something like half the sum demanded— it was a million pounds-plus—if the rest could be raised privately. Even that much comfort could not of course be relied upon until approval was given by the full Council. They would meet on the 24th November. Meanwhile, the Policy and Resources Committee recommended that the Council provide £300,000 towards the total cost.

The time was extremely short, the required sum extremely large. Whatever was to be done must be done at speed. It was decided to organise an Appeal under the auspices of the Friends of Ashdown Forest in co-operation with the Conservators. The Chairman of the Friends, A. W. B. (Bill) James, took on the part of co-ordinator. He, his helpers and a secretary moved into the Centre, settled down in the Committee Room, and fell to.

It is moderately easy to frame an appeal, to set a target, to draw up a timetable. The big problem is how to present it. While The Friends were making their plans, others were working directly and privately, making calls to the wealthy and the influential. The Chairman of Conservators, Anne

Sheldrick, addressed every commoner. The results of these two approaches were dynamic, the contributions amazingly generous.

An understandable tension gripped those earliest days and spread about the neighbourhood. Also a certain amount of inevitable controversy. Money raising having become an industry on its own account, there were plenty to urge the employment of a fund-raiser. But professionals of this expensive nature would have been quite unsuitable. £50,000 was the aim, which an experienced practitioner might well have considered small beer. This was a very personal affair, fraught with particular and even intimate worries. Inspired amateurism surely does best at such times—indeed it has often seemed that inspired amateurism does best in most Forest affairs, though that may read as heresy. Like local government, Forest administration at its best is spelled out in dogged devotion stripped of political bias. The need of the moment was for purpose, conviction, optimism and hard slog.

By 15th October the organisation of the Friends' appeal was well in hand, the office had its volunteers for the dull business of folding and tucking letters into envelopes. The press had been alerted and was ready to help. The news began to filter out—to a certain amount of 'Why wasn't I told?' from village voices. On 16th October, in the small hours, there came that great wind that none of us who heard it will forget, blowing from the south with such violence and sheer ferocity that it grabbed all in its path, shaking and twisting and tossing. The roar of disaster increased as it travelled inland for ever unravelling what had been knitted by time, taking with it the landscape patterns of centuries. Ancient trees fell and their progeny with them, never to grow in the place they were destined to inherit. Tops were plucked off and hurled away like litter. Beech and oak, their roots a hundred, a hundred-and-fifty years in the making, screamed as they fell and at once began to die. In these few hours man was excluded, he was nothing; the battle was with older elements than intelligence. How the deer would be fleeing, the fawns at their mothers' tails, the bucks leaping and crashing! Gathered birds were flung with panic crying about the sky, lit as it was not by lightning but by the perpetual livid flashing of pylons sagging and swaying under the weight of fallen trees. And those tamer trees, whose tidier existence was at the roadside, fell on wires that then dragged to the ground the poles on which they were strung. The earth danced and spurted. At times, increasing the high fantasy the moon emerged brilliant from flying cloud. A burning, salt-heavy atmosphere began at once to shrivel and destroy leaves already wilting. And all the time the air was full of twigs and grass, of dead bracken and mosses which piled against banks and spread a muffling quilt on roadways and lawns . . . The word *mammocked*, that Shakespeare knew, seemed one to use when light came to show the Forest's face, twisted and distorted by this mightiest of strokes . . . No bright autumn would spread over Ashdown now, for winter had already come.

As the light increased and the morning struggled into being it was seen that every road through and across and over the Forest was blocked by fallen trees; the villages were cut off; thousands of miles of power cables trailed and looped murderously from snapped or fallen posts; few telephones were working; no one went to school and few could reach their work—but there was plenty for them to do . . .

At the Centre there was a defeated stillness. No light, no heat; no electric typewriter, computer, addressing device. The Appeal was at a standstill.

Disasters nearly always induce an almost hysterical excitement, a 'high' that carries many over the first frightful impact. Do we really delight in horror—and if it were otherwise could such catastrophes be endured? Looking out on the garden that morning it seemed one looked at the worst. That feeling was dissipated by the sight of the Forest itself. The freakish wind, funnelling and boring, had left strange quiet areas of no-change. It was possible to look one way at familiar things, then turn back to such alteration as was difficult to assimilate. Familiar sounds were swallowed, there were no birds, there were no traffic noises. Then, amazingly soon, came the high whining song of chain-saws, the drum-thump of axes. Impossible to measure the slogging, exhausting hours that cleared enough of the roads for life to slide by and get into gear again.

By Saturday a strange calm had descended, a funereal calm of shock and mourning. We were united by the immensity of the thing, far too vast for personal wailing. Turning from our ravaged gardens, battered roofs, shattered greenhouses and looking to the Forest, we experienced the belittling insignificance of the purely personal.

It would be absurd to write as though Ashdown Forest had suffered alone. The entire south-east was stricken. And the morning found us alive—how might it have been if that roaring monster had hammered us twelve hours earlier or later? If the trees that fell had fallen on hundreds of moving cars and the flying slates had found targets in heads and backs, the splintered glass in throats and eyes— if the several damaged schools had been packed with children. There were indeed human casualties but so few that their number must, however brutally, count as a blessing.

As the roads were opened, so we moved from place to place, looking for what was lost, knowing that this destruction was of a sort that could never be entirely mended, that for years to come must show its scars in, at the best, new alignment, slow-growing replacement. And where to start, facing that ruin during the first days? Which tragic graveyard should take precedence? Shall this be saved at the expense of that? Which is the more valuable? How bitter that so many young oaks, perhaps ten years grown, should be tossed and flung among their betters—if only the leaves had already fallen fewer would have suffered . . . And which particular

area were we to decide was worst hit of all? Legsheath, said
some with justification. But Old Lodge, Twyford, Hindleap,
Kidds Hill, Broadstone, Chelwood Gate—all could qualify. It
took ten men an entire day to make a way through to the
main road from Old Lodge. Along the Ridge Road, from
Wych Cross to Coleman's Hatch, the firs of Ashdown Park
stood headless and splintered—the picture there was of a
world war battlefield. Further along, it seemed to be the oak
that had suffered most, with Broadstone a disaster area.
Alongside every road for many days the leaves and other
debris bunched and banked like some strange firefighter's
foam. Whole new vistas were opened in those few hours of
hurricane. The heart was torn out of the Five Hundred Acre
Wood . . . Strangest of all, in those early days, was the way
the great trees, falling on one another across the roads and
hastily beheaded to make a way through, were then held by
their great root blocks. For they were angled like mounted
guns and looked as menacing, half camouflaged by the
salt-burned heads flung down among them. Later, as winter
moved in and the shrivelled leaves finally died and fell, there
appeared in a way an increased desolation. By then we had
grown more or less accustomed to what had happened
without warning, during a very few hours, on that October
morning that would be for ever marked in our calendar.

One consequence of all this can be counted as a benefit. All
over the Forest light has been let in to nourish soil already
rich with humus from season after season of fallen leaves.
Within a very short span we can look for sheets of bluebells,
so speedily do they multiply—as they did when first the
verges on Millbrook were cleared of scrub to improve vision
and help to save deer casualties. Wood anemone should
benefit. Though I mourn a favourite walk now blocked by
fallen birch too unimportant to take up clearance time, the
few wild daffodils there, the one or two clumps of primose
will surely seize their opportunities and flourish undisturbed.
It is good anyway when such small tracks regain their

Fallow deer (*Dama dama*), very much the speciality of the Forest.

Woodlands bordering the Forest heathlands are home to the badger (*Meles meles*).

The tawny owl (*Strix aluco*). The woods on the Forest are important breeding areas.

Cold winters and water pollution have a marked effect on the kingfisher (*Alcedo atthis*).

Silver-studded blue butterfly (*Plebejus argus*) feeding on bell heather. Ashdown Forest is one of its strongholds.

Small red damselfly (*Ceriagrion tenellum*). A nationally rare damselfly found on the Forest in one sphagnum pool.

The dormouse (*Muscardinus avellanarius*) secretive, nocturnal and endearing.

Emperor moth (*Saturnia pavonia*). The female is able to attract the day-flying male over great distances.

Great raft spider (*Dolomedes fimbriates*), one of the largest British spiders. Fully-grown individuals are said to be capable of catching small fish.

The great spotted woodpecker (*Dendrocopos major*); well-established throughout the Forest.

The rare marsh gentian (*Gentiana pneumonanthe*).

Bog asphodel (*Narthecium ossifragum*), once thought to cause brittle bones in animals feeding on the plant.

Cotton grass (*Eriophorum angustifolium*) flourishes in boggy areas of the Forest.

Cross-leaved heath (*Erica tetralix*), above, is the most dominant of the heathers in wet areas.

Heath spotted-orchid (*Dectylorhiza maculata*), left, is commonly found on or near the cut firebreaks.

FIRE !

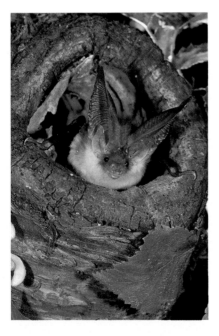

The brown long-eared bat (*Plecoyus auritus*) emerging from its day-time roost.

The Ashdown Forest Centre.

Towards Millbrook and the South Downs.

'A rare and exalting light.'

privacy. Likewise, the great humping roots themselves offer shelter to a good many small creatures—they had moved in in no time at all. And the deer returned unflurried. Where had they hidden? We shall never know; no casualties were ever reported. Only the birds seemed for a month or so to be in short supply. Many must have been shredded by that hot and howling wind . . .

While we were all setting about the business of clearing up our gardens, finding help and paying for it, enduring lack of heat and light, cooking problems and a shortage of hot baths, the power at the Centre was restored—the Appeal was once more under way. The disturbance had shortened the begging time—the 24th November deadline seemed like tomorrow during the third week in October—and surely people would have so much to spend their money on that there would be little left over. Substantial sums were hoped for from those various bodies whose interest lay with the Forest—Barclays, BAT—and from national organisations such as The Countryside Commission, the Council for the Preservation of Rural England and so on. Persons of name and importance with some connection and recollection of Ashdown, residents who had moved away—all were approached. The press, obviously, were enlisted; all the local papers used the story generously—but only one gave the address to which pledges of help should be sent. Once again Pooh went stumping the Forest—well covered by the national press.

It cannot have been easy for those working in a rather chilly room at the Centre to keep up their spirits at a time when everyone around was feeling extremely low. Now they had to wait for results. On this front they had to wait quite a time. People remained storm-stunned, so that it was as if the message had simply not got through—that no one had spirit left to care who bought or sold the ruined Forest or what happened to it once the sale was made. The prospect of success, the hope of £50,000, began to recede. Whatever it may have been that finally roused the neighbourhood, whether the reading of notices and letters or the exchange of views in the village streets and shops, Radio Sussex, Coast to Coast or just Winnie the Pooh, the Friends' Appeal suddenly took off. Both to the Friends and to the Conservators the money began to roll in—from the big bodies, from wealthy sympathisers, from almost anybody who had ever known and loved the Forest, from old residents, holidaymakers, walkers, from next door. Probably the most remarkable thing of all was the fact that as much as half the offerings were in sums of under £25. 'Towards the end of the third week,' wrote the Friends' co-ordinator, in an article in the *Ashdown Forest News*, 'we passed our first target of £50,000.' Sights were raised to £100,000, then to £150,000. The final target was £200,000 and on the evening before that vital Council Meeting the sum promised had reached £175,000. That afternoon the East Sussex County Council unanimously voted the sum recommended by their finance committee. All the hard work was justified, all the personal efforts—like the Teddy Bears' Picnic organised by a ten-year-old and netting £80, like the recruiting poem sent with her contribution by a nun dwelling a few miles away—all the running round with notices, the bearding of motorists in the car parks, the article-writing and the TV appearances of C. R. Milne travelling up from his Devonshire home . . .

So we rejoiced that the Forest would not after all be split up, as it might so easily have been. Councils, as we know, change their personnel and therefore their views—but we could breathe again at least for the present . . .

So we believed until three and a bit more months had passed. In February, the Lord of the Manor, the Earl De La Warr, died suddenly and tragically. No contract had been signed. The eleventh Earl De La Warr inherited the Manor of Duddleswell and with it Ashdown Forest.

CHAPTER TWELVE

And Now . . .?

Walking on the Forest in March, that great rending storm several months behind us, the melancholy that remained had to be accepted. The forest floor was further beaten by the long rains of a sullen winter. The tattered remains of exhausted bracken and sedge grass lay sallow and flat, refusing any hint of regeneration. If the landscape looked exhausted, so, no doubt, did we, for there seemed no promise of spring. It was foggy, the atmosphere fed by the smoke of bonfires which over the months had consumed the corpses of trees unnumbered. Was it ever said that Ashdown is a forest without trees? Even in the aftermath that claim could not have been met, and within weeks re-planting had begun. Yet still in those first months of a year in which death had been piled on destruction, the mist drifted and curled, dispersed and re-formed like smoke from a magic cauldron . . . Walking solitary on the Forest at such a moment must surely match a climber's loneliness: what I have come from has vanished, where I am bound is undisclosed.

The spring did indeed arrive in 1988. It was brief but it was dazzlingly profuse. Perhaps we had a sneaking feeling that the storm could have left some curse behind and that what came into leaf and flower would simply wither away—certainly those lovely days induced a mood almost of hilarity after all the gloom.

By then it was more or less certain that the Forest would, as already planned, become the property of the East Sussex County Council; we learnt that this wish had been expressed and accepted between the late Earl and his heir. The Earl's death, of course, at once set back negotiations for legal reasons, though intentions remained the same. Plans were to be drawn for the setting up of a charitable trust to maintain the Forest as the Act of 1974 already requires—that is, with the primary intention of promoting its conservation and keeping it accessible to the public. The Board of Conservators would still have the day-to-day running of the Forest and the income derived be used solely for the benefit of the Forest. The only positive change, in fact, would lie in the Lordship of the Manor—which would be as it were secularised and in the hands of the proposed trust. The Charity Commissioners, however, could not act to set up the trust until probate was granted to the estates of the late Lord De La Warr.

Delays in such cases are inevitable, even without the special circumstances that befell Ashdown Forest. As the months wore on a number of people became both anxious and critical—as indeed could be expected when one recalls the Ashdown temperament in all its manifestations over the years and its easy infection of newcomers . . . At last, on the 25th November 1988, the signing took place and Ashdown Forest changed hands.

'The Forest is saved for ever!' they cried a hundred years or so ago, with sad confidence. So it may be—but few things are so gloriously certain that they can defy the curious convolutions brought about by time. We cannot pretend that all threats are now withdrawn. Oil will almost certainly be a recurrent problem, there is talk of a by-pass that can only filch some acres of Forest land; as always a benefit to some, a deprivation for others. All this has happened before and the wise and the calm urge a long view. Oil, they say, if indeed it ever comes, will be gone in a matter of seven or ten years. It certainly need not ravage the land as did the iron industry we speak of with such pride. And there is that other assurance— that wild life shelters and prospers in enclosures that were once as hotly disputed as any problem since. If the Forest has lasted so long, surely it may last for ever . . .?

It has, however, only just lasted. There have been many years between crises but each time one has occurred something has changed—as in the 1693 award that cut the grazing in half, as in the administrative alterations of the 1880s when the new authority, the Board of Conservators, was first set up. At those times the ruling tradition was maintained, the feudal pattern—if one can call it so. Now it must go, as the Sackville name must go. The Lordship cannot be destroyed—but it is difficult not to feel a shade of romantic resentment and to cry—What is a lordship without a lord!

What is left now of the Forest's ancient beginnings is the persisting Right of Common.

Because of imponderables bound up in any new regime the commoners of Ashdown Forest had better not slumber. They must remain watchful and keep a keen eye on affairs which, with the best will from all in authority, are bound to threaten differences, however subtle. It is unfortunate indeed that we have few now of what must be called *real commoners,* commoners by inheritance whose names we know, who gained at least some part of their living through attachment to the Forest soil and never forgot how to raise their voices. New commoners, as I am, may be keen, devoted and vigilant, but they and I can never belong in any true sense. However much we may cherish the Forest and strive for its well-being, we can still only hope for adoption. Perhaps that is what we should exploit.

The Friends, the many volunteer workers, inside and out, the owners of properties which have lost their commonable right and who regret it, all those who rushed to contribute to the Forest's salvation in that year of extraordinary disasters, 1988, could they not become as it were honorary commoners? Are they not, indeed, by their actions and sympathies so readily expressed, more or less self-appointed?

The past can seem a burden to some, an irrelevance to be shuffled off, leaving the present unencumbered and vital. For others the past is the parent of today and as such powerful, wise, instructive. Ashdown Forest has once more been snatched from disaster, preserved by a past now centred in the Right of Common, far older than any local lordship. That ancient Right must uphold the Forest's future.

Geology of the Ashdown Forest Area

The Laying Down Of The Weald And Its Minerals

Although this book is about Ashdown Forest, the geology of the forest can best be considered as part of the whole Wealden area. It is an enigma of the Weald that the oldest stratum found on Ashdown Forest is almost as high as the youngest stratum of the chalk Downs surrounding the area. Basically, the Weald is very unstable, the land has been slowly sinking for at least four hundred and fifty million years, apart from a short period of dramatic uprising starting sixty five million years ago. Throughout the initial period of sinking, the level of the land remained more or less constant because, over time, rivers were depositing their sediment over the Weald. The oldest visible stratum in the Weald was laid down one hundred and twenty million years ago, and this is a convenient place to start the story. It must be remembered that England did not exist as we know it, as it was only 4.5 thousand years ago that the coastal outline we see today was finally established.

One hundred and twenty million years ago, several large rivers from high land to the north of the Weald were bringing sediment down to a delta that covered the whole Wealden area. As the flow of water slowed on reaching the delta, the larger sandy sediment was dropped whilst the clays were deposited in deeper water beyond the delta. After some seven hundred feet of sediment had been laid down, not forgetting that it had sunk this same amount, the world's climate became warmer and the ice-caps melted. This extra water raised the sea level and allowed a freshwater lake to cover the Weald, so causing the finer sediment to be deposited in the Wealden area.

This, in a nutshell, is how all the Wealden strata were deposited over fifty five million years, with alternate layers of fine sands and clays.

It will come as no surprise that Wealden geology is defined as 'sedimentary': (rock which has been eroded from an older rock moved by water and deposited at a new place). The earlier rock may have been 'igneous' (natural rock), or 'metamorphic' (sedimentary rock which has been changed by heat and pressure).

The alternate layers of fine and coarse sediment are called 'cyclothems' (cyclic changes in the earth's temperature); and there are minor cyclothems in each stratum.

This effect may be studied on a sandy beach where flowing water will deposit the largest grains of sand first before dropping the fine silt where it slows down on reaching deeper water.

Figure 1 shows the name and relative thickness of each major stratum in the Weald, starting when the Ashdown Sand was being deposited on top of 'Gypsum' in the Purbeck Beds. This, the oldest visible stratum in the Weald, was laid down under saline conditions and is now quarried from the Mountfield area to be used for making plaster board. 'Ashdown Sand', at the bottom of Figure 1, was the forerunner in a period of freshwater conditions in the Weald. As might be expected, it now covers most of Ashdown Forest, with the highest point being over seven hundred and twenty five feet, just north of King's Standing; although Crowborough Beacon is higher at seven hundred and ninety two feet. In places, the top of this sand stratum has been chemically fused together to form 'rock', and accounts for some of the impressive sandstone outcrops in the area. In many places it is possible to see where the rock has been 'worked' to produce building stone.

Next comes the 'Wadhurst Clay', famous for consistant bands of nodular iron ore still to be found towards the bottom of this stratum. Although the ore is a very hard, dense rock, the material was originally laid down as a fine silty sediment which has since hardened.

The majority of the sandstone outcrops in the Weald are formed within the next stratum, 'Lower Tunbridge Wells Sand'. This sandstone is known locally as 'Ardingly Sandstone', and has been much used as a building stone with Philpot's quarry still being worked near West Hoathly. Above this comes a thin stratum of 'Grinstead Clay', where calcareous (lime) 'marl', was dug from the lower levels for improving the soil. Above this is the 'Upper Tunbridge Wells Sand' whose only claim to fame seems to be for brickmaking.

Now comes the 'Weald Clay'; a noticeably low, flat area between

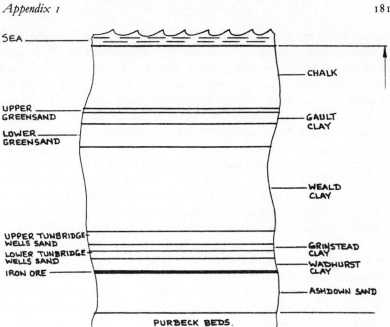

FIGURE 1. SECTION THROUGH THE WEALD 65 MILLION YEARS AGO.

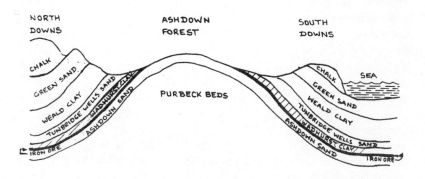

FIGURE 3. A SECTION THROUGH THE WEALD TODAY.

the high central Weald and the Greensand Ridge (next stratum) and in many places suitable for brickmaking. There are several outcrops of iron ore mainly around Crawley and the Western Weald. White silica sand from this stratum was used by the fourteenth to seventeenth century Wealden glass-makers' working on the Surrey/Sussex border near Kirdford. It is also famous for 'Horsham Stone', a thin layer of sandstone that was used as a roofing material on the more important Wealden houses.

The remaining strata were laid down under saline conditions, starting with the 'Lower Greensand'. This forms the 'Greensand Ridge', a ring of hills inside the Chalk Downs (next stratum) with the highest point being almost a thousand feet at Leith Hill in Surrey. This stratum is commercially profitable, around Redhill in Surrey, from sand and fuller's earth. This latter material was used in the woollen industry to absorb grease during the fulling and felting process. It is now used as a bonding agent in moulding sand for castings and various tasks in the petro-chemical and food industry. The 'Gault Clay' comes next, again suitable for brick making, and along which the southern part of the M25 motorway runs, and then 'Upper Greensand'. A building stone called 'firestone' was mined from this in the Betchworth, Reigate, Merstham and Godstone districts. These mines are now being mapped, and it shows that the useful seam was only about five feet thick in the central area, petering out to the east and west. Although the stone does not weather well, it was used in the building of Westminster Abbey, Nonsuch Palace, St. Mark's and St. Phillip's churches, Reigate and St. Matthews, Redhill. Another, 'hearthstone', was also mined in later times for use as hearth and step whitener.

Finally comes the 'Chalk'. This material forms the North and South Downs surrounding the Weald; joining up in the western Weald beyond Petersfield. The Chalk is over one thousand feet thick and was laid down over the whole Wealden area in deep water and well away from land; hence the absence of any sands or clays. The Downs are breached by several rivers: Adur, Arun, Cuckmere, Medway, Mole, Ouse, Great Ouse and Wey; each has eroded its way down through the chalk over millions of years. The highest point is eight hundred and thirteen feet at Ditchling Beacon on the South Downs.

Some levels of the chalk have been used in the past as marl for improving the soil. Chalk was also heated in kilns to produce 'quick lime', which, after 'slaking' with water was used as lime for agriculture or mortar for building; while today it forms the basis of cement. After the last ice-age, ten thousand years ago, flint in the Chalk was worked by Mesolithic and Neolithic Man to make his tools. Flint has also been used locally as a building stone, with the more important houses and churches being built of 'knapped' flint to produce a decorative stone-work.

This is the final stratum to cover the whole Wealden area, by which time nearly five thousand feet of sediment had been laid down over fifty five million years.

The Rising Up of the Weald

Some sixty five million years ago the sinking of the Weald was reversed and a large area centring on Handcross, some eight miles west of Ashdown Forest, was raised up. This happened at a time when the Alps were being formed and dinosaurs began to die out. The uprising took place over many millions of years, but at the same time the action of frost, wind and water on the fractured surface was wearing the dome down. At this time the Chalk covered dome might have been eight to ten thousand feet high. Eventually the Weald started to sink again, and over the succeeding millions of years the combination of weathering and sinking has transformed Wealden geology into a form capable of supporting the contrasting scenery that we see today. Figure 2 shows a simplified plan of today's Wealden geology.

It may now be seen from Figure 3, that the Wealden enigma has been solved. All the strata laid down since the Purbeck Beds have been brought to the surface all around the Weald by the uprising *and* later erosion.

During the last two million years there have been several ice-ages interspersed by warmer times. During the cold periods the sea level dropped by up to three hundred feet due to the water being 'locked up' as snow and ice: when the weather warmed, the sea level rose, occasionally one hundred feet above its present level. It was during these warmer periods that various minor strata were laid down on the North and South Chalk Downs. After the last ice-age, ten thousand years ago, the sea level rose again to produce the English Channel; prior to this there had been a 'land-bridge' to the Continent.

During the early nineteenth century, Dr Gideon Mantell of Lewes, one of the first geologists, discovered and explained

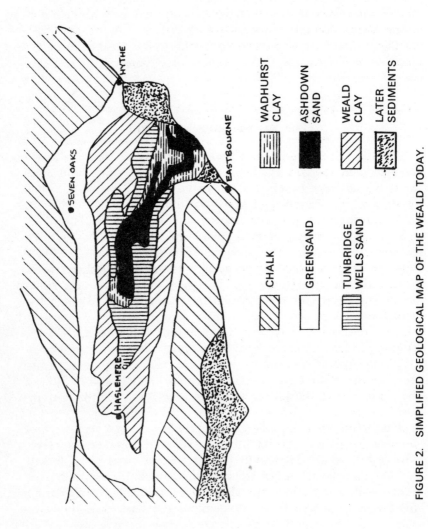

FIGURE 2.   SIMPLIFIED GEOLOGICAL MAP OF THE WEALD TODAY.

the Wealden dinosaur fossil 'Iguanodon'. It was found in a claypit at Cuckfield, and since then numerous fossils have been found throughout the Weald. Over the years, much has been discovered about Wealden geology and many of the strata are named after the locality where they were first studied. All this work has culminated in the production of 'geological maps', from which it is now possible to predict where outcrops of various minerals may be found.

Geological Aspects of the Ashdown Forest Area Shown on the Map

The seams of Wealden iron ore are usually about six inches thick and they were dug from either large open-cast pits or via vertical shafts ten to twenty feet in diameter and up to thirty feet deep. These latter pits were back-filled and may be seen in woodland as numerous water-filled depressions, due to the soil having settled.

Two rare outcrops of iron ore occur locally in the Ashdown Sand, one beside the Nutley to Camp Hill road, and the other in Pippingford Park. Many of the ponds along the Coleman's Hatch to Hartfield road are also mine pits whilst on the north side of Weir Wood Reservoir, near the dam, signs of the back-filled pits may be seen in the wood.

Many earthen dams were built in the area to hold back water to power the blast furnaces and conversion forges; although only Oldlands Furnace pond remains in water. Weir Wood was one of the last earthen reservoir dams to be thrown up in England.

On the road from Nutley to Chelwood Gate it is possible to see, in the valley to the north, where the south-east flowing Millbrook was 'captured' from flowing south, millions of years ago. It now flows east, then north to the Medway, whilst its old course may be seen as a slight dip, high up on the Nutley to Camp Hill road and as a very deep valley to the south.

The road from Gill's Lap to Newbridge descends in three stages due to three levels of harder sandstone. Each level has caused the land surface to level out before dipping down to the softer soil below.

There are many wild, inpenetratable places on Ashdown Forest where no one seems to have been for years. Further investigation will usually reveal that these are due to the handiwork of man in his search for minerals; be it clay for bricks, stone for building, iron ore for the furnaces or water being stored to operate water-wheels to drive his machinery. After a while it becomes apparent that, in reality, Man has already trodden on every square foot of Ashdown Forest over the last eight to nine thousand years.

BRIAN HERBERT

APPENDIX 2

Iron Technology on Ashdown Forest

Iron was being smelted and worked on Ashdown by the first century AD. The industry expanded under the Romans but the method of smelting was essentially the same and the product was wrought (malleable) iron. It was made in a bloomery furnace using the *Direct* process. This process continued in use until the sixteenth century.

Towards the end of the fifteenth century, a new method of smelting iron was introduced into Ashdown from northern France. This overlapped and eventually superseded the earlier process, continuing for another three centuries. This *Indirect* process was so called because it required two stages to produce wrought iron. In the first stage, pig (cast) iron, which is an alloy of iron and carbon, was produced from a blast furnace; in the second stage, pig iron was converted into wrought in a conversion forge.

Wrought iron is pure and can be shaped under a hammer when hot; pig iron is too brittle for hammering but in its molten form it can be cast into moulds. Cannon and shot were better in quality and more quickly made of cast iron, so this introduction was of particular benefit to the armaments trade.

The raw materials for smelting by either process were the same and, at least initially, were all abundantly available in the locality. Ironsmelting needed a pure fuel, charcoal, which was made from small trees and branches or, later, coppiced woods. Iron ore was easy to find in stream banks where the water had cut through the geological layers. The seams thus located were followed and dug out.

Stone and clay were there for building furnaces, small or large, and for the latter process bricks were also made from the local clay to line the furnace hearths. Such diggings have left the land pockmarked with numerous ponds and hollows which can still be seen on almost any country walk; slag from furnaces and forges

187

litters our fields and copses, and the water-powered ironworks have left their own unique legacy of furnace and forge ponds still in water or broken banks across flat silted valleys where they once were.

The Bloomery Process. In early times, a bloomery furnace would have been built of stone and clay near to where iron ore had been found. Excavations on the Forest have shown that these little furnaces were set at one end of a small oval pit, the sides of which helped to support the furnace stock. The inside measurement of such a furnace was about 0.5 m and it is thought that its height would have been about a metre (no complete furnaces have been found). The front of the furnace, facing the open pit, was supported by stone and the inside was lined with clay. There was an opening near the base to allow molten slag to run out of the furnace during ironsmelting. A bellows nozzle, protected by a clay tuyere, was inserted through another opening.

After pre-heating the furnace, small pieces of charcoal and pre-roasted iron ore were charged into the top and air was blown into it from the bellows. This air served two purposes: firstly to heat the fire to a temperature of around 1000°C, at which the slag would melt away from the iron, and secondly to form carbon monoxide inside the furnace. This reducing gas releases solid metal from iron ore.

The metal bloom thus formed still had slag mixed with it. After it was taken from the furnace it had to be reheated and hammered to consolidate it into a useful piece of wrought iron.

Each bloomery hearth would have been capable of producing up to 25 kg of iron a day. If larger amounts were required, a number of furnaces were operated at the same time. A group of three such furnaces was excavated at Cowpark, following the discovery of slag and other debris on the surface. Nearby, there were traces of forging hearths and an anvil. A few hundred yards away are the remains of Garden Hill Romano-British hillfort where there is also evidence of ironworking. Other small sites have been found in the immediate neighbourhood of the hillfort, which suggests that the industry may have been organised from there. Many of the small sites found in the Ashdown area have proved to be Romano-British but, strangely, only one furnace that is Saxon. This was similar in many ways to the earlier furnaces but instead of the slag being run out of the furnace, it was allowed to accumulate in its base.

We know that in other parts of the country, bloomery furnaces increased in size during the Middle Ages and that water-power was used to drive bellows and hammers. Field evidence suggests that this may also have happened in the Ashdown Forest area. Some water-powered bloomeries may later have been converted into blast furnaces or conversion forges and no doubt much evidence has been overlaid by later remains. There may have been a stage when iron blooms made in small furnaces were consolidated using a water-powered hammer: much larger iron articles could have been made by this means. However, the use of water-power meant that capital was needed to finance the building of dams and water-courses, workshops and storehouses. The way was being paved for the introduction of a new, large-scale process from the Continent. Indeed, it could be claimed that the Industrial Revolution began on Ashdown.

The Blast Furnace. An ironworks using the *Indirect* process was built at Newbridge in 1496. All that remains there now is a bank which once held the stream in check to make a pond and a mixture of bloomery, blast furnace and forge slags and cinders spread about the ground. Evidence from archaeological excavations of other sites, contemporary paintings and documents suggests the following description of the blast furnace:

A square, stone building about six metres high. Its overall outside measurement was much the same as its height, for the walls had to be double-skinned and filled with rubble to take temperatures which might reach 1400°C. Inside the furnace hearth was about 60 cm square and above this the chimney at first widened and then narrowed towards the top. Two arches occupied adjacent sides of the building, each with an opening into the stack. One allowed the furnace master to attend the fire and to let out slag and iron when necessary; the other allowed air to be blown in from two large pairs of bellows operating off the shaft of a waterwheel. Rough housing, either thatched or tiled, surrounded the furnace, giving shelter to the workers and a place where tools could be kept and moulds made.

Water was led from the pond through the dam to serve the waterwheel, after which it was channelled away from the working area; eventually it rejoined the surplus water which was allowed to leave the pond via a sluice, weir and spillway.

The excavation of a later furnace at Pippingford showed that it was built quite close to the dam (or 'bay' as it was then known) and that it was filled via a charging ramp. This was attached to a spur on the bay and would have led to the loading platform at the top of the furnace.

Before a furnace was put into blast, iron ore and charcoal were stockpiled, for a blast furnace might be in operation for many weeks. Iron ore was weathered and often roasted in heaps, different sorts being mixed together; charcoal had to be stored under cover. When all was ready, a fire would be built in the hearth and when the furnace was hot enough it could be loaded with charcoal and iron ore.

As the filling of raw materials gradually dropped towards the hearth, the heat from the fire melted the iron ore and it dripped into the hearth, iron accumulating underneath the slag which floated above it. From time to time, the furnace master would tap off the slag, thus leaving more room in the hearth for molten iron. About once a day, the hearth would be full of iron. Casting could then take place into previously prepared moulds. About a tonne a day was made.

Sand moulds were adequate for such simple shapes as firebacks and grave slabs but more complicated goods required skill and just the right proportions of clay, loam and other ingredients. The exact nature and quantities of these materials was a closely guarded secret. The superiority of Wealden cannon after 1543 was attributed to the excellence of the moulds into which they were cast. These new one-piece cannon became the foundation of a prosperous armaments industry, which not only manufactured guns but vast quantities of 'shot' of various sizes.

D. M. MEADES

The Trees of Ashdown Forest

Ashdown Forest is a specialised environment which has largely been created by man, on the basic rock formulation known as Ashdown Sandstone. This a very fine grained sandstone lying pretty close to the surface, and it breaks down into a whitish silt. Once broken down it tends to become fairly impervious to water. This combined with frequent fires creates very acid conditions with the result that a pan forms which worsens drainage. The original tree crop was undoubtedly oak (*quercus*) whose leaf fall created a fertile humus which inclined to counteract the effects of bad drainage. But as a result of burning there is now very little opportunity for oak leaf to accumulate, and such as there is is very easily blown away. The result has been increased encroachment by bracken, heather and birch, followed by pine. Nowadays the heather phase of the ecological cycle is deliberately prolonged by management entailing the removal of young trees.

Because of the acid conditions on the Forest, certain lime-loving species such as ash, sycamore, thorn, whitebeam and to some extent yew, are infrequently found.

There are two main growing areas on Ashdown Forest: the tip, or plateau, where the only effective free crop is birch or pine, and the lower slopes and the wet places where oak, beech, holly, sallow, alder and buckthorn are found. There are also some sweet chestnut, mainly on the fringes.

OAK (*Quercus*)

The type of oak growing on the Forest tends to be stunted and bushy-topped. Forest oak is very little use as timber, its shape preventing it from being sawn effectively. Oak is without doubt the No. 1 food plant for caterpillars of moths and butterflies, which in their turn feed any amount of birds. A great deal of oak still survives as coppice and it undoubtedly used to be grown and used for charcoal, being cut every twenty- five years or so. Oak coppice is quite an attractive crop; the pity is that large areas may get burnt every five to ten years, just before they can become established. Much of this coppice root stock must be over two hundred years old. There are patches of fast-grown oak covering 10% or so of the Forest which could grow into timber and live up to two hundred years.

BEECH *(Fagus)*

Normally, beech is at its best on chalk soil. But a strain exists on Ashdown that grows very large and bushy-topped and seems to appreciate sandstone. The timber is usually dark, as against the white of chalk beech; for this reason it is not particularly valuable. Beech leaf litter also tends to encourage acidic conditions. The largest beech are probably only a hundred and fifty years old and the tree itself is usually considered mature at one hundred, when it should be felled and replaced. Most of the Forest beech sadly perished in the hurricane of 16th October 1987, and the survivors' fate seem uncertain. Replacement at such times is essential.

SWEET CHESTNUT *(Castania sativa)*

There is usually a sprinkling of large chestnut among the oaks on the lower bracken slopes. As timber it has the same faults as oak, namely an inherent tendency to shake. It is comparatively fast growing and should be encouraged. It is long-lived and seldom rots. Sweet Chestnut does not suffer unduly from windblow.

PINE *(Pinus sylvestris)*

The Ashdown Forest pine is rather akin to the Caledonian pine and is in fact always alluded to as Scots pine. By and large it grows as a bushy-topped tree and survives fires and strong winds. The shape of most of the Forest examples is very attractive. Left to themselves they seed freely and have to be contained. Without doubt, the pine would grow as a tall straight tree if contained in plantations. This would not be considered suitably attractive, however, even with the added advantage of timber value. The clumps originally planted as viewpoints have been renewed from time to time, and the oldest Forest pine are around eighty years old.

BIRCH *(Betula)*

The most prolific of the Forest trees, but seldom living over forty years. Birch, however, has the great advantage of regenerating after fires, and its shape and attractive bark, and its autumn colouring make it a great popular favourite. If given the chance it would succeed in improving the soil over great areas. The seed is very fine and blows everywhere, which is a disadvantage when it comes to managing heather. The main use for birch has been as firewood, but these days it is in great demand both for wood turnery and pulpwood.

HOLLY *(Ilex)*

Very much at home on the Forest, where it grows to quite a size, forty feet or so. Holly probably lives no longer than sixty years. Apart from its splendid berries, it offers only a very hard and heavy wood, rarely used for anything other than firewood, and even that rather second rate. As a shelter for bird life it stands alone, and it is also host to the lovely little Holly Blue butterfly, which is particularly abundant on Ashdown.

SALLOW *(Salix)*

A fast grown, short lived willow (40 years) that abounds on the Forest. It likes bog and badly drained ground. The catkins are a great glory in the spring, so that single trees show up at a considerable distance. Otherwise, it tends to be a rather dull and useless tree, having no attributes for foliage, timber or wood-burning—though it is, of course, one of the trees covered by the commoners' ancient *estovers*. It is also one of the most popular host plants for insects, and nurtures many spectacular species of moth caterpillars, such as puss-moths.

ALDER (*Alnus*)

Found in the valley bottoms by streams, the alder is quite a pioneer species that establishes itself readily in wet conditions. Its dark green glossy leaves and catkins are attractive, and it lives rather longer than sallow—say fifty years—and coppices readily. It is still used in wood turnery. Historically, it used to be bought for the manufacture of hat boxes, being a soft wood and easily sawn. Its main property when freshly cut is to turn a gorgeous shade of orange that lasts for a few weeks. It is a poor firewood and useless as a host plant.

ALDER (*Buckthorn*)

This is a small shrub-like tree, seldom exceeding ten feet, that is very common amongst the birch on Ashdown Forest. It has small insignificant flowers in June that seem to be super-attractive to bees, and the hum from these bushes when in flower is quite remarkable. The fruit is a small black berry. Its other great property is to be the food plant of the Yellow Brimstone butterfly. It is because of the number of alder buckthorn trees on the Forest that the Brimstones are so numerous.

ASPEN (*Populus tremula*)

Locally common. The aspen is a small poplar seldom growing more than thirty feet in height or older than thirty years. It is distinguished by its silvery leaves that shake in the slightest breeze. A white softwood, it is of no value other than as a second-rate firewood. It has one peculiarity, however; cut one down and a hundred suckers will shoot up all round. As the early growth of these suckers is extremely rapid, a thicket of aspen is quickly formed that is very difficult to get rid of.

MOUNTAIN ASH, or ROWAN (*Fraxinus*)

A very attractive small tree found locally on the Forest. Its pinnate leaves are golden in the autumn, and its red berries in August are a delight. It seldom exceeds thirty-eight feet, although occasionally a big one can reach fifty feet and some sixty years in age. Its timber is too small to be of any value and it is not a top quality firewood. The wood is white with a dark heart that is quite hard. The rowan has many cousins from all over the world, some of which have been imported and used with effect as garden trees.

CRAB APPLE (*Malus sylvestris*)

One of the rarer Forest trees is the wild crab-apple. Some of the Forest specimens are quite large and lusty—up to forty feet. They produce a splendid show of pink and white blossom in April and considerable crops of quite large green apples in the autumn. These are much enjoyed by deer.

WILD CHERRY or GEAN (*Prunus avium*)

Not a common species on the Forest, it is however a widespread Sussex tree and exists on the Forest edge where the soil is deeper and richer. The cherry is a much sought after timber tree. It grows quite tall, sixty feet plus, and makes a spectacular show in spring with its white blossom. It often provides good autumn colour. Unfortunately, this is one of the species that was badly blown in the 1987 hurricane.

JOHN GENT

The Wildlife of the Forest

MAMMALS

Hedgehog	+
Mole	+
Common shrew	+
Pigmy shrew	+ +
Water shrew	+
Wolf	E(C15)
Fox	+ +
Brown bear	E(C10)
Pine marten	—
Stoat	+
Weasel	+
Polecat	—
Ferret	+ (feral)
Mink	+ (feral since 1950)
Badger	+ +
Otter	—
Wild cat	—
Red-necked wallaby	—
Wild boar	E(C17)
Red deer	+ (escape from deer farm)
Sika deer	+ (feral since 1890 and escapes)
Fallow deer	+ +
Roe deer	+
Muntjac deer	+
Chinese water deer	—
Brown hare	+
Rabbit	+ +
Red squirrel	—
Grey squirrel	+ + (feral since 1890)

Beaver	—(C12)
Dormouse	+
Harvest mouse	+ +
Wood mouse	+ +
Yellow-necked mouse	+ +
House mouse	+
Black rat	—
Brown rat	+ +
Bank vole	+ +
Field vole	+
Water vole	+

> − does not occur + less common or rare + + common E extinct, followed by century it became extinct

NOTES ON MAMMAL LIST

Proper surveys of small mammals have not been carried out; the list is drawn from known habits and distributions.

Roe deer and brown hares are not generally found on the Forest, but are found on adjacent farmland.

Dormouse numbers are probably declining due to loss of hazel coppice.

MAMMALS — BATS

No extensive bat surveys have been carried out on the Forest. The following list is drawn up from British bats, which, from their known habits and distribution, may be expected to be found on the Forest.

Barbastelle	Very rare
Bechstein's	Very rare
Brandt's	
Brown long-eared	Common
Daubenton's	
Leisler's	Very rare
Natterer's	
Noctule	Common
Pipistrelle	Common
Serotine	
Whiskered	

BIRDS

*denotes species that may occur as casuals.

Grey heron	House martin	Firecrest
Mandarin duck	Great spotted	Spotted flycatcher
Mallard	woodpecker	Long-tailed tit
Hen harrier	Lesser spotted	Marshtit
Sparrowhawk	woodpecker	Willow tit
Buzzard	Green woodpecker	Coal tit
Kestrel	Meadow pipit	Blue tit
Hobby	Tree pipit	Grey tit
Merlin*	Skylark	Nuthatch
Red-legged partridge	Pied wagtail	Treecreeper
Grey partridge*	Grey wagtail	Great grey shrike
Pheasant	Wren	Red backed shrike*
Water rail	Dunnock	Golden oriole*
Moorhen	Robin	Jay
Lapwing	Redstart	Magpie
Woodcock	Nightingale	Jackdaw
Snipe	Whinchat	Crow
Jack snipe*	Stonechat	Rook
Curlew	Wheatear	Starling
Black-headed gull	Blackbird	House sparrow
Stock dove	Redwing	Tree sparrow*
Collared dove	Fieldfare	Chaffinch
Turtle dove	Song thrush	Goldfinch
Woodpigeon	Mistle thrush	Siskin
Cuckoo	Grasshopper	Greenfinch
Tawny owl	warbler	Linnet
Barn owl	Whitethroat	Redpoll
Little owl	Lesser whitethroat	Bullfinch
Short-eared owl*	Blackcap	Crossbill
Nightjar	Wood warbler	Hawfinch
Kingfisher	Chiffchaff	Yellow hammer
Swift	Willow warbler	Reed bunting
Swallow	Goldcrest	Corn bunting*

BUTTERFLIES

Brimstone	common
Clouded yellow	migrant
Comma	common
Common blue	common
Dark green fritillary	rare
Dingy skipper	uncommon
Gatekeeper	common
Grayling	rare
Green-veined white	common
Grizzled skipper	uncommon
High brown fritillary	rare
Holly blue	common
Large skipper	common
Large white	common
Meadow brown	common
Orange tip	common
Painted lady	common
Peacock	common
Pearl-bordered fritillary	uncommon
Purple emperor	uncommon
Purple hairstreak	uncommon (probably overlooked)
Red admiral	common
Ringlet	common
Silver-studded blue	common
Silver-washed fritillary	rare
Small copper	common
Small heath	common
Small pearl-bordered fritillary	uncommon
Small tortoiseshell	common
Small skipper	common
Small white	common
Speckled wood	common
Wall (Hedge brown)	uncommon
White admiral	uncommon

MOTHS

SOME OF THE MANY MOTHS FOUND ON
ASHDOWN FOREST

Angle shades
Antler
Autumnal moth
Birch mocha
Bordered white
Brown silver-lines
Chestnut
Clouded border
Common quaker
Coxcomb prominent
Cream wave
Dark sword grass
December
Double-striped pug
Early thorn
Elephant hawk
Emperor
Engrailed
Eyed hawk
Feathered thorn
Five spot burnet
Frosted green
Great prominent
Grey birch
Green brindled crescent
Heath rustic
Hebrew character
Herald
Iron prominent
Knot-grass
Lesser swallow prominent
Lime hawk

Lunar marbled brown
Marbled brown
Mottled umber
Northern winter
November
Nut-tree tussock
Oak hook-tip
Oak eggar
Pale oak beauty
Pale tussock
Peach blossom
Pebble hook-tip
Pebble prominent
Peppered
Puss
Red lined quaker
Satellite
Scalloped hazel
Scalloped hook-tip
Seraphim
Shuttle-shaped dart
Silver Y
Small engrailed
Spruce carpet
Streak
Streamer
Swallow prominent
Twin spot quaker
Yellow-lined quaker
Yellow underwings
Winter moth

DRAGONFLIES AND DAMSELFLIES

Aeshna cyanea	Southern hawker
Aeshna grandis	Brown hawker
Aeshna mixta	Scarce hawker
Anax imperator	Emperor dragonfly
Calopteryx virgo	Beautiful demoiselle
Ceriagrion tenellum	Small red damselfly
Coenagrion puella	Azure damselfly
Cordulegaster boltonii	Golden-ringed dragonfly
Cordulia aenea	Downy emerald
Enallagma cyathigerum	Common blue damselfly
Erythromma najas	Red eyed damselfly
Ischnura elegans	Blue-tailed damselfly
Libellula depressa	Broad bodied chaser
Libellula quadrimaculata	Four spotted chaser
Lestes sponsa	Emerald damselfly
Platycnemis pennipes	White legged damselfly
Pyrrhosoma nymphula	Large red damselfly
Somatochlora metallica	Brilliant emerald
Sympetrum sanguineum	Ruddy darter
Sympetrum striolatum	Common darter

AMPHIBIANS AND REPTILES

Common frog	Palmate newt
Toad	Smooth newt
Adder	Slow worm
Grass snake	Common lizard
Great crested newt	

HEATHLAND PLANTS

Anagallis tenella	Bog pimpernel
Calluna vulgaris	Ling heather
Carex binerva	Two nerved sedge
Cladonia species	lichens
Cuscuta epithymum	Dodder
Dactylorhiza maculata	Heath spotted-orchid
Erica cinerea	Bell heather
Erica tetralix	· Cross-leaved heath
Euphrasia anglica	English sticky eyebright
Euphrasia nemorosa	Common eyebright
Frangula alnus	Alder buckthorn
Funaria hygrometrica	'fire moss'
Galium saxatile	Heath bedstraw
Genista anglica	Petty whin
Gentiana pneumonanthe	Marsh gentian
Hypericum pulchrum	St. John's wort
Hypnum cupressiforme	'feather moss'
Juncus squarrosus	Heath rush
Molinia caerulea	Purple moor grass
Nardus stricta	Mat grass
Odontites verna	Red bartsia
Osmunda regalis	Royal fern
Pedicularis palustris	Lousewort
Pinus sylvestris	Scots pine
Polygala serpyllifolia	Heath milkwort
Pteridium aquilinum	Bracken
Rumex acetosella	Sheep's sorrel
Salix repens	Creeping willow
Serratula tinctoria	Saw-wort
Scutellaria minor	Lesser skullcap
Sieglingia decumbens	Heath grass
Sorbus aria	Whitebeam
Sorbus aucuparia	Mountain ash
Sphagnum compactum	'cushion' bog moss
Ulex minor	Dwarf gorse
Vaccinium myrtillus	Bilberry

WOODLAND PLANTS

Anemone nemorosa	Wood anemone
Betula pendula	Silver birch
Betula pubescens	Hairy birch
Carex paniculata	Tussock sedge
Corydalis claviculata	Climbing corydalis
Fagus sylvatica	Beech
Ilex aquifolium	Holly
Leucobryum glaucum	'white fork moss'
Malus sylvestris	Crab apple
Melampyrum pratense	Common cow-wheat
Mnium hornum	'*thread moss*'
Narcissus pseudonarcissus	Wild daffodil
Neottia nidus-avis	Bird's-nest orchid
Oxalis acetosella	Wood sorrel
Polytrichum spp.	'*star mosses*'
Prunus avium	Wild cherry
Quercus cerris	Turkey oak
Quercus petraea	Sessile oak
Quercus robur	Pedunculate oak
Taxus baccata	Yew
Teucrium corodonia	Woodsage
Thelypteris limbosperma	Lemon-scented fern
Thelypteris palustris	Marsh fern
Wahlenbergia hederacea	Ivy-leaved bell-flower

WATER PLANTS

Alnus glutinosa	Alder
Callitriche spp.	Starworts
Caltha palustris	Marsh marigold
Eleocharis palustris	Common spike-rush
Elodea canadensis	Canadian pondweed
Glyceria fluitans	Flote grass
Iris pseudocorus	Yellow flag
Lemna trisulca	Ivy-leaved duckweed
Lycopus europaeus	Gipsywort

Mentha aquatica	Water mint
Nardia compressa	a liverwort
Nymphaea alba	White water lily
Potamogeton spp.	Pondweeds
Sparganium spp.	Bur-reeds
Typha latifolia	Bulrush
Veronica beccabunga	Brooklime

BOG PLANTS

Carex echinata	Star sedge
Carex panicea	Carnation sedge
Cirsium dissectum	Meadow thistle
Dactylorhiza incarnata	Early marsh orchid
Drosera intermedia	Long-leaved sundew
Drosera rotundifolia	Round-leaved sundew
Eriophorum angustifolium	Cotton grass
Hydrocotyle vulgaris	Marsh pennywort
Lycopodium inundatum	Marsh club-moss
Menyanthes trifoliata	Bogbean
Mitrula paludosa	Bog beacon
Narthecium ossifragum	Bog asphodel
Polytrichum spp.	'star mosses'
Sphagnum spp.	'bog mosses'
Rhynchospora alba	White beaked-sedge
Trichophorum cespitosum	Deer grass
Viola palustris	Marsh violet

SCRUB PLANTS

Achillea ptarmica	Sneezewort
Agrimonia eupatoria	Agrimony
Anthriscus sylvestris	Cow parsley
Centaurium erythraea	Centaury
Cirsium palustre	Marsh thistle
Crataegus monogyna	Hawthorn
Cytisus scoparium	Broom

Epilobium angustifolium	Rosebay willowherb
Eupatorium cannabinum	Hemp agrimony
Heracleum sphondylium	Hogweed
Pulicaria dysenterica	Fleabane
Prunus spinosa	Blackthorn
Rubus fruticosus	Blackberry
Rubus idaeus	Raspberry
Ulex europaeus	Gorse
Valeriana officinalis	Valerian

INTERESTING ROADSIDE PLANTS

Briza media	Quaking grass
Campanula rotundifolia	Harebell
Epipactis helleborine	Broad-leaved helleborine
Epipactis purpurea	Violet helleborine
Linum catharticum	Fairy flax
Listera ovata	Twayblade
Ophioglossum vulgatum	Adder's tongue
Orchis mascula	Early purple orchid
Spiranthes spiralis	Autumn ladies'-tresses

NOTES ON PLANT LISTS

1. The lists are not complete and are intended only to give the reader an idea of the flora of the Forest.
2. No distinction has been made between very rare and very common plants.
3. Species are by no means confined to the habitat group where I have listed them.

SOME PLANTS WHICH HAVE PROBABLY DISAPPEARED FROM THE FOREST IN RECENT TIMES

Genista pilosa	Hairy greenweed
Hammarbya paludosa	Bog orchid
Lycopodium clavatum	Stag's horn clubmoss
Pyrola rotundifolia	Round-leaved wintergreen
Thelypteris phegopteris	Beech fern

A SELECTION OF THE FUNGI FOUND ON ASHDOWN FOREST

(so far, the total list exceeds 100 species with many more identified only to genus level)

Agaricus sylvaticus	*Cortinarius sanguineus*	*Nectria cinnabarina*
Aleuria aurantia	*Hericium clathroides*	*Oudemansiella mucida*
Amanita citrina	*Hydnum repandum*	*Paxillus involutus*
Amanita fulva	*Hygrophoropsis auratiaca*	*Phallus impudicus*
Amanita muscaria	*Hygrocybe conica*	*Pholiota squarrosa*
Armillaria mellea	*Inocybe maculata*	*Piptoporus betulinus*
Auricularia auricula	*Laccaria amethystina*	*Ramaria flava*
Boletus badius	*Lactarius deliciosus*	*Russula claroflava*
Boletus calopus	*Lactarius piperatus*	*Russula emetica*
Bulgaria inquinans	*Lactarius turpis*	*Russula mairei*
Chlorosplenium	*Lepiota crstata*	*Sparassis crispa*
aeruginascens	*Lycoperdon pyriforme*	*Suillus bovina*
Clathrus archeri	*Marasmius oreades*	*Trametes versicolor*
Clavulina cristata	*Mycena spp.*	*Xylaria hypoxylon*
Coprinus comatus		

CHRIS MARRABLE

Note on grazing experiment

Much of the valuable heathland habitat on the Forest is being lost to invading birch, pine and bracken. To help control this, the Conservators are intending to fence an experimental area of one hundred acres to allow commoners' animals safe grazing. The area will be carefully monitored to ensure that the grazing intensity is beneficial to heathland flora and fauna. The fence will have gates wherever it crosses a ride or path and there will be no restrictions on public access.

The experiment will begin in the summer of 1989.

The Society of the Friends of Ashdown Forest

(Registered Charity No.205245)

The Friends of Ashdown Forest came into being in 1961. The Society was the brainchild of Ursula Ridley of West Hoathly, a lady of great spirit whose activities and interest in local affairs and local history were not interrupted even by blindness. At that time she was a member of the Board of Conservators, and the first exploratory meeting of what was to be The Friends took place at her house. The first chairman was R. J. Lumsden, whose daughter, Anne Lumsden, was a Conservator for many years as well as being a local farmer. The committee of nine included David Streeter, already an ardent conservationist, and Nick Cranfield of Broadstone Farm. The Marchioness of Aberdeen, then Lady Dudley Gordon, turned from a committee member into Chairman on the death of R. J. Lumsden—one of few commoners commemorated in stone on the Forest itself. The Society soon became a registered charity. It prospered from the start, for its aims were just coming into urgent prominence—not only conservation as such, but the preservation of the Forest itself, its wild life, its amenities for public enjoyment.

The Friends were pledged to the support of the Conservators and over the years they have contributed an impressive amount of practical assistance. The first Land Rover to be used by the Conservators came through the Friends. Any number of technical aids have followed. The Friends, too, were responsible for the Four Counties Dial that commemorates the Queen's Silver Jubilee of 1977. They made themselves responsible for the Macmillan Clump in the Birch Grove area, and they planted Friends' Clump in 1973, the 'Year of the Tree'.

In 1987, it became necessary to raise a very large sum of money to assist the purchase of the Forest by the East Sussex County Council from the late Earl De La Warr and so avert the threat of possible partition. The Friends joined with the Conservators in organising an Appeal that was magnificently successful.

There are at present five hundred paid-up members of the Friends of Ashdown Forest contributing anything from a minimum of £5 annually; many contribute a great deal more. No membership of such an organisation is ever too big. Membership forms can always be obtained from the Ashdown Forest Centre, or they will be posted on request. The aims of the Society remain as vital as when it was formed in the '60s; in fact, as time goes on the support of the Friends becomes ever more desirable, valuable and urgent.

The Society of the Friends of Ashdown Forest,
    Ashdown Forest Centre
    Wych Cross
    Forest Row
    E. Sussex RH18 5JN

APPENDIX 6

Personal Recollections

The Reeve's Tale: 1

My great-grandfather was Reeve to the Earl of Guildford: that
was in 1850. In 1880 my grandfather came to Maresfield Park as
Reeve for Sir John Shelley. Then in 1912 my father got the job on
the Forest of Ranger and Reeve—he was on a month's trial and he
stayed forty-six years! He retired in 1960 and I took over. The wage
was 12/- a week, so it was week-end work. People came for a
permit to cut heather or dig stone, and if I was not there then my
wife was able to issue the permit. Then at week-ends I went round
to see they'd cut in the right place. When you got a permit for
cutting heather and gorse, anything that could be cut with a sickle
or scythe was allowed. Anything too big to be cut in that way
belonged to the Lord of the Manor, Earl de la Warr. The gorse
used for litter was what we used to call *dog furze*—that's the kind
that grows low among the heather, around autumn.

During my father's years as Reeve he had some awkward times.
There were some tramps settled in at Pound Gate and Father went
to move them on. Ten men surrounded him, all carrying whips—
and those whips had good hard brass handles to hit with. Father
wondered what was going to happen next, as a man had been killed
on the Forest in a fight with tramps. What happened was that a
woman came to the door of one of the 'vans. She had a gun and
she threatened the tramps. She shouted out—'I shoot the first one
that hits the Ranger!' So they let him get on with his business.

Then there were tramps at Fairwarp. Several times Father called
and warned Harry Walters he would be summoned for being on
Forest ground. One time Harry rushed at him with a pitchfork.
There had to be a court case. But Harry got a shrewd man from
Brighton to speak for him. He was a man the poachers used when
they were in trouble with the magistrate. Well, when Father got up

in court and made his statement, this man said to him in a loud manner—'Is it a well-known fact that the County Council have got a snow plough rotting at Duddleswell—on Forest ground?' Father had to think what to answer and this Mr Carter called out—'Come on, come on—you know where I mean.' Father had to think pretty fast before answering, and then he said—'The County Council has the right to deposit roadway materials beside the roadway.' That meant on Forest ground, so that saved the day.

Father was also Beadle to the Lord of the Manor and had to collect rents and other money, and see that people put out fodder for the deer—they had to do that in return for their common rights. Some time in the '20s a commoner, Jesse Ridley, used to go to Forest Row with his cart and collect pig swill, and when he was on his way back home, he'd stop and cut birch, being a commoner, and throw it on the cart. One day Father was coming by Cherry Garden on his bicycle and he saw Jesse Ridley. So he stopped to watch him. Every so often Jesse'd stop, and he'd got a handful of old sprout plants—no sprouts on them, just the old stalks—and he'd stick the stalks into the holes where he'd cut his birch.

So Father called out to him—'Jesse! What are you on, then, Jesse?'

'Well,' said Jesse, 'fodder for the deer.'

'Not much fodder on 'em!'

Now Jesse had a very old law book, and any time he had to answer for what he was doing, he'd slap it open and read from it—he knew a lot of it by heart. So now he stood up and said in a big voice, every word clear, 'The law does not state how *much* fodder I need give!'

Another thing the Beadle had to do was collect what they called *heriot*. That was when someone died and the property was to change hands. Heriot was paid on copyhold land; in 1936 all copyhold land became freehold by law. But in those days the heriot depended on the property—whether it was rich or not, I suppose, and how big or how small. Heriot could be anything from 'the best beast' to furniture—right down to one chicken, or even a red rose. When Father was Beadle he had to go and collect heriot from Sheffield Park when Lord Sheffield died. Sheffield Park was most freehold but some copyhold. It was 'best beast' there and when Father looked around he couldn't see what he'd call a best beast—so he picked on the best horse in the stable. Of course, by that time they didn't take the beast itself; Father valued it and they paid the due in money.

Then another job for the Reeve or the Beadle—before the Enclosure Act of 1886, that was—came when people threw out their boundary and claimed a bit of Forest that wasn't their right. 'Couldn't we pay a bit more rent?' they'd say. That might be only 1/- or 1/6, or if it was freehold perhaps £20. This was a matter for the Lord of the Manor. If he thought there was reason in it, then he'd let the land be kept. The tenant became 'tenant at will'—that is at the will of the Lord of the Manor.

Later on there was a certain Chairman of the Board of Conservators that was very strict about encroaching on to the Forest. There was a man built his garage with no more than three inches encroaching, but the Ranger was sent to put things right. He sawed a bit off the garage in one corner—that was all that was on the Forest—and you can see where he did it to this day!

F. KIRBY

The Reeve's Tale: 2

Twenty years ago somebody was interested in purchasing the trees on the Forest—not with the object of cutting them down, but to purchase them so that they could be preserved for all time. So Strutt & Parker sent one of their agents and I went with him, and we had about three days, measuring and valuing the timber. Well, we started down at the bottom of Priory Road, the Forest Row end, worked our way round the palings of Kidbrooke Park and up to Hindleap Warren—there are some beautiful trees along that way. Then we went to Legsheath. There, there was about thirty oaks, not good quality, and the beech was old and had had its best days. But there was one tree there—there's only two that I know of on the Forest—and that was a larch tree. A well-grown larch tree, and there's another one at Greenwood Gate. They're the only two I've ever seen on the Forest, and I should think those trees were anything from eighty to a hundred years old.

Well, then we made our way to Sutton's Farm, Twyford. There we found some good oak, there was about a hundred and fifty to two hundred. Next we were at The Vachery, it's all fir round there and there was just about two hundred and twenty oak. The fir was all young growing trees and when they're left they grow into good thick trees, they have to grow straight up to the light. Then we went to Pippingford, being close by. There the trees were bigger, there was about ninety fir trees there, and six oaks, and ten

chestnut. They were quite good trees, apart from the oak they'd
had the fire through the bottom of them—that spoilt the trees, you
see; they'd been scorched. After Pippingford we came across to the
Nutley side, down to Rough Ground. Believe it or not, there's some
very good oak down there. There were sixty-seven oak trees then
and fifty-five young tellers to grow into good trees. Then we went
up to the Marlpits. Well, there's quite a lot of oaks in there but
they'd had the fire through and that scorched the bottoms. Then
there was Beech View—there was some decrepit old oak up there.

After all that we went along the Groombridge Road to the Five
Hundred. We didn't go right on down into the Five Hundred, but
I know what it's like there, very similar to Legsheath, the beech
have had their day. The oldest trees on the Forest are at Legsheath
and the Five Hundred, you could call them some of the old original
forest trees. Going down through the Five Hundred road till you
come out to the Forest again, on the left there is Iron Latch Gate,
that goes into Buckhurst Park. There was a lot of good trees there,
young trees then, but unfortunately some of the chestnut wanted
cutting years ago. Because when they get old, they get what we call
'ring-shakes'; that's when the tree's cut down and you find it's all
rings cracked round the base, so if you put a saw to it it just falls
apart. Then there was just St. John's, where there's good fir, and
it's easy to get in and out there because of the roads the army left
after the war.

That's twenty years ago, but the only trees that'd fall would be
the beech—oak just stands till its hollow. With the beech, once one
tree goes down it lets the wind in to the next one and then it either
blows a great limb off of that or else blows it right over. They
nearly always go down when they're in leaf. If you get a lot of wet
weather and the ground gets water-logged and the tree's all out in
leaf, it's like a big sail, and as the wind blows it loosens the roots
up. You seldom get them falling in the dead of winter.

The beech down Twyford Lane suffered through the war. It
wasn't the best beech—it was what we'd call stub trees. That's
when the tree's been cut once and let grow. Well, during the war
the Army parked their tanks a bit off the road among the beeches,
and then they washed the tanks down with diesel, and the diesel
got into the roots of the beech and killed them—four or five we
had to cut down there. Some they cut down there lately I'd say
could have lasted another ten, fifteen years.

All that timber, in 1964, was valued at about four thousand
pounds—at today's prices I suppose it'd be nearer twenty.

There's lots of wood now but the talk's all of oil. Which reminds
me that when my father started as a Ranger in 1912, one of his first
jobs was to attend to a coal mine! It was being dug up at the top
of Kidd's Hill. These men had got down quite a way, and there was
a professor there and my father asked him, 'Do you think they'll
ever find coal there, then?'. 'Oh yes', he said, 'If you draw a line
from Belgium to Kent and then to Wales, anywhere in that line
you'll find coal'. Father said they'd got down about fifty feet before
the Board of Conservators had it stopped. I suppose it was some
government plan, or something. As for oil—I think the Forest
should stay as its been for thousands of years.

F. KIRBY

Ranged Forest for 36 years

(Mr Fred Kirby of Nutley sends this clipping from the *Courier*
about his father, just short of his retirement in 1947.)

The only time that Ranger Herbert Kirby does not feel at home in
the 6,500 acres of Ashdown Forest is when there is a fog. He
admitted this to a *Courier* reporter who visited him at his home in
Nutley.

'I find my way about at night by the stars', he said. 'Often I stand
still and listen for the sound of traffic on a certain road. I find that
wind direction is another good way of getting my bearings. But
fog—well that sometimes gets me worried'.

Mr Kirby, whose retirement early next year was announced at a
recent meeting of the Conservators of Ashdown Forest, recalled
an incident during the first World War when he was out on patrol
in no-man's-land.

'Suddenly I found that I was lost', he said. 'Luckily I had made
a note of the direction of the wind before I set out, so I managed
to get back. Since that occasion I have always made a note of the
way the wind is blowing before going out into the Forest at night'.

For 36 years Mr Kirby has been ranging Ashdown Forest, a
record for any Ranger since the formation of the Board of
Conservators, and yet he confesses that he does not like staying in
one job too long!

'Before I came to Ashdown Forest I worked for 19 years in
Maresfield Park', he remarked. 'I said when I left the Park that I
would never work for so long at one job again. But I did. The

Forest got a hold on me and I've stayed here all these years'.

Mr Kirby reckons he has helped to deal with several thousand fires in the Forest.

'The fires today are not as big as those we used to have years ago', he said. 'For one thing, the undergrowth is not so thick and high as it used to be. I can remember fires which spread over an area of 1,500 acres. In those days we had to beat out the flames with what help we could muster. Today we can call out the NFS and get help from the Army if necessary'.

Mr Kirby recalled the fact that two years ago two children were burned after they had kicked a phosphorous smoke cannister which they found lying in the Forest.

'I thought I would go and see if there were any more lying about in the area. Sure enough, I found one. I did not move it, but got in touch with the military authorities. A sergeant-major came along and exploded the bomb by throwing a heavy stick at it'.

Visitors to the Forest are more tidy in their habits today, thinks Mr Kirby.

'Before the war', he said, 'the Forest used to be littered with waste paper and empty bottles. The paper shortage and salvage drives during the war were a blessing in disguise. I had never seen the Forest look so tidy before'.

Mr Kirby said that on one occasion when he was out in the middle of the Forest he noticed some freshly-turned soil underneath a holly bush.

'I knew at once that something had been buried there. At that time a lot of young girls had been reported missing from various parts of the country, so I hurried back to the village and told the police of my discovery. A constable returned with me to the spot and we started digging. We got down to about a foot and the spade struck a wooden box. Carefully we raised the lid. Inside was something covered by a brown blanket. Underneath the blanket was a woollen cardigan. We removed the cardigan and saw a woman's silk blouse. Slowly I pulled the blouse out of the box, revealing the body of . . . an old Airedale dog'.

Mr Kirby is Kentish by birth—he was born in Dover 65 years ago—but for the past 55 years he has lived and worked in Sussex. After his retirement he will continue to live in his cottage The Highlands at Nutley, overlooking the hills and hollows of the Forest he knows and loves so well.

'I shall have my garden to look after', he said, 'but I expect I shall find it a bit small after the Forest'.

The Forester's Tale: 1

Years ago the snow used to be worse than now. Up at Duddleswell, where the nursery is now, there was a snow-plough. Mr Collins lived there then and he used to pull it down the road to Lampool Corner and clear all the snow away. He fastened his horse to it. Everyone then, locals, used to go tracing on the Forest for rabbits and different things to eat, and I was one of them who did that. No one thought to stop us. It was not anything like it is now. You could go out and do what you liked on the Forest. There was no firebreaks cut then and the fires was as bad as they are now—but we never had no fire-engines come out. We used to back-burn the fires and put them out by that method. There used to be one forest Ranger and that was Mr Fred Kirby's father. He was the forest Ranger and he used to come out on his bicycle to all these fires.

It really makes me laugh when people start shouting about forest fires the way they are today. It really is laughable, people make such a fuss over a forest fire and they need only back-burn it from the rides that's been cut. *Then* it was only footpaths we'd burn it from. If they was to back-burn it they'd never have all this bother. What with the firemen, and this, that and the other, look what gets spent on the Forest as regards to that sort of thing. I mean, there was nothing spent then.

There used to be a lot of grazing on the Forest—there was stock always—sheep, cows. Old Mr Barclay at Duddleswell, he kept a herd of milking cows. He'd ride round on a horse, to keep them in. Two of them had bells and you could always hear Barclay round with his cows, which was really wonderful. And there were horses out grazing on the Forest. They never bothered about them when the fires was on—they just moved out the way. You see, the Forest used to be burnt off a lot more than now, for the grazing, and the consequence of it was short stuff. Now it's left and left and not burnt and not burnt, and it's taller and taller—so if there's a fire it really gets going. That's all there is to it. I mean, the amusing part of it is—and I do laugh a bit when they say about people getting hurt—I've lived on Ashdown Forest all my life, which is way over sixty years, and I've never known anyone to get burnt, or a house get burnt. I've known hedges to get burnt—but not anything like people say.

Mr Kirby, he used to be wonderful. He'd always know where to put a match, light it and back-burn it and one thing and another—oh, he was wonderful. I think if they had to do a little controlled burning of the Forest they wouldn't have so much bother as they're having now. It's nearly time they came to it, because there's a lot of people would help with it that know something about it. A lot of firemen—well, I mean, they don't know what back-burning is.

Father was a great woodsman. He did a lot of wooding— chestnut post cutting and all this, and he was the one looked after Oldlands estate. He used to cut all the trees, and of course they used to cut their own wood out—board, and stuff, posts and all that. He was put in charge of all the wood cut down and I went with him quite a lot, helping him with posts and stuff. Also we used to have to catch all the rabbits for the estate bloodhounds; I went with him to help catch those.

You could wood where you liked on the Forest. It was not the same as it is now, where if you cut a stick they're after you. At that time you could cut where you liked and what you liked, and there was plenty. Round about August and so on, father used to go cutting bracken and litter. Now litter consisted of heather and gorse and a little bracken, and a farmer down at Nursery Lane used to come and get it, and it was sold to him for ten-shilling a load. We'd help him lump it up for taking away, when we was boys.

There wasn't so many deer then as now, but around Old Lodge there were the red deer; whether they originated from Oldlands or not, I don't know. They had them at Oldlands when I was working there—whether they let them out or what, I can't say. Oldlands had them from Buxted Park, because we had to go and help get them and take them to Oldlands.

Oldlands was a really lovely place to work, everyone knew what they were doing. I left Fairwarp school at fourteen and the first two years after that I was working in the greenhouses, and then I spent the next two years out on the pleasure gardens. Then the war came, and I was called up into the Army in 1939.

BILL COLEMAN

The Forester's Tale: 2

On Sundays there used to be two things in the summertime. One was to go down to Lampool corner and wait for the coaches to come through, and they used to throw us out money; and then in the afternoon we went to Sunday school, and we used to spend our time at that.

Bell-ringing—that was in the latter part of my life, when I was round about sixteen or seventeen; there was a whole peal of us, ringing Sunday mornings, Sunday nights, and it was great fun. When anyone died the bell would be tolled by the Vicar, the number of strokes was the number of years the dead person had lived. If we was somewhere and we heard the bell tolling then we would count up. Some people used to be quite an age and we would count them all up. There was a coffin path at Putlands, where the coffin was carried from the Forest up through the farm and out at the top and down along the main road. They carried all coffins then by bearers.

All this was a long time before the radio station; because the radio station was put up after I went into the army. I went in in 1939 and that was put up after, during the war.

Hunting on the Forest—there used to be quite a lot of hunting on the Forest—Eridge Hunt, Surrey and Burstow—Eridge used to do all this part of the Forest (Fairwarp area) before Surrey and Burstow took over; Southdown hunted Furnace wood.

Fairwarp school was an adorable place. There was between 90 and a 100 children there, and there were three classes. At playtime we'd go out on the Forest and play, cricket or anything like that; we used to play everything out on the Forest. It was a great school. I think it was a real pity that it ever closed.

Transport—well, there was no buses came up this road for quite a long time. I remember this road when it was flint—when I was very young, that was. Then they tarmacked it and we used to play tops on the road between the school and the church—we played all those sorts of games after they put the asphalt on—tops and wheeling, marbles, conkers. Wheeling is done with an ordinary wheel with no spokes and we used to travel it along with a stick, we'd have wooden wheels or bicycle wheels. At Five Ash Down there was a dump, and we'd walk through Hendall and go over there and pick these old wheels out, and frames, and bring them all back home and make a bicycle out of them. That's how we used to make our bicycles. The first proper bicycle I ever had was when I started work and Mother bought it for me, and that was bought in Uckfield at Eve's for three pound five. That was the first bicycle ever I had which was really a good one.

Every year we went hop-picking when we was children, and Father used to work between the oast-houses to dry the hops and we worked out in the hop-garden. We had to pick so many hops before we was allowed to play. After that, Mother let us out and we had to go to the oast-house every night to get the baked potatoes. The farm was Brotherwood's Farm, between Five Oak Green and Paddock Wood. We used to go there every year, either by cart—horse and cart—any method in that way, and then when we came back we would have to wait for Mother because she used to go round Tunbridge Wells and buy our boots and shoes or trousers or anything like that—she rigged us up out of the money she'd earned.

Every year we had an outing to Brighton, and Mr Allit, down at Boringwheel, used to take us to Uckfield Station in his horse and waggon and we'd go by train, then, to Brighton. He used to pick us up from the train coming back. But in latter years we had a Maidstone & District coach to pick us up. Mother paid our fare and we used to have about two and six to spend—we went on the piers and different places in Brighton. The school-teachers took us and it used to be an enjoyable outing.

Camp Hill and King's Standing were always there as I can remember, because we'd go to King's Standing Clump (that was when I played in the band) on a Sunday evening and have the Sunday service up there and the vicar from Fairwarp used to take it, and we used to go up with the band and play the hymns and different things, and it used to be wonderful.

I can never remember the games outside the Beacon, but my father told me a lot about it because he used to live then where Mr Sainsbury lives now. He played cricket there and he'd go to the Old Fox the opposite side of the road for a drink. I can remember the pavilion, which was a tin pavilion, going from the Beacon here to Nutley sports ground until they had the new one.

I remember uncle Shepherd and Dad, they had a dog which they used to send with messages between the two of them: my uncle lived in Larkshill where Mr and Mrs Billings live now—he had a little bungalow there, he lived there for quite a few years. Father moved from where Mr Sainsbury is now down to Well Cottage where we used to live. Then when we was old enough we used to come across to Larkshill and knock up crocks for the chickens— like plates or cups which are broken. We used to set there and knock them all up, and feed them to the chickens, because chickens need shell for their eggs and the crocks make shell—so that's what we used to knock up.

Local shops—well, at Fairwarp you could get practically everything you wanted. Shoes, boots, coal, chicken food—there wasn't anything you couldn't go in there and get. A bale of hay, you could go and get. Everything was there except bread. Now bread used to come round with a horse and cart from Buxted, round about three or four times a week. There was an old chap by the name of Green who came round on a three-wheeler push-bike, with cakes, they made them all at Buxted and they used to come through here. Milk—Mr Cottingham, down at Lampool Corner, you know the oast house there. He'd come round with the old horse and cart and take it out of the churn, a pint or a half-pint, whatever it was. He used to pay you a visit every morning, until Mr Osborne took over. Bill Osborne down at Spring Garden took over, but there was a chap before that, a Mr Maynard, but he didn't do it all that many years.

Meat—that used to be from Mr Bailey at Maresfield. He had a butcher's shop and delivered meat round here—he used to go and get the sage for making sausages off my mother-in-law . . . I remember things like that—yes.

BILL COLEMAN

Ashdown Park Memorial School

I first went to Ashdown Park Memorial School just as World War One had ended in 1918 and stayed for three years. My sister, Molly, followed me at the school from 1923 until 1929.

The Head Teacher, during our time, was Miss Gilliam whom Molly correctly describes as elderly, with grey straight hair taken back in a bun—a good teacher, strict but fair, whom we held in some awe. The junior teacher was Miss Oakley from Chelwood Gate. Molly says two or three nuns from the Convent occasionally came to talk to the school but the main interest was taken in the jars of boiled sweets they brought. I do not remember even the latter!

School curriculum was simple. Books were scarce at the end of the war. In fair weather our time was often effectively employed in weeding the school garden or gathering fire wood under the tall trees opposite. That area was known as 'High Beeches' then. We never went far into Broadstone Warren although that, like the Hindleap and Press Ridge Warrens, all belonged to Mr Douglas

Freshfield who lived at Wych Cross Place. My father was his head
gardener until he died in 1934. The 1200 acre estate was then sold.

My sister says the walk between Wych Cross and school seemed
much more than a long mile. Yet the children who struggled up
from the Coleman's Hatch area had a longer one and often some
came bare foot. Various carpet slippers were kept in a huge box in
front of the window. These were worn by one and all in winter and
on wet days, any size, colour odd or otherwise.

I remember no organised sporting activities, yet by magic, at the
mysteriously appointed seasons, marbles, hoops, tops, conkers,
hop-scotch came upon us.

The long, twice daily treks to and from school occasioned
incidents at times. I remember, periodically, seeing old Spikey
Brown, the forest ranger, trudging along pushing his bike—he
would be going to move-on some overstaying gypsies. Less often
we would see old Crazy Mary along the roadside, minding her own
business. Nature was closer to us—the colourful leaves, flowers,
grasses, heather, bracken and the wortleberries to make our
mouths black—also the insects, butterflies and little animals. I
remember treading, in the long grass, on an assumed snake's nest
and disturbing a family of young adders (a local man, Mr Cork, had
died from a snake bite some years before). I was frightened and ran
home. Once or twice some of us fell through the ice on Wych
Cross Pond—then opposite the Roebuck—muddy, but not deep.
The old well by the gate to Wych Cross Place, the sole supply of
water for the cottages around, was always a source of interest as the
bucket fell deeply to splash into the water far below. I believe there
was a well near the school too.

I fnd my sister's conclusion quite apt—'I would not say they
were such happy days, a struggle more against lonely roads, dark
winter days, and with very few playmates.'

**BARNETT FIELD AND
MOLLY PREECE (*neé* FIELD)**

APPENDIX 7

Some Sources

Ashdown Forest archives:
The Raper Papers
Minute Books of the Convservators of Ashdown Forest 1886–1988

The Sussex Archeological Collections
Sussex Notes & Queries

Ashdown Forest   J. K. Irons (unpublished thesis)

Ashdown Forest   Garth Christian

The Sussex Landscape   Peter Brandon
History of Sussex   T. W. Horsfield
History of Sussex   Mark Anthony Lower
Unknown Sussex   Donald Maxwell

History of the British Iron & Steel Industry   H. R. Schubert
Wealdon Iron   Ernest Straker
The Iron Industry of the Weald   Henry Cleere & David Crossley
The Queen's Gunstone Maker   Edmund Teesdale

Smuggling in Sussex   Mary Waugh
Bricks & Tiles   M. Beswick

Nutley Windmill   Simon Wright & Frank Gregory

Historical Collections from Danehill, Forest Row, Hartfield, Withyham etc.

General Index

Bird Watching & Preservation Society, 126
Blackcock, 50
Bolebrook at Hartfield, 114
Boleyn, Anne, 135
    Sir Thomas, 16, 135
Boringwheel Mill, Cackle Street, 114
Bowyer, John & Denise, of Parrock, 111
Brakes, (bracken) cutting of, 39, 41, 42, 68
Brett, John, 37, 38
Bradford, Esq. Thomas, 119, 127
    William, 127
Brandon, Peter, *The Sussex Landscape*, 13
Brickyards, 113
British Petroleum (BP), 164, 165
Broadstone Warren, Manor Charitable Trust, 17, 172, 80
Brooker, John, 47, 49, 50
Burgess, William, 89
Buss, nephew of Edward Heaver, 50
Buxted, Parish of, 19, 105, 109
    Levett, William, 113

California, International University of, 121
Camden, William, 106 *Britannia*
Camp Hill, 133, 139, 160
Car Parks, 3, 15, 36, 147
The Castle Stewarts, 130, 136
Centenary Celebrations, 155, 156
Chapel Wood, 117, 124
Charles II, 28, 126, 130
Chelwood Gate, 152, 172
Chelwood Vachery (or Vechery or Vaccary), 123, 125, 129, 131, 157
    B.A.T.'S, 124, 173
Christian, Garth, 1967, *Ashdown Forest*, 29
    see Martha Baker, 54, 159
Cleer, Henry & David Crossley, *The Iron Industry of the Weald*, 108
    Wealden Iron Research Group (WIRG), 109
Clerks to the Board of Conservators, William Augustus Raper, 1885;
    Mr. H. Fovargue follows, 72, 75; Peter Williams, solicitor, 75;
    Lt. Comdr. Peter Angell, 4th in 100 years, 76;
    Lt. Col. J. R. Nicholls, OBE
Cobbett, William, *Rural Rides*, 104, 105, 112
Colchester, Lord, (Rt. Hon. Charles Abbott) Speaker of the House, 48, 113, 122
Coleman's Hatch, 119, 141, 172
    church, 121
    village hall, 165
Comber, Steve, of Comber & Sons, 143
Commoner (Customary Tenant), 2
Commoners' Committee, 77, 79, 85
Commons, Grisling, 24; Horney, 19; Piltdown, 24; St. John's, 19;
    Stumblewood, 19
    Protection Act of, 67

Pettit, Joseph, 109
Pevsner, Nikolaus, *Buildings of England, Sussex*, 122, 132
Pigs, 76
Pilbream, William, 45
Pippingford Park (or Pippingworth, Pippinford, or Pypynford), 23, 75, 126,
    127—129, 130, 131
Pope, John, of Hyndall (Hendall), 24
Predators, 97, 98

Ragg, Alfred R., 139
    Manor Charitable Trust, 140
    Isle of Thorns, 139
    Broadstone Warren, 140
    Hindleap Warren, 140
The Rangers, 40, 80–84, 96, 147
    Mr. Kirby, 74 and Ranger Hatchett, 68
Raper, William Augustus, 43–57, 75, 113, 114
Richard II, 21
The Ridge Road, 17, 172
Riding, 81
    Act of 1974 permit issue, 100
Riding code, 148
Right of Common, 1, 23, 177
Roebuck Hotel, 120, 166
Roman Forest, called Anderida, 14
Roman road, 14
Rural England, The Council for the Preservation of, 173
Rystwood, 152

Sackville Family, 11
    Margaret, neé Dallingridge, 21
    Thomas, Earl of Dorset, Master of the Forest, 28, 167
    Robert, Earl of Dorset, 28
    Richard, son of Robert, 167
    Lords of the Manor of Duddleswell, 167
    Earls of Dorset become Dukes, 167
    Vita Sackville-West, Sissinghurst, 156
    See Arabella Diana, Dowager Duchess of Dorset, 167
    her daughter marries a De La Warr, 167, 177
Sackville-West, Vita of Sissinghurst, 156
St. Richard de Wych, 120, 121
Saleshurst, Monks of, (Sidneys of Penshurst), 22
Samuel, Sir Stuart, 124
Schubert, H. R., *The Story of the British Iron and Steel Industry*, 108, 109
Scott, Brigadier "Tim", 159
Sewell, William Esq. of Twyford Lodge, 35, 37
Sheep, 76, 93
Sheffield, Earl of, 55
Sheffield Park, 123
Sheldrick, Anne, Chairman of the Conservators, 168, 169

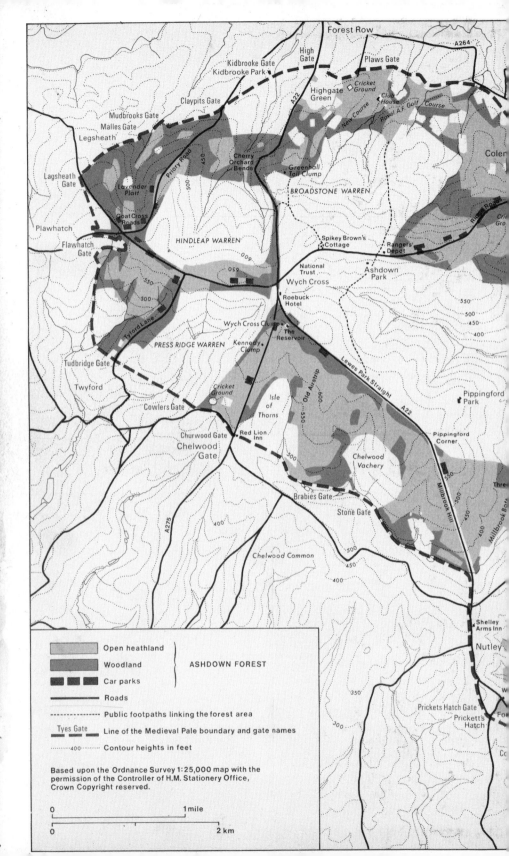